The Simple Plant-Based Cookbook for Beginners

Over 180 Easy and Flavourful Recipes of Healthy, Nutrient-Rich Dishes for a No-Processed Food Lifestyle, Featuring a 56-Day Meal Plan

By Steven Gable

Disclaimer

The information provided in this cookbook, *"The Simple Plant-Based Cookbook for Beginners: Over 180 Easy and Flavourful Recipes of Healthy, Nutrient-Rich Dishes for a No-Processed Food Lifestyle, Featuring a 56-Day Meal Plan"* is for general informational and educational purposes only. The recipes and nutritional advice provided herein are not intended to diagnose, treat, cure, or prevent any disease or health condition. Always consult with a healthcare professional or registered dietitian before making significant changes to your diet, especially if you have any existing medical conditions.

The author, Steven Gable, does not claim to be a medical professional, and the advice offered in this book is based on personal research and experience. The nutritional values provided are estimates and may vary depending on the specific products and measurements used.

Every effort has been made to ensure that the information in this book is accurate and up-to-date. However, the author and publisher assume no responsibility for errors, omissions, or contrary interpretations of the subject matter herein. The reader is responsible for their own health and wellbeing and should use their own discretion when trying new foods or recipes.

By using this cookbook, you agree to take full responsibility for your actions and decisions related to your dietary and lifestyle choices.

Author: Steven Gable
Year: 2025

Table of Contents

Main Dishes   **47**

Embracing the Plant-Based Diet

Exploring the Plant-Based Diet

A plant-based diet is a way of eating that emphasizes foods derived from plants. This includes not only vegetables and fruits but also whole grains, nuts, , legumes, seeds, oils, and beans. A plant-based diet doesn't necessarily mean that you are vegetarian or vegan and completely avoid meat or animal products. Rather, you are choosing more of your foods from plant sources.

The philosophy behind a plant-based diet is simple: consuming whole, unprocessed, or minimally processed plant foods, while limiting or eliminating animal products, refined foods, and artificial ingredients. This approach to eating is often associated with many health benefits, for example lower risk of chronic diseases like diabetes and cancer, weight management and improved heart health.

However, a plant-based diet is not just about what you eat; it's also about how you think about food. This diet encourages you to focus on foods in their most natural, nutrient-rich form, which are free from additives and preservatives. It's about choosing foods that nourish your body and support long-term health.

Plant-Based Diets: Pros and Cons

Like any diet, a plant-based diet has its advantages and disadvantages. Understanding these can help you make an informed decision about whether this way of eating is right for you.

Pros:

Nutrient Density: Plant-based diets are rich in antioxidants, fiber, vitamins and minerals which can help to improve overall health, boost immunity, and prevent chronic diseases. Consuming a wide variety of plants ensures you get a broad spectrum of nutrients.

Heart Health: Studies have shown that a plant-based diet is able to significantly reduce the risk of cardiovascular diseases. The reason is naturally low levels of saturated fats and cholesterol, at the same time being high in heart-healthy fats from nuts, seeds, and avocados.

Weight Management: Plant-based diet is often lower in calories and higher in fiber than diet that includes animal products, making it easier to manage your weight. Fiber helps you feel full longer, reducing overall calorie intake.

Environmental Impact: Reducing the consumption of animal products can lessen your carbon footprint. Fewer resources are required by a plant-based diet, such as land and water, as well as fewer greenhouse gasses are generated compared to a diet heavy in meat and dairy.

Ethical Considerations: A plant-based diet is a more humane choice, avoiding the ethical dilemmas associated with animal farming and slaughter.

Cons:

Nutrient Deficiencies: A plant-based diet, if not well-planned, can cause deficiencies in vital nutrients such as vitamin B12, iron, calcium, omega-3 fatty acids, and protein.

Social Challenges: Adopting a plant-based diet can be challenging in social situations, especially if you're dining out or attending events with limited plant-based options. It may require more effort to find suitable foods.

Increased Meal Preparation: A plant-based diet often involves more cooking and preparation time since processed and convenience foods are usually avoided. For some, this might be a barrier due to a lack of cooking skills or time constraints.

Cost: While fruits, vegetables, and grains are generally affordable, specialty items like organic produce, nuts, seeds, and plant-based meat substitutes can be more expensive. This can make the diet seem costly, though it's possible to manage expenses with careful planning.

Learning Curve: Switching to a plant-based diet can require significant research and education, especially for those who are used to a diet rich in animal products. Understanding how to combine foods to obtain all essential amino acids and nutrients is key.

Plant-Based Diet Shopping List & Budget-Friendly Tips

Here's a basic shopping list to get you started on a plant-based diet. These items can be mixed and matched to create a variety of delicious and nutritious meals.

Fruits:	Vegetables:	Grains:	Legumes:
Apples	Leafy greens (spinach, kale, lettuce)	Brown rice	Black beans
Bananas		Quinoa	Chickpeas
Berries	Cruciferous vegetables (broccoli, cauliflower, Brussels sprouts)	Oats	Lentils
Oranges		Barley	Kidney beans
Grapes		Millet	Peas
Avocados	Root vegetables (sweet potatoes, carrots, beets)		Edamame
Dried fruits (dates, apricots, raisins)	Peppers		
	Tomatoes		
	Cucumbers		
	Mushrooms		
	Onions and garlic		

Nuts and Seeds:	**Herbs and Spices:**	**Other Essentials:**
Almonds	Basil	Tofu
Walnuts	Oregano	Tempeh
Chia seeds	Cumin	Plant-based milks (almond,
Flaxseeds	Turmeric	soy, oat)
Pumpkin seeds	Cinnamon	Olive oil
Sunflower seeds	Rosemary	Coconut oil
Nut butters (almond	Paprika	Nutritional yeast
butter, peanut butter)		Soy sauce or tamari

Plant-based diet costs can vary greatly depending on your food choices, where you live, and whether you buy organic or specialty products. However, with careful planning, it can be quite affordable.

Buy in Bulk: Purchasing staples like grains, beans, and nuts in bulk can save money. These items have a long shelf life and are often cheaper per unit when bought in larger quantities.

Seasonal Produce: Buying vegetables and fruits in season can significantly reduce costs. Seasonal produce is often fresher, more flavorful, and less expensive.

Frozen and Canned Options: Frozen vegetables and fruits are often just as nutritious as fresh ones and are usually cheaper. Canned beans and vegetables can also be economical and convenient options, just be sure to choose low-sodium varieties.

Limit Processed Foods: While plant-based meat substitutes and specialty products are convenient, they are often expensive. Focusing on whole foods like beans, lentils, grains, and seasonal produce can help keep costs down.

Cook at Home: Preparing meals at home is usually less expensive than eating out or buying pre-made meals. Batch cooking and meal prepping can save time and money.

Tips for Plant-Based Diet Beginners

Starting a plant-based diet can be both exciting and daunting. Here are some tips to help you make a smooth transition:

Start Slow: Don't feel like you need to overhaul your entire diet overnight. Start by including more plant-based meals into your weekly routine and gradually reduce your intake of animal products.

Educate Yourself: Learn about the nutritional specifics of a plant-based diet, such as how to get enough protein, iron, calcium, and vitamin B12. This knowledge will help you make balanced choices and avoid deficiencies.

Experiment with Recipes: Try new recipes and explore different cuisines that are naturally plant-based, such as Mediterranean, Indian, or Thai. This will keep your meals satisfying and interesting.

Prepare for Cravings: If you find yourself craving certain non-plant-based foods, look for plant-based alternatives. There are many delicious recipes for plant-based versions of burgers, cheeses, and desserts.

Plan Ahead: Meal planning can make it much easier to follow a plant-based diet, especially on busy days. Having ready-to-eat meals and snacks on hand will help you avoid the temptation of convenience and processed foods.

Join a Community: Connect with others who are following a plant-based diet, whether online or in person. This can provide support, recipe ideas, and motivation.

Listen to Your Body: Pay attention to how your body responds to the changes in your diet. Everyone's nutritional needs are different, so adjust your diet as needed to ensure you're feeling your best.

Transitioning to a plant-based diet is a rewarding journey that can significantly benefit your health, the environment, and your wallet. By focusing on whole, unprocessed foods and learning how to create balanced, nutritious meals, you can enjoy the many advantages of a plant-based lifestyle. Remember, it's not about perfection, but about making more informed, healthful choices that align with your values and goals.

56-Day Nutrition-balanced Meal Plan

	Week 1	Week 2	Week 3	Week 4
Sunday	**Breakfast:** Overnight Chia Pudding with Fresh Berries, p.15 **Lunch:** Mediterranean Chickpea Salad, p.30 **Dinner:** Sweet Potato & Chickpea Curry, p.47 **Snack:** Spicy Roasted Chickpeas, p.99	**Breakfast:** Chocolate Almond Overnight Oats, p.17 **Lunch:** Lentil & Veggie Salad, p.42 **Dinner:** Lentil & Vegetable Stir-Fry, p.69 **Snack:** Baked Cinnamon Apples, p.108	**Breakfast:** Cinnamon Raisin Overnight Oats, p.17 **Lunch:** Zucchini & Corn Salad, p.34 **Dinner:** Moroccan Spiced Chickpea Stew, p.90 **Snack:** Lemon Cashew Energy Balls, p.110	**Breakfast:** Zucchini & Carrot Hash Browns, p.29 **Lunch:** Pear & Arugula Salad, p.37 **Dinner:** Sweet Potato & Kale Skillet, p.66 **Snack:** Stuffed Figs with Almonds, p.111
Monday	**Breakfast:** Apple Cinnamon Overnight Oats, p.16 **Lunch:** Quinoa & Black Bean Salad, p.30 **Dinner:** Stuffed Bell Peppers, p.47 **Snack:** Stuffed Dates with Walnuts, p.100	**Breakfast:** Mango & Coconut Chia Pudding, p.16 **Lunch:** Ratatouille Salad, p.40 **Dinner:** Vegetable & Tofu Stir-Fry, p.56 **Snack:** Apple Slices with Almond Butter and Chia Seeds, p.99	**Breakfast:** Berry Green Smoothie, p.20 **Lunch:** Spinach & Quinoa Salad, p.38 **Dinner:** Moroccan Spiced Vegetable Tagine, p.74 **Snack:** Peanut Butter Oat Bars, p.109	**Breakfast:** Apple Cinnamon Overnight Oats, p.16 **Lunch:** Roasted Veggie & Quinoa Salad, p.45 **Dinner:** Moroccan Lentil Soup p.80 **Snack:** Dark Chocolate Covered Strawberries, p.112
Tuesday	**Breakfast:** Banana Almond Smoothie Bowl, p.20 **Lunch:** Avocado & Tomato Salad, p.31 **Dinner:** Cauliflower & Chickpea Tacos, p.49 **Snack:** Baked Plantain Chips, p.102	**Breakfast:** Peanut Butter & Banana Oatmeal, p.18 **Lunch:** Greek Salad, p.38 **Dinner:** Sweet Potato & Black Bean Enchiladas, p.53 **Snack:** Vegan Sushi Rolls, p.105	**Breakfast:** Quick Quinoa Porridge with Almond Butter, p.25 **Lunch:** Avocado & Corn Salad, p.41 **Dinner:** Cauliflower & Chickpea Stew, p.92 **Snack:** Chocolate-Dipped Coconut Bars, p.106	**Breakfast:** Almond Butter & Cacao Nib Smoothie, p.23 **Lunch:** Spinach & Strawberry Salad, p.32 **Dinner:** White Bean & Kale Stew, p.86 **Snack:** Pumpkin Seed Clusters, p.105
Wednesday	**Breakfast:** Blueberry Oat Pancakes, p.18 **Lunch:** Roasted Beet & Arugula Salad, p.33 **Dinner:** Butternut Squash & Black Bean Chili, p.50 **Snack:** Nutty Granola Clusters, p.102	**Breakfast:** Raw Apple Cinnamon "Cereal", p.19 **Lunch:** Summer Vegetable Salad, p.44 **Dinner:** Stuffed Acorn Squash, p.54 **Snack:** Pineapple & Coconut Bites, p.103	**Breakfast:** Strawberry Banana Smoothie, p.21 **Lunch:** Mixed Bean Salad, p.35 **Dinner:** Tomato & Basil Stuffed Eggplant, p.66 **Snack:** Mango Sorbet, p.111	**Breakfast:** Peanut Butter & Banana Oatmeal, p.18 **Lunch:** Kale & Sweet Potato Salad, p.32 **Dinner:** Butternut Squash & Black Bean Burritos, p.65 **Snack:** Nutty Granola Clusters, p.102
Thursday	**Breakfast:** Spinach & Mushroom Tofu Scramble, p.23 **Lunch:** Spinach & Strawberry Salad, p.32 **Dinner:** Mushroom & Spinach Stuffed, Portobello Mushrooms, p.49 **Snack:** Sweet Potato Fries, p.101	**Breakfast:** Green Avocado Smoothie, p.22 **Lunch:** Roasted Brussels Sprouts & Quinoa Salad, p.45 **Dinner:** Spicy Lentil & Spinach Stuffed Sweet, Potatoes, p.57 **Snack:** Zucchini Fritters, p.104	**Breakfast:** Pineapple Coconut Smoothie Bowl, p.22 **Lunch:** Ginger & Carrot Salad, p.39 **Dinner:** Curried Cauliflower & Chickpeas, p.52 **Snack:** Raspberry Chia Jam with Vegan Banana Bread, p.113, p.112	**Breakfast:** Raw Apple Cinnamon "Cereal", p.19 **Lunch:** Cucumber & Avocado Salad, p.42 **Dinner:** Eggplant & Tomato Stew, p.88 **Snack:** Vegan Banana Bread, p.112

Friday	**Breakfast:** Coconut Milk Rice Pudding, p.15 **Lunch:** Kale & Sweet Potato Salad, p.32 **Dinner:** Spaghetti Squash with Tomato Basil Sauce, p.52 **Snack:** Crispy Baked Tofu Cubes, p.104	**Breakfast:** Almond Butter & Cacao Nib Smoothie, p.23 **Lunch:** Beet & Carrot Salad, p.41 **Dinner:** Vegetable Paella, p.58 **Snack:** Pumpkin Seed Clusters, p.105	**Breakfast:** Quick Peanut Butter Banana Sweet Potato Toast, p.26 **Lunch:** Cabbage & Carrot Salad, p.36 **Dinner:** Green Bean & Tofu Stir-Fry, p.61 **Snack:** Vegan Pumpkin Pie Bites, p.114	**Breakfast:** Mango & Coconut Chia Pudding, p.16 **Lunch:** Asparagus & Tomato Salad, p.36 **Dinner:** Spicy Tofu & Broccoli Stir-Fry, p.68 **Snack:** Lemon Cashew Energy Balls, p.110
Saturday	**Breakfast:** Pumpkin Spice Smoothie, p.21 **Lunch:** Cucumber & Dill Salad, p.31 **Dinner:** Thai Peanut Sweet Potato Noodles, p.54 **Snack:** Energy Balls, p.101	**Breakfast:** Warm Spiced Apples with Almonds & Raisins, p.24 **Lunch:** Arugula & Pear Salad, p.43 **Dinner:** Sweet Potato & Lentil Shepherd's Pie, p.60 **Snack:** Vegan Chocolate Chip Cookies, p.109	**Breakfast:** Spinach & Mushroom Tofu Scramble, p.23 **Lunch:** Quinoa & Roasted Veggie Bowl, p.50 **Dinner:** Baked Falafel with Tahini Sauce, p.55 **Snack:** Crispy Baked Tofu Cubes, p.104	**Breakfast:** Pumpkin Spice Smoothie, p.21 **Lunch:** Sweet Potato & Black Bean Salad, p.39 **Dinner:** Spicy Chickpea & Spinach Stew, p.89 **Snack:** Coconut Rice Pudding, p.115

	Week 5	Week 6	Week 7	Week 8
Sunday	**Breakfast:** Mushroom & Spinach Quesadilla (Using Collard Greens as Wraps), p.29 **Lunch:** Mango & Black Bean Salad, p.35 **Dinner:** Red Bean & Corn Chili, p.64 **Snack:** Kale Chips, p.100	**Breakfast:** Cauliflower & Turmeric Breakfast Rice, p.25 **Lunch:** Mixed Bean Salad, p.35 **Dinner:** Green Bean & Tofu Stir-Fry, p.61 **Snack:** Crispy Baked Tofu Cubes, p.104	**Breakfast:** Sweet Potato & Spinach Breakfast Bowl, p.27 **Lunch:** Cabbage & Carrot Salad, p.36 **Dinner:** Roasted Tomato & Garlic Soup, p.77 **Snack:** Zucchini Fritters, p.104	**Breakfast:** Blueberry Oat Pancakes, p.18 **Lunch:** Greek Salad, p.38 **Dinner:** Vegetable Paella, p.58 **Snack:** Sweet Potato Fries, p.101
Monday	**Breakfast:** Spinach & Mushroom Tofu Scramble, p.23 **Lunch:** Broccoli & Cauliflower Salad, p.34 **Dinner:** Spicy Lentil & Spinach Stuffed Sweet Potatoes, p.57 **Snack:** Pineapple & Coconut Bites, p.103	**Breakfast:** Raw Veggie & Nut Breakfast Salad, p.28 **Lunch:** Cucumber & Avocado Salad, p.42 **Dinner:** Eggplant & Tomato Stew, p.88 **Snack:** Stuffed Figs with Almonds, p.111	**Breakfast:** Quick Peanut Butter Banana Sweet Potato Toast, p.26 **Lunch:** Chickpea & Avocado Wraps, p.59 **Dinner:** Lentil & Vegetable Bolognese, p.69 **Snack:** Mango Sorbet, p.111	**Breakfast:** Almond Butter & Cacao Nib Smoothie, p.23 **Lunch:** Kale & Sweet Potato Salad, 32 **Dinner:** Moroccan Spiced Vegetable Tagine, p.74 **Snack:** Nutty Granola Clusters, p.102
Tuesday	**Breakfast:** Avocado & Tomato Stuffed Bell Peppers, p.27 **Lunch:** Beet & Carrot Salad, p.41 **Dinner:** Stuffed Zucchini Boats, p.62 **Snack:** Homemade Trail Mix, p.103	**Breakfast:** Warm Spiced Apples with Almonds & Raisins, p.24 **Lunch:** Roasted Beet & Walnut Salad, p.46 **Dinner:** Moroccan Spiced Chickpea Stew, p.90 **Snack:** Peanut Butter Oat Bars, p.109	**Breakfast:** Green Avocado Smoothie, p.22 **Lunch:** Roasted Brussels Sprouts & Quinoa Salad, p.45 **Dinner:** Curried Cauliflower & Chickpeas, p.52 **Snack:** Raw Vegan Brownies, p.107	**Breakfast:** Warm Spiced Apples with Almonds & Raisins, p.24 **Lunch:** Asparagus & Tomato Salad, p.36 **Dinner:** Spicy Tofu & Broccoli Stir-Fry, p.68 **Snack:** Dark Chocolate Covered Strawberries, p.112

Wednesday	**Breakfast:** Sweet Potato & Spinach Breakfast Bowl, p.27 **Lunch:** Asparagus & Tomato Salad, p.36 **Dinner:** Roasted Carrot & Chickpea Bowl, p.63 **Snack:** Chocolate Avocado Pudding, 106	**Breakfast:** Almond Butter & Cacao Nib Smoothie, p.23 **Lunch:** Kale & Apple Salad, p.43 **Dinner:** Spaghetti Squash with Roasted Tomato Sauce, p.60 **Snack:** Dark Chocolate Covered Strawberries, p.112	**Breakfast:** Mushroom & Spinach Quesadilla, p.29 **Lunch:** Sweet Potato & Black Bean Salad, p.39 **Dinner:** Butternut Squash & Black Bean Burritos, p.65 **Snack:** Chocolate-Dipped Coconut Bars, p.106	**Breakfast:** Quick Quinoa Porridge with Almond Butter, p.25 **Lunch:** Roasted Beet & Arugula Salad, p.33 **Dinner:** Spicy Lentil & Spinach Stuffed Sweet Potatoes, p.57 **Snack:** Coconut Rice Pudding, p.115
Thursday	**Breakfast:** Kale & Sweet Potato Breakfast Skillet, p.28 **Lunch:** Celery & Apple Salad, p.40 **Dinner:** Lentil & Mushroom Shepherd's Pie, p.72 **Snack:** Lemon Cashew Energy Balls, p.110	**Breakfast:** Pineapple Coconut Smoothie Bowl, p.22 **Lunch:** Tomato & Basil Salad, p.44 **Dinner:** Sweet Potato & Kale Skillet, p.66 **Snack:** Coconut Macaroons, p.110	**Breakfast:** Cauliflower & Turmeric Breakfast Rice, p.25 **Lunch:** Ginger & Carrot Salad, p.39 **Dinner:** Spicy Roasted Cauliflower & Quinoa, p.71 **Snack:** Vegan Pumpkin Pie Bites, p.114	**Breakfast:** Spinach & Mushroom Tofu Scramble, p.23 **Lunch:** Avocado & Corn Salad, p.41 **Dinner:** Baked Falafel with Tahini Sauce, p.55 **Snack:** Chocolate Avocado Pudding, p.106
Friday	**Breakfast:** Zucchini & Carrot Hash Browns, p.29 **Lunch:** Chickpea & Avocado Salad, p.37 **Dinner:** Cauliflower Rice & Veggie Bowl, p.63 **Snack:** Berry Coconut Popsicles, p.108	**Breakfast:** Quick Quinoa Porridge with Almond Butter, p.25 **Lunch:** Roasted Veggie & Quinoa Salad, p.45 **Dinner:** Moroccan Lentil Soup, p.80 **Snack:** Vegan Pumpkin Pie Bites, p.114	**Breakfast:** Pumpkin Spice Smoothie, p.21 **Lunch:** Mango & Black Bean Salad, p.35 **Dinner:** Green Lentil & Kale Stuffed Peppers, p.65 **Snack:** Crispy Baked Tofu Cubes, p.104	**Breakfast:** Mushroom & Spinach Quesadilla, p.29 **Lunch:** Cabbage & Carrot Salad, p.36 **Dinner:** Eggplant & Tomato Stew, p.88 **Snack:** Berry Coconut Popsicles, p.108
Saturday	**Breakfast:** Chickpea Omelette with Spinach, p.24 **Lunch:** Summer Vegetable Salad, p.44 **Dinner:** Baked Falafel with Tahini Sauce, p.55 **Snack:** Vegan Banana Bread, p.112	**Breakfast:** Spinach & Mushroom Tofu Scramble, p.23 **Lunch:** Arugula & Pear Salad, p.43 **Dinner:** Stuffed Bell Peppers, p.47 **Snack:** Caramelized Pears with Walnuts, p.113	**Breakfast:** Sweet Potato & Black Bean Breakfast Tacos, p.26 **Lunch:** Spinach & Strawberry Salad, p.32 **Dinner:** Tomato & Basil Stuffed Eggplant, p.66 **Snack:** Almond Butter Stuffed Dates, p.114	**Breakfast:** Green Avocado Smoothie, p.22 **Lunch:** Mixed Bean Salad, p.35 **Dinner:** Red Lentil & Carrot Soup, p.76 **Snack:** Lemon Cashew Energy Balls, p.110

Breakfast

Overnight Chia Pudding with Fresh Berries

 Servings: 2

 Prep. time: 5 min

 Setting time: 4 hours or overnight

Nutritional Information (Per Serving):

Calories: 290 kcal, Protein: 7g, Carbohydrates: 30g, Fats: 16g, Fiber: 14g, Cholesterol: 0mg, Sodium: 70mg, Potassium: 320mg

Ingredients

- 1/4 cup chia seeds
- 1 cup unsweetened almond milk (or any plant-based milk)
- 1 tablespoon maple syrup (optional, for sweetness)
- 1/2 teaspoon vanilla extract
- 1/4 teaspoon ground cinnamon
- 1/2 cup fresh berries (e.g., blueberries, strawberries, raspberries)
- 2 tablespoons sliced almonds
- 1 tablespoon hemp seeds
- 1 tablespoon unsweetened shredded coconut
- 1 tablespoon cacao nibs (optional)
- Fresh mint leaves (optional, for garnish)

Directions:

1. Combine in a medium-sized bowl or jar almond milk, maple syrup, the chia seeds, vanilla extract, and ground cinnamon.
2. Mix the ingredients well to ensure that the chia seeds are evenly dispersed and not clumping together.
3. Let the mixture rest for about 5 minutes, then mix again to break up any clumps that may have formed.
4. Cover the bowl/jar and place it in the refrigerator to set for at least 4 hours, or preferably overnight. The chia seeds will soak up the liquid and swell, resulting in a pudding-like texture.
5. Once the chia pudding has set, give it a good stir to ensure a smooth texture.
6. Divide the pudding evenly between two bowls or jars.
7. Top each serving with fresh berries, sliced almonds, hemp seeds, shredded coconut, and cacao nibs if using.
8. Garnish with fresh mint leaves.
9. Serve the chia pudding cold, straight from the refrigerator.

Coconut Milk Rice Pudding

 Servings: 4

 Prep. time: 5 min

 Total time: 30 min

Nutritional Information (Per Serving):

Calories: 320 kcal, Protein: 4g, Carbohydrates: 52g, Fats: 13g, Fiber: 2g, Cholesterol: 0mg, Sodium: 25mg, Potassium: 200mg

Ingredients

- 1 cup uncooked white rice (preferably short-grain or jasmine)
- 2 cups full-fat coconut milk
- 1 cup water
- 1/4 cup maple syrup (or any natural sweetener)
- 1 teaspoon vanilla extract
- 1/2 teaspoon ground cinnamon
- Pinch of salt

Directions:

1. Combine the coconut milk, rice, and water in a medium-sized saucepan. Boil over medium heat, stirring occasionally.
2. Reduce the heat to low when it starts boiling, cover the saucepan, and let it simmer for 20 minutes, stirring occasionally to prevent sticking.
3. After the rice is tender and most of the liquid is absorbed, stir in the vanilla extract, maple syrup, ground cinnamon, and a pinch of salt.
4. Keep cooking for an additional 5 minutes, stirring until the pudding reaches a creamy consistency.
5. Divide the rice pudding into four bowls. Serve warm or chilled, topped with your choice of fresh fruit, shredded coconut, chopped nuts, or an extra sprinkle of cinnamon.

Mango & Coconut Chia Pudding

Servings: 4 **Prep. time:** 5 min **Setting time:** 4 hours or overnight

Nutritional Information (Per Serving):

Calories: 300 kcal, Protein: 5g, Carbohydrates: 28g, Fats: 20g, Fiber: 10g, Cholesterol: 0mg, Sodium: 15mg, Potassium: 350mg

Ingredients

- 1/4 cup chia seeds
- 1 cup full-fat coconut milk
- 1 tablespoon maple syrup (optional, for sweetness)
- 1/2 teaspoon vanilla extract
- 1 ripe mango, diced
- 2 tablespoons unsweetened shredded coconut
- Toppings (Optional): Sliced fresh mango, Toasted coconut flakes, Chopped nuts (e.g., almonds or cashews)

Directions:

1. In a mixing bowl, combine the chia seeds, coconut milk, maple syrup, and vanilla extract. Stir well to ensure the chia seeds are evenly distributed.
2. Let the mixture sit for 5 minutes, then stir again to break up any clumps. Cover the bowl and refrigerate for at least 4 hours or overnight until the pudding is set and thickened.
3. Just before serving, dice the ripe mango. You can blend half of the mango to create a smooth mango puree if desired, leaving the other half diced for texture.
4. Layer the chia pudding and diced mango (or mango puree) in serving glasses or bowls. Start with a layer of chia pudding, followed by a layer of mango, and repeat.
5. Sprinkle unsweetened shredded coconut on top, and add any additional toppings like toasted coconut flakes or chopped nuts.
6. Serve the Mango & Coconut Chia Pudding chilled. It's perfect as a refreshing breakfast, snack, or dessert.

Apple Cinnamon Overnight Oats

Servings: 2 **Prep. time:** 5 min **Setting time:** 4 hours or overnight

Nutritional Information (Per Serving):

Calories: 240 kcal, Protein: 6g, Carbohydrates: 40g, Fats: 6g, Fiber: 8g, Cholesterol: 0mg, Sodium: 80mg, Potassium: 320mg

Ingredients

- 1 cup rolled oats
- 1 cup unsweetened almond milk (or any plant-based milk)
- 1 apple, grated or finely chopped
- 1 tablespoon chia seeds
- 1 tablespoon maple syrup (optional, for sweetness)
- 1 teaspoon ground cinnamon
- 1/2 teaspoon vanilla extract
- 1/4 teaspoon ground nutmeg (optional)
- Pinch of salt

Directions:

1. In a medium-sized bowl/jar, combine the almond milk, rolled oats, grated apple, chia seeds, maple syrup, ground cinnamon, vanilla extract, nutmeg (if using), and a pinch of salt.
2. Mix well to ensure all ingredients are evenly mixed.
3. Cover the bowl/jar with a lid or plastic wrap and place it in the refrigerator for at least 4 hours (preferably overnight) allowing the oats to soak and absorb the liquid.
4. In the morning, give the oats a good stir. If the oats mixture is too thick, add almond milk to reach your desired consistency.
5. Divide the oats into two servings and add your favorite toppings such as chopped nuts, raisins, sliced apple or an extra sprinkle of cinnamon.

Cinnamon Raisin Overnight Oats

Servings: 2   **Prep. time:** 5 min   **Setting time:** 4 hours or overnight

Nutritional Information (Per Serving):

Calories: 240 kcal, Protein: 6g, Carbohydrates: 43g, Fats: 6g, Fiber: 7g, Cholesterol: 0mg, Sodium: 80mg, Potassium: 290mg

Ingredients

- 1 cup rolled oats
- 1 cup unsweetened almond milk (or any plant-based milk)
- 2 tablespoons raisins
- 1 tablespoon chia seeds
- 1 tablespoon maple syrup (optional, for sweetness)
- 1 teaspoon ground cinnamon
- 1/2 teaspoon vanilla extract
- Pinch of salt

Directions:

1. In a medium-sized bowl or jar, mix the rolled oats, almond milk, raisins, chia seeds, vanilla extract, maple syrup, ground cinnamon, and a pinch of salt.
2. Mix the ingredients well.
3. Cover the bowl/jar with a lid or plastic wrap and place in the refrigerator for at least 4 hours, (preferably overnight) to allow the flavors to meld and the oats to soak.
4. In the morning, stir the oats again. If the mixture is too thick, thin it out by adding a bit more almond milk to achieve the desired consistency.
5. Divide the oats into two servings and top with additional raisins, chopped nuts, sliced banana, or an extra sprinkle of cinnamon as desired.

Chocolate Almond Overnight Oats

Servings: 2   **Prep. time:** 5 min   **Setting time:** 4 hours or overnight

Nutritional Information (Per Serving):

Calories: 300 kcal, Protein: 8g, Carbohydrates: 38g, Fats: 14g, Fiber: 8g, Cholesterol: 0mg, Sodium: 80mg, Potassium: 380mg

Ingredients

- 1 cup rolled oats
- 1 cup unsweetened almond milk (or any plant-based milk)
- 2 tablespoons almond butter
- 1 tablespoon chia seeds
- 1 tablespoon cocoa powder (unsweetened)
- 1 tablespoon maple syrup (optional, for sweetness)
- 1/2 teaspoon vanilla extract
- Pinch of salt
- Sliced almonds
- Dark chocolate shavings or chips
- Sliced banana or berries
- Additional almond butter drizzle

Directions:

1. In a medium-sized bowl/jar, combine almond milk, the rolled oats, cocoa powder, almond butter, chia seeds, maple syrup, vanilla extract, and a pinch of salt.
2. Stir thoroughly to ensure the almond butter and cocoa powder are well incorporated.
3. Seal the bowl/jar with a lid or plastic wrap and place it in the refrigerator for at least 4 hours (preferably overnight) to let the oats soak and take in the flavors.
4. In the morning, give the oats a good stir. If the mixture is too thick, add almond milk to reach your desired consistency.
5. Divide the oats into two servings and top with sliced almonds, dark chocolate shavings, sliced banana, or any additional toppings of your choice.

Peanut Butter & Banana Oatmeal

 Servings: 2   **Prep. time:** 5 min   **Total time:** 15 min

Nutritional Information (Per Serving):

Calories: 320 kcal, Protein: 9g, Carbohydrates: 45g, Fats: 12g, Fiber: 7g, Cholesterol: 0mg, Sodium: 150mg, Potassium: 550mg

Ingredients

- 1 cup rolled oats
- 2 cups unsweetened almond milk (or any plant-based milk)
- 1 ripe banana, sliced
- 2 tablespoons natural peanut butter
- 1 tablespoon maple syrup (optional, for sweetness)
- 1/2 teaspoon ground cinnamon
- 1/2 teaspoon vanilla extract
- Pinch of salt

Directions:

1. Mix the rolled oats and almond milk in a medium saucepan. Heat over medium until it reaches a boil, then reduce to a simmer.
2. Stir in the sliced banana, allowing it to soften and naturally sweeten the oats. Cook for 5-7 minutes, stir occasionally, until the oats are creamy and thickened.
3. Stir in the peanut butter, maple syrup (if using), ground cinnamon, vanilla extract, and a pinch of salt. Mix well until the peanut butter is fully incorporated and the oatmeal is smooth.
4. Divide the oatmeal between two bowls. Top with additional banana slices, chopped nuts, chia seeds, or a drizzle of peanut butter as desired.

Blueberry Oat Pancakes (using whole oats)

 Servings: 4 (8 pancakes) **Prep. time:** 10 min   **Total time:** 25 min

Nutritional Information (Per Serving):

Calories: 210 kcal, Protein: 5g, Carbohydrates: 38g, Fats: 5g, Fiber: 5g, Cholesterol: 0mg, Sodium: 100mg, Potassium: 290mg

Ingredients

- 1 1/2 cups rolled oats
- 1 cup unsweetened almond milk (or any plant-based milk)
- 1 ripe banana
- 1 tablespoon ground flaxseed (optional)
- 1 tablespoon maple syrup (optional, for sweetness)
- 1 teaspoon baking powder
- 1/2 teaspoon vanilla extract
- Pinch of salt
- 1/2 cup fresh or frozen blueberries
- Coconut oil or olive oil for cooking
- Fresh blueberries for toppings
- Maple syrup for toppings
- Chopped nuts (e.g., almonds, walnuts) for toppings

Directions:

1. In a blender, combine the rolled oats, almond milk, ripe banana, ground flaxseed (if using), vanilla extract, maple syrup, baking powder, and a pinch of salt.
2. Blend until the mixture is smooth and well-combined. Let the batter rest for 5 minutes to thicken.
3. Gently mix the blueberries into the batter using a spoon or spatula.
4. Preheat a non-stick skillet (griddle) over medium heat and lightly grease it with coconut oil or olive oil.
5. Pour 1/4 cup of batter onto the skillet for each pancake. Cook for 2-3 minutes, until bubbles form on the top, then flip and cook for another 2-3 minutes until they are golden brown.
6. Serve the pancakes warm with toppings of your choice, like fresh blueberries, maple syrup, or chopped nuts.

Apple & Walnut Oatmeal

Servings: 2   **Prep. time:** 5 min   **Total time:** 15 min

Nutritional Information (Per Serving):

Calories: 300 kcal, Protein: 7g, Carbohydrates: 45g, Fats: 11g, Fiber: 7g, Cholesterol: 0mg, Sodium: 50mg, Potassium: 300mg

Ingredients

- 1 cup rolled oats
- 2 cups water or unsweetened almond milk
- 1 apple, diced (preferably a sweet variety like Honeycrisp or Fuji)
- 1/4 cup chopped walnuts
- 1 tablespoon maple syrup (optional, for sweetness)
- 1 teaspoon ground cinnamon
- 1/4 teaspoon ground nutmeg (optional)
- Pinch of salt
- 1 teaspoon vanilla extract
- Additional chopped walnuts, Sliced apple, Drizzle of maple syrup for toppings (optional)

Directions:

1. In a medium saucepan, bring the water or almond milk to a gentle boil. Add the rolled oats, diced apple, cinnamon, nutmeg (if using), and a pinch of salt.
2. Lower the heat to low and let it simmer for 5-7 minutes, stirring occasionally, until the oats are cooked and the apple pieces are soft.
3. Once the oats are cooked, stir in the chopped walnuts, maple syrup, and vanilla extract. Mix well to evenly distribute the flavors.
4. Divide the oatmeal into two bowls. Top with additional chopped walnuts, sliced apple, and a drizzle of maple syrup if desired.

Raw Apple Cinnamon "Cereal"

Servings: 2   **Prep. time:** 10 min   **Total time:** 10 min

Nutritional Information (Per Serving):

Calories: 320 kcal, Protein: 7g, Carbohydrates: 36g, Fats: 19g, Fiber: 9g, Cholesterol: 0mg, Sodium: 5mg, Potassium: 350mg

Ingredients

- 2 medium apples, diced (preferably a sweet variety like Honeycrisp or Gala)
- 1/4 cup raw walnuts, chopped
- 1/4 cup raw almonds, chopped
- 2 tablespoons raw pumpkin seeds
- 2 tablespoons raw sunflower seeds
- 1 tablespoon chia seeds
- 1 teaspoon ground cinnamon
- 1 tablespoon unsweetened shredded coconut (optional)
- 1/2 cup unsweetened almond milk (or any plant-based milk)
- 1 teaspoon maple syrup (optional, for sweetness)

Directions:

1. In a large bowl, combine the diced apples, chopped walnuts, chopped almonds, pumpkin seeds, sunflower seeds, chia seeds, ground cinnamon, and shredded coconut (if using). Mix well to evenly distribute the ingredients.
2. Pour the almond milk over the apple mixture. Stir gently to combine. If you prefer a sweeter cereal, add the maple syrup and mix it in.
3. Divide the cereal into two bowls. Top with additional nuts, seeds, fresh berries, or a drizzle of almond butter if desired.

Banana Almond Smoothie Bowl

 Servings: 2   **Prep. time:** 10 min   **Total time:** 20 min

Nutritional Information (Per Serving):
Calories: 410 kcal, Protein: 10g, Carbohydrates: 50g, Fats: 21g, Fiber: 10g, Cholesterol: 0mg, Sodium: 60mg, Potassium: 720mg

Ingredients

- 2 large ripe bananas, peeled and frozen
- 1/4 cup raw almonds (soaked overnight for easier blending)
- 1/2 cup unsweetened almond milk (or any plant-based milk)
- 1 tablespoon almond butter
- 1 tablespoon chia seeds
- 1 tablespoon flaxseed meal
- 1/2 teaspoon vanilla extract
- 1/4 teaspoon ground cinnamon
- 1/2 tablespoon maple syrup (optional, for extra sweetness)

Directions:

1. The night before, soak 1/4 cup of raw almonds in water. This step is required to help soften almonds, making them easier to blend and more digestible. Drain and rinse the almonds before using them in the recipe.
2. Combine the soaked almonds, frozen bananas, almond milk, almond butter, chia seeds, flaxseed meal, vanilla extract, ground cinnamon, and maple syrup (if using) in a high-speed blender.
3. Blend on high until smooth and creamy, stopping to scrape down the sides if necessary. The consistency should be thick enough to eat with a spoon. If the mixture is too thick, add a little more almond milk until the desired consistency is reached.
4. Divide the smoothie base between two bowls.
5. Arrange the toppings on top of the smoothie base in an appealing manner.
6. Serve the smoothie bowls immediately while cold and fresh.

Berry Green Smoothie

 Servings: 2   **Prep. time:** 5 min   **Total time:** 5 min

Nutritional Information (Per Serving):
Calories: 250 kcal, Protein: 6g, Carbohydrates: 35g, Fats: 10g, Fiber: 8g, Cholesterol: 0mg, Sodium: 80mg, Potassium: 700mg

Ingredients

- 1 cup spinach leaves (fresh or frozen)
- 1/2 cup kale leaves (fresh or frozen, stems removed)
- 1 cup mixed berries (fresh or frozen; e.g., strawberries, blueberries, raspberries)
- 1 ripe banana
- 1 tablespoon chia seeds
- 1 tablespoon almond butter
- 1 cup unsweetened almond milk (or any plant-based milk)
- 1 teaspoon maple syrup (optional, for sweetness)
- Ice cubes (optional, for a chilled smoothie)

Directions:

1. In a blender, combine the spinach, kale, mixed berries, banana, chia seeds, almond butter, and almond milk.
2. Blend on high until smooth. If desired, add ice cubes and blend again until the smoothie is chilled and frothy.
3. Taste the smoothie. If you prefer it sweeter, add the maple syrup and blend briefly to incorporate.
4. Pour the smoothie into two glasses. Top with additional fresh berries, a sprinkle of chia seeds, sliced banana, or a drizzle of almond butter if desired

Strawberry Banana Smoothie

Servings: 2   **Prep. time:** 5 min   **Total time:** 5 min

Nutritional Information (Per Serving):

Calories: 210 kcal, Protein: 5g, Carbohydrates: 30g, Fats: 9g, Fiber: 6g, Cholesterol: 0mg, Sodium: 80mg, Potassium: 500mg

Ingredients

- 1 cup fresh or frozen strawberries, hulled
- 1 ripe banana
- 1 cup unsweetened almond milk (or any plant-based milk)
- 1 tablespoon flaxseeds (optional, for added omega-3s)
- 1 tablespoon almond butter (optional, for creaminess and protein)
- 1 teaspoon maple syrup (optional, for additional sweetness)
- Ice cubes (optional, for a chilled smoothie)
- Toppings (Optional): Fresh strawberry slices, Banana slices, A drizzle of almond butter

Directions:

1. If using fresh strawberries, hull and slice them. Peel the banana.
2. In a blender, combine the strawberries, banana, almond milk, flaxseeds, almond butter, and maple syrup.
3. Blend on high until smooth. For a thicker, colder smoothie, add ice cubes and blend again until frothy.
4. Pour the smoothie into two glasses. Top with fresh strawberry slices, banana slices, or a drizzle of almond butter if desired

Pumpkin Spice Smoothie

Servings: 2   **Prep. time:** 5 min   **Total time:** 5 min

Nutritional Information (Per Serving):

Calories: 220 kcal, Protein: 4g, Carbohydrates: 35g, Fats: 8g, Fiber: 6g, Cholesterol: 0mg, Sodium: 70mg, Potassium: 550mg

Ingredients

- 1 cup canned pumpkin puree (unsweetened)
- 1 ripe banana
- 1 cup unsweetened almond milk (or any plant-based milk)
- 1 tablespoon maple syrup (optional, for sweetness)
- 1/2 teaspoon pumpkin pie spice
- 1/4 teaspoon ground cinnamon
- 1 tablespoon chia seeds (optional, for added fiber and omega-3s)
- 1/2 teaspoon vanilla extract
- Ice cubes (optional, for a chilled smoothie)

Directions:

1. Peel and slice the ripe banana. Measure out the canned pumpkin puree and other ingredients.
2. In a blender, combine the pumpkin puree, banana, almond milk, maple syrup, pumpkin pie spice, ground cinnamon, chia seeds (if using), and vanilla extract.
3. Blend on high until smooth and creamy. If you prefer a colder, thicker smoothie, add ice cubes and blend again until frothy.
4. Pour the smoothie into two glasses. Optionally, top with a sprinkle of pumpkin pie spice, chopped nuts, or a drizzle of almond butter for extra flavor and texture.

Green Avocado Smoothie

Servings: 2

Prep. time: 5 min

Total time: 5 min

Nutritional Information (Per Serving):

Calories: 280 kcal, Protein: 4g, Carbohydrates: 32g, Fats: 15g, Fiber: 10g, Cholesterol: 0mg, Sodium: 50mg, Potassium: 750mg

Ingredients

- 1 ripe avocado
- 1 cup fresh spinach leaves
- 1 ripe banana
- 1 cup unsweetened almond milk (or any plant-based milk)
- 1 tablespoon chia seeds (optional, for added fiber and omega-3s)
- 1 tablespoon lemon juice (freshly squeezed)
- 1 teaspoon maple syrup or agave nectar (optional, for sweetness)
- Ice cubes (optional, for a chilled smoothie)

Directions:

1. Cut the ripe avocado in half, remove the pit, and scoop out the flesh.
2. Peel and slice the ripe banana. Measure out the spinach, almond milk, chia seeds (if using), and lemon juice.
3. In a blender, combine the spinach, avocado, banana, almond milk, chia seeds (if using), lemon juice, and maple syrup (if using).
4. Blend on high until smooth and creamy. Add ice cubes if you prefer a colder and thicker smoothie, and blend again until frothy.
5. Pour the smoothie into two glasses. Optionally, garnish with fresh spinach leaves, sliced avocado, or a sprinkle of chia seeds
6.
7. Nutrient Density: The avocado adds healthy fats and a creamy texture, while spinach contributes iron and vitamins. Chia seeds boost fiber and omega-3s.
8. Blending Technique: Ensure a thorough blend for a smooth, creamy consistency. Adding ice cubes makes the smoothie colder and thicker.

Pineapple Coconut Smoothie Bowl

Servings: 2

Prep. time: 10 min

Total time: 10 min

Nutritional Information (Per Serving):

Calories: 350 kcal, Protein: 5g, Carbohydrates: 45g, Fats: 17g, Fiber: 7g, Cholesterol: 0mg, Sodium: 80mg, Potassium: 650mg

Ingredients

- 1 cup frozen pineapple chunks
- 1 ripe banana, sliced
- 1/2 cup coconut milk (canned, full-fat or light)
- 1/4 cup unsweetened shredded coconut
- 1 tablespoon chia seeds
- 1 teaspoon vanilla extract
- 1 tablespoon maple syrup or agave nectar (optional, for sweetness)
- Toppings: fresh pineapple slices, sliced banana, a handful of granola, additional shredded coconut, fresh mint leaves (optional)

Directions:

1. Combine the frozen pineapple chunks, sliced banana, coconut milk, shredded coconut, chia seeds, vanilla extract, and maple syrup (if using) in a blender.
2. Blend on high until smooth and creamy. If the mixture is too thick, add more coconut milk or a splash of water or to achieve a desired consistency.
3. Pour the smoothie into two bowls. Smooth out the top with a spoon.
4. Place fresh pineapple slices, sliced banana, granola, additional shredded coconut, and fresh mint leaves (if using) on top of the smoothie base.
5. Enjoy immediately for the best flavor and texture.

Almond Butter & Cacao Nib Smoothie

 Servings: 2

 Prep. time: 5 min

 Total time: 5 min

Nutritional Information (Per Serving):

Calories: 290 kcal, Protein: 7g, Carbohydrates: 30g, Fats: 17g, Fiber: 8g, Cholesterol: 0mg, Sodium: 90mg, Potassium: 600mg

Ingredients

- 1 ripe banana, sliced
- 1 cup unsweetened almond milk (or any plant-based milk)
- 2 tablespoons almond butter
- 1 tablespoon raw cacao nibs
- 1 tablespoon chia seeds (optional, for added fiber and omega-3s)
- 1 tablespoon maple syrup or agave nectar (optional, for sweetness)
- 1/2 teaspoon vanilla extract
- Ice cubes (optional, for a chilled smoothie)

Directions:

1. Slice the banana and measure out the almond milk, almond butter, cacao nibs, chia seeds (if using), and vanilla extract.
2. In a blender, combine the banana, almond milk, almond butter, cacao nibs, chia seeds (if using), vanilla extract, and maple syrup (if using).
3. Blend on high until smooth and creamy. For a thicker and colder smoothie, add ice cubes and blend again until frothy.
4. Pour the smoothie into two glasses. Optionally, top with additional cacao nibs, sliced banana, a drizzle of almond butter, or a sprinkle of granola.

Nutrient Boost: Chia seeds and cacao nibs add fiber, omega-3s, and antioxidants. Almond butter provides healthy fats and protein.
Blending Tip: Blend until completely smooth to ensure a creamy texture. Adjust the thickness by adding more or less liquid as needed.

Spinach & Mushroom Tofu Scramble

  Servings: 2

Prep. time: 10 min

 Total time: 20 min

Nutritional Information (Per Serving):

Calories: 220 kcal, Protein: 16g, Carbohydrates: 10g, Fats: 14, Fiber: 4g, Cholesterol: 0mg, Sodium: 280mg, Potassium: 630mg

Ingredients

- 1 block (14 oz) firm tofu, drained and pressed
- 1 tablespoon extra virgin olive oil (or avocado oil)
- 1/2 cup onion, finely chopped
- 2 cloves garlic, minced
- 1 cup mushrooms, sliced (cremini or button mushrooms)
- 2 cups fresh spinach, chopped
- 1/2 teaspoon turmeric powder (for color and added nutrition)
- 1/2 teaspoon ground cumin
- 1/2 teaspoon smoked paprika
- 1 tablespoon nutritional yeast (optional, for a cheesy flavor)
- Salt and pepper to taste
- 1/4 teaspoon black salt (Kala Namak, optional for an "eggy" flavor)

Directions:

1. Begin by draining and pressing the tofu to remove excess water. Wrap it in a clean kitchen towel and place a heavy object on top for 10 minutes.
2. After pressing, crumble the tofu into small pieces with your hands or a fork, aiming for a scrambled egg-like texture.
3. Heat olive oil in a large non-stick skillet over medium heat. Add chopped onions and sauté for 2-3 minutes until they soften.
4. Add minced garlic and cook for another minute.
5. Add sliced mushrooms and sauté for about 5 minutes, stirring occasionally, until they brown and release their moisture.
6. Move the vegetables to one side of the skillet and add the crumbled tofu to the other.
7. Sprinkle the tofu with turmeric, ground cumin, and smoked paprika, stirring well to coat evenly. Cook for 3-4 minutes.
8. Add chopped spinach and cook for 1-2 minutes until wilted. Season with pepper, salt, and black salt (if using).
9. Mix everything together until well combined and heated through.
10. Divide the tofu scramble onto two plates and serve hot.

Chickpea Omelet with Spinach

 Servings: 2   **Prep. time:** 10 min   **Total time:** 20 min

Nutritional Information (Per Serving):

Calories: 270 kcal, Protein: 10g, Carbohydrates: 32g, Fats: 10g, Fiber: 7g, Cholesterol: 0mg, Sodium: 400mg, Potassium: 700mg

Ingredients

For the Chickpea Flour Batter:
- 1 cup chickpea flour (also known as besan or garbanzo bean flour)
- 1 1/4 cups water
- 1 tablespoon nutritional yeast (optional, for a cheesy flavor)
- 1/2 teaspoon turmeric powder
- 1/2 teaspoon ground cumin
- 1/2 teaspoon paprika
- 1/4 teaspoon garlic powder
- 1/4 teaspoon onion powder
- Salt and black pepper to taste

For the Filling:
- 1 cup fresh spinach leaves, chopped
- 1/2 cup diced tomatoes
- 1/4 cup finely chopped onions
- 1/4 cup chopped bell pepper (any color)
- 1 tablespoon olive oil (for cooking)
- Optional: 1/4 cup sliced black olives or chopped mushrooms

Directions:

1. In a mixing bowl, whisk together the chickpea flour, paprika, water, nutritional yeast (if using), turmeric, cumin, garlic powder, salt, onion powder, and black pepper until smooth. Let the batter rest for about 5 minutes to thicken slightly.
2. Warm 1 tablespoon of olive oil in a non-stick skillet over medium heat. Sauté the onions and bell pepper for 3-4 minutes until they soften. Add the tomatoes and spinach, and cook for 2 minutes until the spinach wilts.
3. If using, add olives or mushrooms and cook for another 1-2 minutes. Season with a pinch of salt and pepper.
4. In the same skillet, pour half of the chickpea flour batter and spread it evenly. Cook over medium heat for about 3-4 minutes, or until the edges start to firm up and bubbles appear on the surface.
5. Carefully flip the omelet using a spatula and cook for another 2-3 minutes until golden brown and cooked through.
6. Transfer to a plate and repeat with the remaining batter.
7. Place the cooked omelets on plates. Spoon the cooked vegetable filling onto one half of each omelet, fold over, and serve.

Warm Spiced Apples with Almonds & Raisins

 Servings: 2   **Prep. time:** 10 min   **Total time:** 20 min

Nutritional Information (Per Serving):

Calories: 230 kcal, Protein: 4g, Carbohydrates: 34g, Fats: 10g, Fiber: 5g, Cholesterol: 0mg, Sodium: 20mg, Potassium: 300mg

Ingredients

- 2 large apples (such as Gala or Fuji), peeled, cored, and sliced
- 1/4 cup raisins
- 1/4 cup chopped almonds
- 1 tablespoon coconut oil or olive oil
- 1 teaspoon ground cinnamon
- 1/2 teaspoon ground nutmeg
- 1 tablespoon pure maple syrup or agave nectar (optional, for extra sweetness)
- 1/2 teaspoon vanilla extract (optional)
- 1/4 cup water or apple juice (for steaming)
- Pinch of sea salt

Directions:

1. Heat the coconut oil (or olive oil) over medium heat in a medium skillet.
2. Add the sliced apples and cook for about 3-4 minutes until they start to soften, stirring occasionally.
3. Sprinkle the ground cinnamon, nutmeg, and a pinch of sea salt over the apples.
4. Mix well to coat the apples with the spices.
5. If using, add the maple syrup or agave nectar and vanilla extract. Stir to combine.
6. Add the raisins and chopped almonds to the skillet.
7. Pour in the water or apple juice to help create a bit of steam and enhance the flavor.
8. Continue to cook for an additional 3-4 minutes, or until the apples are tender and the raisins are plump. Stir occasionally.
9. Divide the warm spiced apples with almonds and raisins between two bowls.
10. Serve immediately as a warm breakfast, snack, or dessert.

Cauliflower & Turmeric Breakfast Rice

 Servings: 2

 Prep. time: 10 min

 Total time: 25 min

Nutritional Information (Per Serving):

Calories: 180 kcal, Protein: 4g, Carbohydrates: 18g, Fats: 10g, Fiber: 6g, Cholesterol: 0mg, Sodium: 400mg, Potassium: 600mg

Ingredients

- 1 medium cauliflower, riced (about 4 cups)
- 1 tablespoon olive oil
- 1/2 cup finely chopped onions
- 2 cloves garlic, minced
- 1/2 teaspoon ground turmeric
- 1/2 teaspoon ground cumin
- 1/4 teaspoon paprika
- 1/4 teaspoon black pepper
- 1/2 teaspoon sea salt (adjust to taste)
- 1/4 cup chopped fresh parsley or cilantro (optional, for garnish)
- 1/4 cup diced bell pepper (any color) (optional, for added color and nutrients)
- Juice of 1/2 lemon (optional, for a fresh tangy flavor)

Directions:

1. Remove the leaves from the cauliflower, stem them and cut it into florets. Rice the cauliflower by processing until it resembles the size of grains of rice using a food processor or box grater. Set aside.
2. In a large non-stick skillet, heat the olive oil over medium heat.
3. Add the finely chopped onions and cook for about 3-4 minutes until they become translucent and soft.
4. Add the garlic (minced) and cook for another 1 minute until fragrant. Add the riced cauliflower to the skillet. Mix well to combine with the onions and garlic.
5. Season with ground turmeric, cumin, paprika, black pepper, and sea salt. Stir to evenly coat the cauliflower with the spices.
6. Cook the mixture over medium heat, stir occasionally, for about 8-10 minutes until the cauliflower is tender and has a rice-like texture. If using diced bell pepper, add it during the last 5 minutes of cooking.
7. Stir in the lemon juice, if desired, for a fresh tangy flavor.
8. Garnish with cilantro or chopped parsley if desired.
9. Serve hot as a light meal or nutritious breakfast.

Quick Quinoa Porridge with Almond Butter

 Servings: 2

 Prep. time: 5 min

 Total time: 15 min

Nutritional Information (Per Serving):

Calories: 290 kcal, Protein: 8g, Carbohydrates: 35g, Fats: 14g, Fiber: 6g, Cholesterol: 0mg, Sodium: 90mg, Potassium: 450mg

Ingredients

- 1 cup cooked quinoa (preferably pre-cooked or cooked in advance; if starting from raw, cook 1/2 cup quinoa in 1 cup water for about 15 minutes)
- 1 cup unsweetened almond milk (or any plant-based milk)
- 2 tablespoons almond butter
- 1 tablespoon maple syrup or agave nectar (optional, for sweetness)
- 1/2 teaspoon ground cinnamon
- 1/4 teaspoon vanilla extract
- Pinch of salt
- Fresh fruit or nuts for topping (optional, e.g., sliced banana, berries, or chopped almonds)

Directions:

1. If not using pre-cooked quinoa, rinse 1/2 cup of raw quinoa under cold water. In a saucepan, combine with 1 cup water. Heat over medium until it reaches a boil, then lower the heat and let it simmer for approximately 15 minutes, or until quinoa is cooked and water is absorbed. Fluff with a fork.
2. Combine the almond milk, cooked quinoa, almond butter, maple syrup (if using), ground cinnamon, vanilla extract, and a pinch of salt in a medium saucepan, .
3. Heat over medium, stirring often until the mixture is heated through and has a creamy consistency, about 5-7 minutes.
4. Divide the porridge between two bowls. Top with nuts or fresh fruits if desired.
   Nutrient Optimization: Cooking quinoa with almond milk adds creaminess and a boost of calcium and vitamins. Almond butter contributes healthy fats and protein.
   Consistency: Adjust the amount of almond milk to achieve your desired porridge thickness. If too thick, add more almond milk and reheat briefly.

Sweet Potato & Black Bean Breakfast Tacos (Lettuce Wraps)

Servings: 4   **Prep. time:** 10 min   **Total time:** 30 min

Nutritional Information (Per Serving):
Calories: 220 kcal, Protein: 6g, Carbohydrates: 30g, Fats: 9g, Fiber: 10g, Cholesterol: 0mg, Sodium: 220mg, Potassium: 750mg

Ingredients

- 1 large sweet potato, peeled and diced (about 2 cups)
- 1 tablespoon olive oil
- 1/2 teaspoon smoked paprika
- 1/2 teaspoon ground cumin
- 1/2 teaspoon garlic powder
- Salt and pepper to taste
- 1 can (15 oz) black beans, drained and rinsed
- 1/4 cup red onion, finely chopped
- 1/4 cup fresh cilantro, chopped
- 1 tablespoon lime juice
- 8 large lettuce leaves (e.g., romaine or butter lettuce)
- 1 avocado, sliced
- Hot sauce or salsa (optional)

Directions:

1. Set the oven to preheat at 400°F (200°C).
2. In a bowl, mix the sweet potato (diced) with olive oil, smoked paprika, cumin, garlic powder, salt, and pepper.
3. APlace the sweet potatoes in a single layer on a baking sheet and roast for 20 minutes, stir halfway through, until they are tender and slightly crispy.
4. While the sweet potatoes are roasting, in a medium bowl, combine the black beans, red onion, cilantro, lime juice, salt, and pepper. Mix well and set aside.
5. Lay out the lettuce leaves on a serving platter.
6. Spoon the roasted sweet potatoes and black bean mixture onto each lettuce leaf.
7. Top with avocado slices and a drizzle of hot sauce or salsa if desired.
8. Serve the tacos immediately while the sweet potatoes are warm

Quick Peanut Butter Banana Sweet Potato Toast

Servings: 2   **Prep. time:** 10 min   **Total time:** 10 min

Nutritional Information (Per Serving):
Calories: 290 kcal, Protein: 6g, Carbohydrates: 42g, Fats: 11g, Fiber: 7g, Cholesterol: 0mg, Sodium: 85mg, Potassium: 710mg

Ingredients

- 1 large sweet potato (approximately 8-10 inches long)
- 2 tablespoons natural peanut butter (no added sugar or oil)
- 1 medium banana, sliced
- 1 teaspoon chia seeds (optional, for extra nutrition)
- 1/2 teaspoon cinnamon
- 1 teaspoon maple syrup or agave nectar (optional, for sweetness)

Directions:

1. Wash and dry the sweet potato thoroughly.
2. Cut the sweet potato lengthwise into 1/4-inch thick slices to create a "toast" base.
3. Toaster Method: Place the sweet potato slices in a toaster and toast on high for 2-3 cycles, until they become soft but remain firm enough to hold toppings. (Toasting time may vary based on your toaster.)
4. Oven Method: Preheat the oven to 400°F (200°C). Arrange the slices on a baking sheet and bake for 10 minutes, flipping them halfway through.
5. As the sweet potato slices are roasting or baking, cut the banana into thin rounds.
6. If using chia seeds, sprinkle them over the peanut butter for added texture and nutrition.
7. Once the sweet potato slices are cooked, spread 1 tablespoon of peanut butter over each slice.
8. Place the banana slices evenly on top of the peanut butter.
9. Sprinkle each toast with a pinch of cinnamon and drizzle with maple syrup or agave nectar if desired.
10. Serve the sweet potato toasts immediately, while warm.

Avocado & Tomato Stuffed Bell Peppers

Servings: 4

Prep. time: 15 min

Total time: 15 min

Nutritional Information (Per Serving):

Calories: 220 kcal, Protein: 4g, Carbohydrates: 16g, Fats: 17g, Fiber: 8g, Cholesterol: 0mg, Sodium: 160mg, Potassium: 770mg

Ingredients

- 4 large bell peppers (any color)
- 2 ripe avocados, diced
- 1 cup cherry tomatoes, quartered
- 1/4 cup red onion, finely chopped
- 1/4 cup fresh cilantro, chopped
- 1 lime, juice
- 1 tablespoon extra virgin olive oil
- 1/4 teaspoon ground cumin
- 1/4 teaspoon sea salt
- 1/4 teaspoon ground black pepper
- 1 tablespoon nutritional yeast (optional for a cheesy flavor)
- 1/4 cup sunflower seeds or pumpkin seeds (optional for added crunch)

Directions:

1. Wash the bell peppers thoroughly.
2. Prepare the bell peppers for stuffing by slicing off the tops, and importantly, removing the seeds and membranes inside. Set the bell peppers aside.
3. Combine the diced avocados, finely chopped red onion, quartered cherry tomatoes, and fresh cilantro in a large mixing bowl.
4. Drizzle the lime juice and olive oil over the mixture.
5. Sprinkle the ground cumin, sea salt, black pepper, and nutritional yeast (if using) over the filling.
6. When mixing, be gentle to maintain the texture of the avocados, ensuring all the ingredients are well combined.
7. Spoon the avocado and tomato mixture into each bell pepper, filling them to the top.
8. If using, sprinkle sunflower or pumpkin seeds on top for added crunch and texture.
9. Serve the stuffed bell peppers immediately, or chill them in the refrigerator for a relaxed and refreshing dish.

Sweet Potato & Spinach Breakfast Bowl

Servings: 2

Prep. time: 10 min

Total time: 30 min

Nutritional Information (Per Serving):

Calories: 250 kcal, Protein: 5g, Carbohydrates: 40g, Fats: 9g, Fiber: 8g, Cholesterol: 0mg, Sodium: 270mg, Potassium: 810mg

Ingredients

- 2 medium sweet potatoes, peeled and diced (about 3 cups)
- 2 cups fresh spinach, chopped
- 1/2 cup cooked quinoa (optional for added protein and texture)
- 1/4 cup red onion, finely chopped
- 1 tablespoon extra virgin olive oil
- 1/4 teaspoon ground turmeric
- 1/4 teaspoon smoked paprika
- 1/4 teaspoon garlic powder
- 1/4 teaspoon sea salt
- 1/4 teaspoon ground black pepper
- 1 tablespoon fresh lemon juice
- 1 tablespoon tahini (optional for drizzling)
- 1 tablespoon chopped fresh parsley or cilantro (optional for garnish)
- 1/4 avocado, sliced (optional for topping)

Directions:

1. Preheat your oven to 400°F (200°C).
2. Place sweet potatoes (diced) on a baking sheet, drizzle with olive oil, and sprinkle with turmeric, garlic powder, smoked paprika, black pepper, and sea salt.
3. Toss the sweet potatoes until evenly coated, then place them in a single layer on the baking sheet.
4. Roast in the oven for 20 minutes or until tender and lightly browned, turning once halfway through.
5. While the sweet potatoes are roasting, heat a small amount of water in a large skillet over medium heat.
6. Add the chopped red onion and sauté until softened, about 2-3 minutes.
7. Add the spinach (chopped) and cook until wilted, about 2-3 minutes.
8. Season with a pinch of salt and pepper, and remove from heat.
9. Divide the cooked quinoa (if using) between two bowls.
10. Top each bowl with the roasted sweet potatoes and sautéed spinach.
11. Drizzle with fresh lemon juice and tahini (if using) for added flavor.
12. Garnish with chopped parsley or cilantro and avocado slices if desired.

Kale & Sweet Potato Breakfast Skillet

Servings: 2   **Prep. time:** 10 min   **Total time:** 30 min

Nutritional Information (Per Serving):

Calories: 250 kcal, Protein: 4g, Carbohydrates: 32g, Fats: 12g, Fiber: 8g, Cholesterol: 0mg, Sodium: 280mg, Potassium: 800mg

Ingredients

- 1 large sweet potato, peeled and diced (about 2 cups)
- 2 cups kale, chopped and tough stems removed
- 1/2 red bell pepper, diced
- 1/4 red onion, finely chopped
- 1 tablespoon extra virgin olive oil
- 1/2 teaspoon ground cumin
- 1/4 teaspoon smoked paprika
- 1/4 teaspoon garlic powder
- 1/4 teaspoon sea salt
- 1/4 teaspoon ground black pepper
- 1/2 avocado, sliced (optional for topping)
- 1 tablespoon fresh lemon juice
- 1 tablespoon nutritional yeast (optional for a cheesy flavor)
- 1 tablespoon chopped fresh parsley or cilantro (optional for garnish)

Directions:

1. Heat 1 tablespoon of olive oil in a large skillet over medium heat.
2. Add sweet potatoes (diced) to the skillet and sauté for about 10 minutes, stirring occasionally, until they begin to soften and turn golden brown.
3. Season with ground cumin, smoked paprika, garlic powder, sea salt, and black pepper. Stir to coat the sweet potatoes evenly, releasing a tantalizing aroma.
4. Add red onion (chopped) and bell pepper to the skillet. Cook for another 5 minutes until the onion becomes translucent and the bell pepper softens.
5. Stir in the kale (chopped) and cook for an additional 3-5 minutes, until the kale wilts and everything is heated through.
6. Remove the skillet from heat and drizzle with fresh lemon juice for a bright flavor.
7. If using, sprinkle the nutritional yeast over the dish for a cheesy, savory touch.
8. Divide the skillet mixture between two plates or bowls.
9. Top with avocado slices and garnish with chopped parsley or cilantro if desired.

Raw Veggie & Nut Breakfast Salad

Servings: 2   **Prep. time:** 10 min   **Setting time:** none

Nutritional Information (Per Serving):

Calories: 290 kcal, Protein: 7g, Carbohydrates: 23g, Fats: 21g, Fiber: 7g, Cholesterol: 0mg, Sodium: 180mg, Potassium: 800mg

Ingredients

- 1 cup shredded raw carrots (about 2 medium carrots)
- 1 cup shredded raw beetroot (about 1 medium beetroot)
- 1 cup cherry tomatoes, halved
- 1 cup thinly sliced cucumber
- 1/2 cup thinly sliced red bell pepper
- 1/2 cup raw almonds, roughly chopped
- 1/4 cup pumpkin seeds
- 1/4 cup fresh parsley or cilantro, chopped

For the Dressing:

- 2 tablespoons extra-virgin olive oil
- 1 tablespoon apple cider vinegar
- 1 teaspoon Dijon mustard
- 1 teaspoon maple syrup or agave nectar (optional, for sweetness)
- 1 clove garlic, minced

Directions:

1. Peel and shred the raw carrots and beetroot using a grater or food processor. Place them in a large bowl.
2. Cut the cherry tomatoes in half and place them in the bowl.
3. Thinly slice the cucumber and red bell pepper and add them to the same bowl.
4. Gently toss the vegetables to mix them together.
5. Roughly chop the raw almonds and add them, along with the pumpkin seeds, to the bowl.
6. In a small bowl or jar, whisk together olive oil, apple cider vinegar, Dijon mustard, maple syrup (if using), minced garlic, salt, and pepper until fully blended.
7. Drizzle the dressing over the vegetable and nut mixture.
8. Mix everything thoroughly to ensure the salad is evenly coated with the dressing.
9. Sprinkle chopped parsley or cilantro on top and give the salad one last toss.
10. Divide the salad evenly between two serving bowls.
11. Serve immediately, or refrigerate for up to an hour to let the flavors develop.

Zucchini & Carrot Hash Browns

Servings: 4   **Prep. time:** 15 min   **Total time:** 30 min

Nutritional Information (Per Serving):

Calories: 130 kcal, Protein: 3g, Carbohydrates: 11g, Fats: 8g, Fiber: 3g, Cholesterol: 0mg, Sodium: 250mg, Potassium: 370mg

Ingredients

- 2 medium zucchinis, grated (about 2 cups)
- 2 medium carrots, grated (about 1 cup)
- 1 small onion, finely chopped
- 1/4 cup chickpea flour (or any gluten-free flour)
- 1/4 cup nutritional yeast (optional for a cheesy flavor)
- 1/4 teaspoon garlic powder
- 1/4 teaspoon onion powder
- 1/4 teaspoon ground black pepper
- 1/2 teaspoon salt
- 2 tablespoons olive oil or avocado oil (for frying)

Directions:

1. Grate zucchinis and carrots, then squeeze out excess moisture from the zucchini using a clean towel.
2. Combine the grated zucchini, grated carrots, and chopped onion in a large mixing bowl.
3. Combine with chopped onion in a bowl. Add chickpea flour, nutritional yeast (optional), and spices, mixing until the mixture holds together.
4. Heat 1 tablespoon of oil in a large non-stick skillet over medium heat.
5. Take a small handful of the mixture (about 1/4 cup) and shape it into a patty. Repeat with the remaining mixture.
6. Place the patties in the skillet, pressing down gently with a spatula.
7. Cook the hash browns for 3-4 minutes on each side, or until golden brown and crispy. Add more oil to the skillet as needed for subsequent batches.
8. After cooking, place the hash browns on a paper towel-lined plate to absorb any excess oil.
9. Serve the hash browns hot, topped with fresh herbs, a squeeze of lemon juice, or your favorite plant-based sauce.

Mushroom & Spinach Quesadilla (Using Collard Greens as Wraps)

Servings: 2   **Prep. time:** 10 min   **Total time:** 25 min

Nutritional Information (Per Serving):

Calories: 180 kcal, Protein: 6g, Carbohydrates: 16g, Fats: 11g, Fiber: 7g, Cholesterol: 0mg, Sodium: 120mg, Potassium: 740mg

Ingredients

- 4 large collard green leaves, stems removed
- 1 tablespoon olive oil or avocado oil
- 1 cup mushrooms, sliced (cremini or button)
- 1 cup fresh spinach, chopped
- 1/2 small onion, finely diced
- 1 clove garlic, minced
- 1/2 teaspoon ground cumin
- 1/2 teaspoon smoked paprika
- Salt and pepper to taste
- 1/4 cup nutritional yeast (optional, for a cheesy flavor)
- 1/2 avocado, sliced
- 1 tablespoon fresh lemon juice

Directions:

1. Carefully remove the tough stems from the collard green leaves.
2. Bring a large pot of water to a boil and briefly blanch the collard greens for 30 seconds. Immediately transfer the leaves to a bowl of ice water to stop the cooking process.
3. In a skillet, heat olive oil and sauté diced onion for 2-3 minutes. Add garlic for 30 seconds, then cook mushrooms for 5-6 minutes until browned.
4. Stir in the chopped spinach, cumin, smoked paprika, salt, and pepper. Cook until the spinach wilts, about 2 minutes.
5. If using nutritional yeast, stir it in at this point to give the filling a cheesy flavor.
6. Remove the skillet from heat and set the filling aside.
7. Lay two collard green leaves flat on a clean surface. Place half of the mushroom and spinach filling onto each leaf, distributing it evenly.
8. Top with avocado slices and a squeeze of fresh lemon juice.
9. Fold the collard green leaves over the filling, tucking in the sides to form a wrap or quesadilla shape.
10. If desired, heat a clean skillet over medium heat and lightly brown the quesadillas on each side for 2-3 minutes to warm through and enhance the flavors. Alternatively, you can enjoy them as-is.
11. Cut the quesadillas in half and serve immediately.

Salads

Mediterranean Chickpea Salad

Servings: 4   **Prep. time:** 15 min   **Setting time:** none

Nutritional Information (Per Serving):

Calories: 280, Protein: 8g, Carbohydrates: 32g, Fats: 12g, Fiber: 8g, Cholesterol: 0mg, Sodium: 330mg, Potassium: 400mg

Ingredients

- 1 can (15 oz) chickpeas (drained and rinsed)
- 1 cup cherry tomatoes (halved)
- 1 cup cucumber (diced)
- 1/2 cup red onion (finely diced)
- 1/4 cup Kalamata olives (sliced)
- 1/4 cup fresh parsley (chopped)
- 2 tablespoons extra-virgin olive oil
- 2 tablespoons lemon juice
- 1 teaspoon dried oregano
- 1/2 teaspoon garlic powder
- Salt and black pepper (to taste)

Directions:

1. Drain and rinse the chickpeas under cold water.
2. Halve the cherry tomatoes.
3. Dice the cucumber.
4. Finely dice the red onion.
5. Slice the Kalamata olives.
6. Chop the fresh parsley.
7. In a large bowl, mix the chickpeas, cherry tomatoes, cucumber, red onion, olives, and parsley.
8. In a separate small bowl, whisk together the dried oregano, olive oil, garlic powder, salt, lemon juice, and black pepper until thoroughly blended.
9. Pour the dressing over the salad and gently toss to evenly coat all the ingredients.
10. Adjust the seasoning with more salt and pepper, if needed.
11. Serve right away, or refrigerate for up to 2 hours to allow the flavors to develop.

Quinoa & Black Bean Salad

Servings: 4   **Prep. time:** 15 min   **Setting time:** 10 min (to allow flavors to meld)

Nutritional Information (Per Serving):

Calories: 290, Protein: 11g, Carbohydrates: 45g, Fats: 8g, Fiber: 9g, Cholesterol: 0mg, Sodium: 220mg, Potassium: 500mg

Ingredients

- 1 cup quinoa (dry)
- 1 can (15 oz) black beans (drained and rinsed)
- 1 cup corn kernels (fresh or frozen)
- 1 cup cherry tomatoes (halved)
- 1/2 cup red bell pepper (diced)
- 1/2 cup red onion (diced)
- 1/4 cup fresh cilantro (chopped)
- 2 tablespoons extra-virgin olive oil
- 2 tablespoons lime juice
- 1 teaspoon ground cumin
- 1/2 teaspoon chili powder
- Salt and black pepper (to taste)

Directions:

1. Rinse 1 cup of quinoa under cold water.
2. Place the quinoa and 2 cups of water in a medium saucepan.
3. Bring the mixture to a boil, then lower the heat, cover, and let it simmer for approximately 15 minutes, or until the quinoa is soft and all the water has been absorbed.
4. Take it off the heat and leave it covered for 5 minutes. Fluff the quinoa with a fork before serving. Allow it to cool to room temperature. Drain and rinse the black beans.
5. If using frozen corn, thaw it by placing it in a colander under cold running water.
6. Halve the cherry tomatoes. Cut the red bell pepper and red onion into small pieces. Finely chop the fresh cilantro.
7. In a large bowl, combine the cooked quinoa, black beans, corn, cherry tomatoes, diced red bell pepper, red onion, and chopped cilantro.
8. In a separate small bowl, whisk together the olive oil, lime juice, ground cumin, chili powder, salt, and black pepper.
9. Scatter the dressing over the salad and gently toss to mix everything together.

Avocado & Tomato Salad

  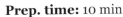

Servings: 4　**Prep. time:** 10 min　**Setting time:** none

Nutritional Information (Per Serving):

Calories: 220, Protein: 3g, Carbohydrates: 16g, Fats: 16g, Fiber: 7g, Cholesterol: 0mg, Sodium: 130mg, Potassium: 650mg

Ingredients

- 2 ripe avocados
- 2 cups cherry tomatoes (halved)
- 1/2 red onion (thinly sliced)
- 1/4 cup fresh basil (chopped)
- 1 tablespoon extra-virgin olive oil
- 1 tablespoon balsamic vinegar
- 1 teaspoon lemon juice
- 1/2 teaspoon dried oregano
- Salt and black pepper (to taste)

Directions:

1. Halve the avocados, remove the pits, and scoop out the flesh. Cut the avocado into small cubes.
2. Slice the cherry tomatoes in half.
3. Thinly slice the red onion.
4. Chop the fresh basil finely.
5. In a large bowl, gently mix together the diced avocado, cherry tomatoes, sliced red onion, and chopped basil.
6. In a small bowl/jar, whisk together the olive oil, balsamic vinegar, lemon juice, dried oregano, salt, and black pepper.
7. Pour the dressing over the salad and toss to combine.
8. Serve immediately to enjoy the freshest flavor, or chill in the refrigerator for up to 30 minutes.

Cucumber & Dill Salad

Servings: 4　**Prep. time:** 10 min　**Setting time:** 10 min (optional for chilling)

Nutritional Information (Per Serving):

Calories: 50, Protein: 1g, Carbohydrates: 5g, Fat: 3g, Fiber: 1g, Cholesterol: 0mg, Sodium: 10mg, Potassium: 200mg

Ingredients

- 2 large cucumbers (thinly sliced)
- 1/4 red onion (thinly sliced)
- 2 tablespoons fresh dill (chopped)
- 2 tablespoons apple cider vinegar
- 1 tablespoon extra-virgin olive oil
- 1 teaspoon lemon juice
- 1/2 teaspoon maple syrup (optional for slight sweetness)
- Salt and black pepper (to taste)

Directions:

1. Thinly slice the cucumbers and red onion. A mandoline slicer is useful for making consistent, thin slices.
2. Chop the fresh dill.
3. In a large bowl, add the cucumbers (sliced), red onion, and chopped dill.
4. Mix together the olive oil, apple cider vinegar, lemon juice, and maple syrup (if using) in a small bowl. Season with black pepper and salt to taste.
5. Drizzle the dressing over the cucumber mixture and toss gently to combine all ingredients evenly.
6. For enhanced flavor, allow the salad to rest in the refrigerator for 10 minutes before serving.
7. Serve the salad chilled as a refreshing side dish.

Spinach & Strawberry Salad

 Servings: 4   **Prep. time:** 10 min   **Setting time:** none

Nutritional Information (Per Serving):

Calories: 110, Protein: 2g, Carbohydrates: 8g, Fats: 8g, Fiber: 2g, Cholesterol: 0mg, Sodium: 20mg, Potassium: 300mg

Ingredients

- 4 cups fresh baby spinach (washed and dried)
- 1 cup fresh strawberries (hulled and sliced)
- 1/4 cup raw walnuts (roughly chopped)
- 1/4 cup red onion (thinly sliced)
- 1 tablespoon balsamic vinegar
- 1 tablespoon extra-virgin olive oil
- 1 teaspoon maple syrup (optional for sweetness)
- Salt and black pepper (to taste)

Directions:

1. Start by thoroughly washing and drying the baby spinach to ensure a clean and fresh salad.
2. Hull and slice the strawberries.
3. Roughly chop the raw walnuts.
4. Thinly slice the red onion.
5. Combine the spinach, sliced strawberries, walnuts, and red onion in a large bowl.
6. In a small bowl, whisk the olive oil, balsamic vinegar, and maple syrup (if desired). Combine the olive oil, balsamic vinegar, and maple syrup (if using) in a small bowl and whisk until smooth. Season with salt and black pepper to taste.
7. Drizzle the dressing over the salad and toss gently to coat all the ingredients evenly.
8. Serve immediately as a fresh, vibrant side dish.

Kale & Sweet Potato Salad

 Servings: 4   **Prep. time:** 10 min   **Total time:** 30 min

Nutritional Information (Per Serving):

Calories: 220, Protein: 4g, Carbohydrates: 30g, Fats: 10g, Fiber: 6g, Cholesterol: 0mg, Sodium: 180mg, Potassium: 530mg

Ingredients

- 2 medium sweet potatoes (peeled and diced)
- 1 tablespoon olive oil (for roasting)
- 1 bunch kale (about 4 cups, stems removed and leaves chopped)
- 1 tablespoon lemon juice
- 1 tablespoon extra-virgin olive oil (for the dressing)
- 1/4 teaspoon salt (for massaging kale)
- 1/4 cup raw pumpkin seeds (optional: lightly toasted)
- 1/4 cup dried cranberries (unsweetened)
- 1/4 teaspoon ground cinnamon (for seasoning sweet potatoes)
- 1/4 teaspoon paprika (for seasoning sweet potatoes)
- Salt and black pepper (to taste)

Directions:

1. Set the oven to preheat, 400°F (200°C).
2. Combine the diced sweet potatoes with 1 tablespoon of olive oil, cinnamon, paprika, and a pinch of salt in a bowl.
3. Lay them out evenly on a baking sheet and roast for 20 minutes, turning them over halfway, until they become tender and slightly crispy.
4. Drizzle the lemon juice, 1 tablespoon of olive oil, and 1/4 teaspoon salt over the kale.
5. Massage the kale with your hands for 2-3 minutes until the leaves soften and become more vibrant in color.
6. Once the sweet potatoes are roasted, let them cool slightly.
7. Add the sweet potatoes, pumpkin seeds, and dried cranberries to the massaged kale.
8. Toss everything together until well combined. Season with salt and black pepper to taste.
9. Divide the salad into bowls or plates and serve immediately.

Apple & Walnut Salad

 Servings: 4   **Prep. time:** 10 min   **Total time:** 10 min

Nutritional Information (Per Serving):

Calories: 220, Protein: 3g, Carbohydrates: 20g, Fats: 16g, Fiber: 4g, Cholesterol: 0mg, Sodium: 30mg, Potassium: 300mg

Ingredients

- 4 cups mixed greens (such as arugula, spinach, or romaine)
- 2 medium apples (cored and thinly sliced)
- 1/2 cup raw walnuts (roughly chopped)
- 1/4 cup dried cranberries (unsweetened)
- 1/4 cup red onion (thinly sliced)
- 1 tablespoon lemon juice (to prevent apple browning)
- 2 tablespoons extra-virgin olive oil (for the dressing)
- 1 tablespoon apple cider vinegar
- 1 teaspoon maple syrup (optional)
- 1/4 teaspoon Dijon mustard
- Salt and black pepper (to taste)

Directions:

1. Thinly slice the apples and toss them with 1 tablespoon of lemon juice to prevent discoloration.
2. In a small bowl, whisk together extra-virgin olive oil, apple cider vinegar, Dijon mustard, and maple syrup (if you choose to use it).
3. Season with salt and/or black pepper to taste.
4. Mix the apple slices, salad greens, walnuts, dried cranberries, and red onion in a large bowl.
5. Spread the dressing over the salad and toss gently to coat all ingredients evenly.
6. Divide the salad into individual bowls or plates and serve right away.

Roasted Beet & Arugula Salad

 Servings: 4   **Prep. time:** 10 min   **Total time:** 50 min

Nutritional Information (Per Serving):

Calories: 210, Protein: 4g, Carbohydrates: 20g, Fats: 14g, Fiber: 5g, Cholesterol: 0mg, Sodium: 85mg, Potassium: 540mg

Ingredients

- 4 medium beets (trimmed and scrubbed)
- 6 cups fresh arugula
- 1/2 cup raw walnuts (roughly chopped)
- 1/4 cup red onion (thinly sliced)
- 1/4 cup balsamic vinegar
- 2 tablespoons extra-virgin olive oil
- 1 teaspoon Dijon mustard
- 1 teaspoon maple syrup (optional)
- Salt and black pepper (to taste)

Directions:

1. Set the oven to preheat, 400°F (200°C).
2. Place each beet, wrapped in a foil, on a baking sheet.
3. Roast in the oven for 35-40 minutes, or until the beets are tender when pierced with a fork.
4. Remove from the oven, unwrap the foil, and let the beets cool.
5. After the beets have cooled, peel off the skin and cut them into wedges.
6. In a small bowl, whisk together balsamic vinegar, extra-virgin olive oil, Dijon mustard, and maple syrup (if you prefer).
7. Season with salt and black pepper to taste.
8. In a large bowl, mix the arugula, beet wedges, walnuts, and red onion.
9. Drizzle the dressing over the salad and toss gently to combine everything.
10. Divide the salad among individual bowls or plates.
11. Serve right away to savor the fresh, vibrant flavors.

Zucchini & Corn Salad

Servings: 4   **Prep. time:** 10 min   **Total time:** 20 min

Nutritional Information (Per Serving):

Calories: 105, Protein: 2g, Carbohydrates: 12g, Fats: 6g, Fiber: 3g, Cholesterol: 0mg, Sodium: 15mg, Potassium: 340mg

Ingredients

- 2 medium zucchinis (sliced into thin rounds)
- 1 cup fresh or frozen corn kernels
- 1/4 cup red bell pepper (diced)
- 1/4 cup red onion (finely chopped)
- 1/4 cup fresh cilantro (chopped)
- 2 tablespoons fresh lime juice
- 1 tablespoon extra-virgin olive oil
- 1/2 teaspoon ground cumin
- Salt and black pepper (to taste)

Directions:

1. Warm a large non-stick skillet on medium heat.
2. Add the zucchini slices and cook on each side for 2-3 minutes until lightly browned and tender. Set aside to cool.
3. In the same skillet, add the corn kernels and cook for 3-4 minutes until they begin to brown slightly. If using frozen corn, make sure it is [thawed, drained, and patted dry] before cooking.
4. Combine the corn, cooked zucchini, diced red bell pepper, red onion, and cilantro in a large mixing bowl.
5. Combine the lime juice, extra-virgin olive oil, ground cumin, salt, and black pepper in a small bowl.
6. Drizzle the dressing over the mixed vegetables and toss thoroughly to coat everything evenly.
7. Serve the salad right away or chill for up to 2 hours to allow the flavors to blend. Enjoy it as a side dish or a light lunch.

Broccoli & Cauliflower Salad

Servings: 4   **Prep. time:** 15 min   **Total time:** 20 min

Nutritional Information (Per Serving):

Calories: 170, Protein: 5g, Carbohydrates: 18g, Fats: 9g, Fiber: 5g, Cholesterol: 0mg, Sodium: 80mg, Potassium: 520mg

Ingredients

- 2 cups broccoli florets (fresh, chopped into bite-sized pieces)
- 2 cups cauliflower florets (fresh, chopped into bite-sized pieces)
- 1/4 cup red onion (finely chopped)
- 1/4 cup sunflower seeds (raw or lightly toasted)
- 1/4 cup dried cranberries (unsweetened)
- 1/4 cup fresh parsley (chopped)
  Dressing:
- 2 tablespoons tahini
- 2 tablespoons fresh lemon juice
- 1 tablespoon apple cider vinegar
- 1 tablespoon maple syrup (optional)
- 1 garlic clove (minced)
- Salt and black pepper (to taste)

Directions:

1. For a slightly tender texture, steam the broccoli and cauliflower for 2-3 minutes until just tender but still crisp. Then, simply transfer to a bowl of ice water to stop cooking and retain the bright color. Drain well. It's that easy!
2. Combine the chopped broccoli, cauliflower, red onion, sunflower seeds, dried cranberries, and parsley in a large mixing bowl.
3. Whisk together the tahini, lemon juice, apple cider vinegar, maple syrup (if using), minced garlic, salt, and black pepper in a small bowl.
4. Add water a little at a time, whisking until the dressing reaches your desired consistency. It should be thick but pourable.
5. Pour the dressing over the broccoli and cauliflower mixture.
6. Toss well to coat all the ingredients evenly with the dressing.
7. Feel free to experiment with different ingredients or adjust the dressing to your taste. This salad is a canvas for your culinary creativity. Serve it immediately or let it sit in the refrigerator for 15-20 minutes to allow the flavors to meld together. This salad can also be made a few hours in advance.

Mixed Bean Salad

Servings: 4   **Prep. time:** 10 min   **Total time:** 10 min

Nutritional Information (Per Serving):

Calories: 300, Protein: 9g, Carbohydrates: 28g, Fats: 17g, Fiber: 10g, Cholesterol: 0mg, Sodium: 200mg, Potassium: 710mg

Ingredients

- 1 cup canned chickpeas (drained and rinsed)
- 1 cup canned black beans (drained and rinsed)
- 1 cup canned kidney beans (drained and rinsed)
- 1/2 cup cherry tomatoes (halved)
- 1/4 cup red onion (finely chopped)
- 1/4 cup cucumber (diced)
- 1/4 cup fresh parsley (chopped)
- 1/4 cup fresh cilantro (chopped)
- 1 avocado (diced)
  Dressing:
- 3 tablespoons extra-virgin olive oil
- 2 tablespoons fresh lemon juice
- 1 tablespoon apple cider vinegar
- 1 teaspoon Dijon mustard
- 1 garlic clove (minced)
- Salt and black pepper (to taste)

Directions:

1. Drain and rinse the canned chickpeas, black beans, and kidney beans. This removes excess sodium and helps the beans blend better with the dressing.
2. Combine chickpeas, black beans, kidney beans, cherry tomatoes, red onion, cucumber, parsley, cilantro, and diced avocado in a large mixing bowl.
3. In a small bowl, whisk the olive oil, lemon juice, apple cider vinegar, Dijon mustard, minced garlic, salt, and black pepper until everything is thoroughly blended.
4. Drizzle the dressing over the bean mixture and gently toss to ensure all ingredients are well coated.
5. Serve the salad right away, or refrigerate it for 15-20 minutes to let the flavors come together. This salad can be enjoyed either as a main dish or a side.

Mango & Black Bean Salad

Servings: 4   **Prep. time:** 15 min   **Total time:** 15 min

Nutritional Information (Per Serving):

Calories: 180 kcal, Protein: 6g, Carbohydrates: 16g, Fats: 11g, Fiber: 7g, Cholesterol: 0mg, Sodium: 120mg, Potassium: 740mg

Ingredients

- 1 cup canned black beans (drained and rinsed)
- 1 large ripe mango (peeled, pitted, and diced)
- 1 red bell pepper (diced)
- 1/2 cup red onion (finely chopped)
- 1/4 cup fresh cilantro (chopped)
- 1 avocado (diced)
- 1/2 cup cherry tomatoes (halved)
- 1 jalapeño pepper (seeded and finely chopped, optional)
  Dressing:
- 3 tablespoons fresh lime juice
- 2 tablespoons extra-virgin olive oil
- 1 tablespoon apple cider vinegar
- 1 teaspoon maple syrup or agave nectar
- Salt and black pepper (to taste)

Directions:

1. Drain and rinse the black beans thoroughly under cold water. This helps remove excess sodium and improves the flavor of the salad.
2. To ensure a balanced taste and even distribution of flavors, it's important to dice the mango, red bell pepper, and avocado. Also, finely chop the red onion, cilantro, and jalapeño pepper (if using) and halve the cherry tomatoes.
3. Combine the black beans, mango, red bell pepper, red onion, cilantro, avocado, cherry tomatoes, and jalapeño pepper in a large mixing bowl. Gently toss to mix.
4. In a small bowl, whisk together the lime juice, olive oil, apple cider vinegar, maple syrup or agave nectar, salt, and black pepper until well combined.
5. Pour the dressing over the salad ingredients. Toss gently to ensure everything is evenly coated with the dressing.
6. For the best flavor, it's recommended to let the salad sit for 10 minutes after preparation. This allows the flavors to meld, creating a more delicious and satisfying dish. Whether enjoyed on its own or as a side dish, this salad is sure to impress.

Asparagus & Tomato Salad

 Servings: 4   **Prep. time:** 10 min   **Total time:** 15 min

Nutritional Information (Per Serving):
Calories: 110, Protein: 3g, Carbohydrates: 8g, Fats: 8g, Fiber: 3g, Cholesterol: 0mg, Sodium: 90mg, Potassium: 350mg

Ingredients

- 1 bunch asparagus (about 1 pound, trimmed and cut into 2-inch pieces)
- 1 pint cherry tomatoes (halved)
- 1/4 cup red onion (finely chopped)
- 2 tablespoons fresh basil (chopped)
- 2 tablespoons fresh parsley (chopped)
  Dressing:
- 2 tablespoons extra-virgin olive oil
- 1 tablespoon balsamic vinegar
- 1 tablespoon fresh lemon juice
- 1 teaspoon Dijon mustard
- 1 clove garlic (minced)
- Salt and black pepper (to taste)

Directions:

1. Bring a pot of water to a boil. Add the asparagus pieces and blanch them for 2-3 minutes until tender-crisp. Blanching helps to preserve the vibrant green color and crisp texture of the asparagus.
2. Once the asparagus is cooked, immediately transfer them to a bowl of ice water. This step not only halts the cooking process but also preserves their bright green color, adding freshness to your salad. Drain well and pat dry.
3. Cut the cherry tomatoes in half and finely chop the red onion.
4. In a small bowl, whisk together the olive oil, balsamic vinegar, lemon juice, Dijon mustard, minced garlic, salt, and black pepper until fully mixed.
5. In a large bowl, combine the blanched asparagus, halved cherry tomatoes, chopped red onion, fresh basil, and parsley.
6. Drizzle the dressing over the salad and gently toss to coat all the ingredients evenly.
7. This salad can be served right away or chilled for a while, making it a versatile option as a light main dish or a refreshing side. The choice is yours!

Cabbage & Carrot Salad

 Servings: 4   **Prep. time:** 15 min   **Total time:** 15 min

Nutritional Information (Per Serving):
Calories: 95, Protein: 2g, Carbohydrates: 12g, Fats: 5g, Fiber: 3g, Cholesterol: 0mg, Sodium: 120mg, Potassium: 300mg

Ingredients

- 3 cups green cabbage (shredded)
- 1 cup carrots (shredded)
- 1/2 cup red bell pepper (diced)
- 1/4 cup red onion (finely chopped)
- 1/4 cup fresh cilantro (chopped)
  Dressing:
- 2 tablespoons apple cider vinegar
- 1 tablespoon extra-virgin olive oil
- 1 tablespoon maple syrup (or agave nectar)
- 1 teaspoon Dijon mustard
- 1 clove garlic (minced)
- Salt and black pepper (to taste)

Directions:

1. Shred the cabbage and carrots using a box grater or a food processor.
2. Cut the red bell pepper into small cubes and finely chop the red onion.
3. Chop the fresh cilantro.
4. In a small bowl, combine the olive oil, apple cider vinegar, olive oil, maple syrup, Dijon mustard, minced garlic, salt, and black pepper, whisking until thoroughly mixed.
5. Combine the shredded cabbage, carrots, diced red bell pepper, and chopped red onion in a large mixing bowl.
6. Drizzle the dressing over the vegetables and mix well to ensure they are evenly coated.
7. Allow the salad to rest for ten minutes to let the flavors blend; this step is optional but suggested for better taste.
8. Serve right away or chill in the refrigerator until ready to serve.

Pear & Arugula Salad

Servings: 4   **Prep. time:** 10 min   **Total time:** 10 min

Nutritional Information (Per Serving):

Calories: 210, Protein: 3g, Carbohydrates: 25g, Fats: 12g, Fiber: 4g, Cholesterol: 0mg, Sodium: 180mg, Potassium: 300mg

Ingredients

- 4 cups arugula (fresh)
- 2 ripe pears (sliced thinly)
- 1/4 cup walnuts (chopped)
- 1/4 cup red onion (thinly sliced)
- 1/4 cup dried cranberries (unsweetened)
- 1/4 cup vegan feta cheese (optional, for added flavor)
  Dressing:
- 2 tablespoons extra-virgin olive oil
- 1 tablespoon balsamic vinegar
- 1 tablespoon lemon juice
- 1 tablespoon maple syrup
- 1 teaspoon Dijon mustard
- Salt and black pepper (to taste)

Directions:

1. Wash and dry the arugula.
2. Thinly slice the pears.
3. Chop the walnuts and slice the red onion into thin strips.
4. Measure the dried cranberries and vegan feta cheese, if using.
5. In a small bowl, whisk together extra-virgin olive oil, balsamic vinegar, lemon juice, maple syrup, Dijon mustard, salt, and black pepper until fully blended.
6. In a large bowl, mix the arugula, pear slices, chopped walnuts, sliced red onion, and dried cranberries.
7. Pour the dressing over the salad and gently toss to ensure all ingredients are evenly coated.
8. If desired, sprinkle vegan feta cheese on top and give the salad one last toss.
9. Let the salad sit for about 5 minutes to allow the flavors to meld, or serve right away.

Chickpea & Avocado Salad

Servings: 4   **Prep. time:** 15 min   **Total time:** 15 min

Nutritional Information (Per Serving):

Calories: 245, Protein: 8g, Carbohydrates: 27g, Fats: 13g, Fiber: 9g, Cholesterol: 0mg, Sodium: 190mg, Potassium: 550mg

Ingredients

- 1 can (15 oz) chickpeas (rinsed and drained)
- 1 large ripe avocado (diced)
- 1 cup cherry tomatoes (halved)
- 1/2 cucumber (diced)
- 1/4 red onion (finely chopped)
- 1/4 cup fresh parsley (chopped)
- 1 tablespoon extra-virgin olive oil
- 1 tablespoon lemon juice
- 1 teaspoon Dijon mustard
- 1 garlic clove (minced)
- Salt and black pepper (to taste)

Directions:

1. Rinse and drain the chickpeas.
2. Cut the avocado and cucumber into small cubes.
3. Halve the cherry tomatoes and finely chop the red onion.
4. Chop the fresh parsley.
5. In a small bowl, whisk together extra-virgin olive oil, lemon juice, Dijon mustard, minced garlic, salt, and black pepper.
6. In a large mixing bowl, combine the chickpeas, diced avocado, cherry tomatoes, cucumber, red onion, and parsley.
7. Drizzle the dressing over the salad and gently toss to evenly coat all the ingredients.
8. You can serve the salad immediately or chill it for a cool, refreshing option.

Greek Salad

Servings: 4   **Prep. time:** 15 min   **Total time:** 15 min

Nutritional Information (Per Serving):

Calories: 170, Protein: 2g, Carbohydrates: 10g, Fats: 14g, Fiber: 3g, Cholesterol: 0mg, Sodium: 320mg, Potassium: 350mg

Ingredients

- 2 cups cherry tomatoes (halved)
- 1 cucumber (diced)
- 1/2 red onion (thinly sliced)
- 1/2 cup Kalamata olives (pitted and sliced)
- 1/4 cup fresh parsley (chopped)
- 1/4 cup fresh mint (chopped)
- 1/4 cup extra-virgin olive oil
- 2 tablespoons red wine vinegar
- 1 teaspoon dried oregano
- Salt and black pepper (to taste)

Directions:

1. Cut the cherry tomatoes in half.
2. Dice the cucumber into small pieces.
3. Thinly slice the red onion.
4. In a large bowl, mix together the halved cherry tomatoes, diced cucumber, sliced red onion, and Kalamata olives.
5. In a small bowl, whisk extra-virgin olive oil, red wine vinegar, dried oregano, salt, and black pepper until well combined.
6. Drizzle the dressing over the salad and toss to coat all the ingredients evenly.
7. Add the chopped parsley and mint, and gently toss once more.
8. Serve immediately or refrigerate for 30 minutes to let the flavors develop.

Spinach & Quinoa Salad

Servings: 4   **Prep. time:** 15 min   **Total time:** 30 min

Nutritional Information (Per Serving):

Calories: 210, Protein: 4g, Carbohydrates: 23g, Fats: 14g, Fiber: 6g, Cholesterol: 0mg, Sodium: 130mg, Potassium: 450mg

Ingredients

- 1 cup quinoa (uncooked)
- 2 cups water (for cooking quinoa)
- 4 cups fresh spinach (washed and chopped)
- 1 cup cherry tomatoes (halved)
- 1/2 cup cucumber (diced)
- 1/4 cup red onion (finely diced)
- 1/4 cup sliced almonds (toasted)
- 1/4 cup fresh parsley (chopped)
- 1/4 cup lemon juice (freshly squeezed)
- 2 tablespoons extra virgin olive oil
- 1 tablespoon apple cider vinegar
- 1 clove garlic (minced)
- 1 teaspoon Dijon mustard
- 1/2 teaspoon sea salt
- 1/4 teaspoon freshly ground black pepper

Directions:

1. In a medium saucepan, bring 2 cups of water to a boil.
2. Add 1 cup of quinoa to the boiling water. Reduce heat to low, cover, and simmer for 15 minutes, or until the quinoa is tender and the water is absorbed.
3. Remove from heat and let the quinoa sit covered for 5 minutes, then fluff with a fork. Allow it to cool to room temperature.
4. While the quinoa is cooling, prepare the vegetables. Halve the cherry tomatoes, dice the cucumber, and finely dice the red onion.
5. Wash and chop the fresh spinach and fresh parsley.
6. In a dry skillet over medium heat, toast the sliced almonds for 3-4 minutes, stirring frequently, until they are golden brown and fragrant. Watch closely to avoid burning. Set aside to cool.
7. In a small bowl, combine the lemon juice, olive oil, apple cider vinegar, minced garlic, Dijon mustard, sea salt, and black pepper, whisking until fully blended. This dressing provides a tangy flavor and helps to balance the richness of the quinoa.
8. In a large bowl, combine the cooled quinoa, chopped spinach, cherry tomatoes, cucumber, red onion, and parsley.
9. Pour the dressing over the salad and toss gently to combine all ingredients evenly.
10. Sprinkle the toasted almonds over the top of the salad just before serving for a crunchy texture.
11. SServe immediately, or refrigerate for up to 2 hours before serving. This salad can be enjoyed cold or at room temperature.

Sweet Potato & Black Bean Salad

Servings: 4   **Prep. time:** 20 min   **Total time:** 30 min

Nutritional Information (Per Serving):

Calories: 280, Protein: 8g, Carbohydrates: 43g, Fats: 9g, Fiber: 9g, Cholesterol: 0mg, Sodium: 280mg, Potassium: 800mg

Ingredients

- 2 medium sweet potatoes (peeled and diced, about 2 cups)
- 1 tablespoon olive oil
- 1/2 teaspoon ground cumin
- 1/2 teaspoon smoked paprika
- 1/4 teaspoon chili powder
- 1/4 teaspoon salt
- 1/4 teaspoon black pepper
- 1 can (15 oz) black beans (rinsed and drained)
- 1 red bell pepper (diced)
- 1/2 red onion (diced)
- 1 cup fresh cilantro (chopped)
- Juice of 1 lime
- 1 tablespoon apple cider vinegar
- 1 avocado (diced, optional for garnish)

Directions:

1. Preheat the oven to 425°F (220°C).
2. Toss the diced sweet potatoes with olive oil, cumin, smoked paprika, chili powder, salt, and black pepper.
3. Spread them on a baking sheet in a single layer.
4. Roast for 20 minutes, stirring halfway through, until tender and slightly caramelized.
5. In a large bowl, combine the rinsed black beans, diced red bell pepper, diced red onion, and chopped cilantro.
6. In a small bowl, whisk together the lime juice, apple cider vinegar, and a pinch of salt and pepper.
7. Once the sweet potatoes are done roasting, let them cool for about 10 minutes.
8. Add the roasted sweet potatoes to the salad base.
9. Pour the dressing over the salad and toss gently to combine.
10. If desired, top with diced avocado for extra creaminess.
11. Serve immediately or refrigerate for up to 2 hours to let the flavors meld.

Ginger & Carrot Salad

Servings: 4   **Prep. time:** 15 min   **Total time:** 25 min

Nutritional Information (Per Serving):

Calories: 130, Protein: 2g, Carbohydrates: 14g, Fats: 8g, Fiber: 4g, Cholesterol: 0mg, Sodium: 270mg, Potassium: 400mg

Ingredients

- 4 medium carrots (peeled and julienned or grated, about 3 cups)
- 1 tablespoon freshly grated ginger
- 2 tablespoons sesame oil
- 2 tablespoons rice vinegar
- 1 tablespoon maple syrup (or agave nectar)
- 1 tablespoon soy sauce (or tamari for gluten-free)
- 1/2 teaspoon ground cumin
- 1/4 teaspoon turmeric
- 1/4 teaspoon black pepper
- 1/4 cup chopped fresh cilantro (for garnish)
- 2 tablespoons sesame seeds (optional, for garnish)

Directions:

1. Peel and julienne or grate the carrots. Place them in a large mixing bowl.
2. In a small bowl, whisk together the freshly grated ginger, sesame oil, rice vinegar, maple syrup, soy sauce, ground cumin, turmeric, and black pepper until well combined.
3. Pour the dressing over the julienned or grated carrots.
4. Toss well to ensure all the carrots are evenly coated with the dressing.
5. If desired, sprinkle with chopped cilantro and sesame seeds.
6. Let the salad sit for about 10 minutes to allow the flavors to meld, though it can be served immediately.

Celery & Apple Salad

Servings: 4   **Prep. time:** 10 min   **Total time:** 20 min (optional for setting)

Nutritional Information (Per Serving):
Calories: 50, Protein: 1g, Carbohydrates: 5g, Fat: 3g, Fiber: 1g, Cholesterol: 0mg, Sodium: 10mg, Potassium: 200mg

Ingredients

- 4 celery stalks (diced, about 2 cups)
- 2 medium apples (diced, with skins on, about 2 cups)
- 1/4 cup raw walnuts (chopped)
- 1/4 cup dried cranberries (unsweetened, optional)
- 2 tablespoons fresh lemon juice
- 1 tablespoon olive oil
- 1 tablespoon maple syrup (or agave nectar)
- 1/2 teaspoon Dijon mustard
- Salt and pepper (to taste)
- 2 tablespoons chopped fresh parsley (for garnish)

Directions:

1. Dice the celery and apples into bite-sized pieces. If using dried cranberries, chop them slightly if they are large.
2. Chop the raw walnuts into small pieces.
3. In a small bowl, whisk together the lemon juice, olive oil, maple syrup, Dijon mustard, salt, and pepper until well combined.
4. In a large mixing bowl, combine the diced celery, apples, walnuts, and dried cranberries (if using).
5. Pour the dressing over the salad and toss everything together until well coated.
6. Garnish with chopped fresh parsley.
7. Let the salad sit for about 10 minutes to allow the flavors to meld, though it can be served immediately.

Ratatouille Salad

Servings: 4   **Prep. time:** 20 min   **Total time:** 30 min

Nutritional Information (Per Serving):
Calories: 180, Protein: 4g, Carbohydrates: 20g, Fats: 10g, Fiber: 6g, Cholesterol: 0mg, Sodium: 150mg, Potassium: 650mg

Ingredients

- 1 medium zucchini (diced, about 1 1/2 cups)
- 1 medium eggplant (diced, about 1 1/2 cups)
- 1 red bell pepper (diced, about 1 cup)
- 1 cup cherry tomatoes (halved)
- 1/2 red onion (diced)
- 2 cloves garlic (minced)
- 2 tablespoons olive oil
- 1 teaspoon dried oregano
- 1 teaspoon dried basil
- Salt and black pepper (to taste)
- 2 tablespoons balsamic vinegar
- 1 tablespoon fresh basil (chopped, for garnish)
- 2 tablespoons pine nuts (toasted, optional for crunch)

Directions:

1. Preheat the oven to 400°F (200°C).
2. Dice the zucchini, eggplant, and red bell pepper. Halve the cherry tomatoes and dice the red onion.
3. On a baking sheet, toss the diced zucchini, eggplant, red bell pepper, and cherry tomatoes with olive oil, minced garlic, dried oregano, dried basil, salt, and black pepper.
4. Spread the vegetables in a single layer on the baking sheet.
5. Roast for 20-25 minutes, stirring halfway through, until vegetables are tender and slightly caramelized.
6. Allow the roasted vegetables to cool for about 10 minutes.
7. In a large bowl, combine the roasted vegetables with diced red onion.
8. In a small bowl, whisk together balsamic vinegar, a pinch of salt, and black pepper.
9. Pour the dressing over the roasted vegetable mixture and toss gently to combine.
10. Garnish with fresh basil and toasted pine nuts (if using).
11. Serve immediately or chill in the refrigerator for a more refreshing taste.

Beet & Carrot Salad

 Servings: 4   **Prep. time:** 15 min   **Total time:** 15 min

Nutritional Information (Per Serving):

Calories: 170, Protein: 3g, Carbohydrates: 13g, Fats: 12g, Fiber: 4g, Cholesterol: 0mg, Sodium: 160mg, Potassium: 350mg

Ingredients

- 2 medium beets (about 1 cup, peeled and grated)
- 2 medium carrots (about 1 cup, peeled and grated)
- 1/4 cup fresh parsley (chopped)
- 1/4 cup sunflower seeds (unsalted, raw or lightly toasted)
- 2 tablespoons extra virgin olive oil
- 1 tablespoon lemon juice (freshly squeezed)
- 1 teaspoon apple cider vinegar
- 1 teaspoon maple syrup (optional, for sweetness)
- 1/4 teaspoon sea salt
- 1/4 teaspoon freshly ground black pepper

Directions:

1. Peel and grate the beets and carrots using a box grater or food processor with a grating attachment. Place the grated vegetables in a large mixing bowl.
2. Chop the fresh parsley and add it to the bowl with the beets and carrots.
3. In a small bowl, whisk together the extra virgin olive oil, lemon juice, apple cider vinegar, maple syrup (if using), sea salt, and freshly ground black pepper until well combined.
4. Pour the dressing over the grated beets, carrots, and parsley.
5. Toss everything together until the vegetables are evenly coated with the dressing.
6. Sprinkle the sunflower seeds over the salad and give it a final toss to distribute them evenly.
7. Serve the salad immediately or chill it in the refrigerator for 10-15 minutes before serving to allow the flavors to meld together.

Avocado & Corn Salad

 Servings: 4   **Prep. time:** 10 min   **Total time:** 10 min

Nutritional Information (Per Serving):

Calories: 210, Protein: 3g, Carbohydrates: 17g, Fats: 17g, Fiber: 7g, Cholesterol: 0mg, Sodium: 150mg, Potassium: 580mg

Ingredients

- 2 ripe avocados (diced)
- 1 1/2 cups corn kernels (fresh or cooked, about 2 ears of corn)
- 1 cup cherry tomatoes (halved)
- 1/4 cup red onion (finely diced)
- 1/4 cup fresh cilantro (chopped)
- 2 tablespoons lime juice (freshly squeezed)
- 1 tablespoon extra virgin olive oil
- 1/4 teaspoon sea salt
- 1/4 teaspoon freshly ground black pepper
- Optional: 1 small jalapeño pepper (seeded and finely chopped for a bit of heat)

Directions:

1. Dice the avocados and place them in a large mixing bowl.
2. Add the corn kernels, halved cherry tomatoes, and finely diced red onion to the bowl with the avocados.
3. Chop the fresh cilantro and add it to the bowl with the other ingredients.
4. In a small bowl, whisk together the lime juice, extra virgin olive oil, sea salt, and freshly ground black pepper until well combined.
5. Pour the dressing over the salad ingredients in the mixing bowl.
6. Gently toss the salad to combine all the ingredients, being careful not to mash the avocados.
7. If you like a bit of heat, add the finely chopped jalapeño to the salad and mix well.
8. Serve the salad immediately as a light meal or side dish. If not serving immediately, cover and refrigerate for up to 30 minutes to allow the flavors to meld.

Cucumber & Avocado Salad

Servings: 4   **Prep. time:** 10 min   **Total time:** 10 min

Nutritional Information (Per Serving):

Calories: 180, Protein: 2g, Carbohydrates: 10g, Fats: 16g, Fiber: 7g, Cholesterol: 0mg, Sodium: 120mg, Potassium: 600mg

Ingredients

- 2 large cucumbers (sliced thinly, about 4 cups)
- 2 ripe avocados (diced)
- 1/4 cup red onion (thinly sliced)
- 1/4 cup fresh dill (chopped)
- 2 tablespoons fresh lemon juice (about 1 lemon)
- 1 tablespoon extra virgin olive oil
- 1/4 teaspoon sea salt
- 1/4 teaspoon freshly ground black pepper

Directions:

1. Wash the cucumbers thoroughly and slice them thinly. If you prefer, you can peel the cucumbers before slicing. Place the sliced cucumbers in a large mixing bowl.
2. Cut the avocados in half, remove the pits, and dice the flesh. Add the diced avocados to the bowl with the cucumbers.
3. Thinly slice the red onion and chop the fresh dill. Add both to the mixing bowl with the cucumbers and avocados.
4. In a small bowl, whisk together the fresh lemon juice, extra virgin olive oil, sea salt, and freshly ground black pepper until well combined.
5. Pour the dressing over the cucumber, avocado, onion, and dill mixture. Gently toss the salad to ensure all ingredients are evenly coated with the dressing. Be careful not to mash the avocado.
6. Serve the salad immediately for the best texture and flavor. If you need to prepare it in advance, you can refrigerate the salad for up to 30 minutes, but it's best enjoyed fresh.

Lentil & Veggie Salad

Servings: 4   **Prep. time:** 15 min   **Total time:** 35 min

Nutritional Information (Per Serving):

Calories: 260, Protein: 12g, Carbohydrates: 35g, Fats: 8g, Fiber: 14g, Cholesterol: 0mg, Sodium: 240mg, Potassium: 600mg

Ingredients

- 1 cup dry green or brown lentils (rinsed and drained)
- 3 cups water
- 1 medium red bell pepper (diced)
- 1 medium cucumber (diced)
- 1 medium carrot (grated)
- 1/2 red onion (finely chopped)
- 1 cup cherry tomatoes (halved)
- 1/4 cup fresh parsley (chopped)
- 2 tablespoons extra virgin olive oil
- 2 tablespoons fresh lemon juice (about 1 lemon)
- 1 tablespoon apple cider vinegar
- 1 teaspoon Dijon mustard
- 1/2 teaspoon sea salt
- 1/4 teaspoon freshly ground black pepper
- 1/4 teaspoon ground cumin

Directions:

1. Place the rinsed lentils and 3 cups of water in a medium saucepan. Bring to a boil, then reduce the heat to a simmer. Cook the lentils uncovered for about 20 minutes, or until they are tender but not mushy. Drain any excess water and let the lentils cool slightly.
2. While the lentils are cooking, dice the red bell pepper and cucumber, grate the carrot, chop the red onion finely, and halve the cherry tomatoes. Place all the prepared vegetables in a large mixing bowl.
3. In a small bowl, whisk together the extra virgin olive oil, fresh lemon juice, apple cider vinegar, Dijon mustard, sea salt, black pepper, and ground cumin until well combined.
4. Once the lentils have cooled to room temperature, add them to the bowl with the vegetables. Pour the dressing over the salad and gently toss to combine all the ingredients. Ensure the lentils and vegetables are evenly coated with the dressing.
5. Chop the fresh parsley and sprinkle it over the salad. Toss lightly to distribute the herbs throughout the salad.
6. Serve the salad immediately or refrigerate it for up to 2 hours to allow the flavors to meld. This salad can be enjoyed cold or at room temperature.

Arugula & Pear Salad

 Servings: 4   **Prep. time:** 10 min   **Total time:** 10 min

Nutritional Information (Per Serving):

Calories: 210, Protein: 3g, Carbohydrates: 22g, Fats: 14g, Fiber: 4g, Cholesterol: 0mg, Sodium: 150mg, Potassium: 280mg

Ingredients

- 4 cups fresh arugula (packed)
- 2 ripe pears (sliced thinly)
- 1/4 cup walnuts (chopped)
- 1/4 cup dried cranberries (unsweetened)
- 1/4 cup pomegranate seeds
- 2 tablespoons extra virgin olive oil
- 1 tablespoon balsamic vinegar
- 1 teaspoon Dijon mustard
- 1 teaspoon maple syrup (optional for sweetness)
- 1/4 teaspoon sea salt
- 1/4 teaspoon freshly ground black pepper

Directions:

1. Rinse and dry the arugula. Place it in a large salad bowl.
2. Wash and thinly slice the pears. To prevent browning, you can lightly toss them in a bit of lemon juice if desired.
3. Chop the walnuts into small pieces.
4. Add the sliced pears, chopped walnuts, dried cranberries, and pomegranate seeds to the bowl with the arugula.
5. In a small bowl, whisk together the extra virgin olive oil, balsamic vinegar, Dijon mustard, maple syrup (if using), sea salt, and black pepper until well combined.
6. Drizzle the dressing over the salad. Gently toss all the ingredients together to ensure the arugula and toppings are evenly coated with the dressing.
7. Serve the salad immediately. This salad is best enjoyed fresh to maintain the crispness of the arugula and the sweetness of the pears.

Kale & Apple Salad

 Servings: 4   **Prep. time:** 15 min   **Total time:** 15 min

Nutritional Information (Per Serving):

Calories: 210, Protein: 4g, Carbohydrates: 23g, Fats: 14g, Fiber: 6g, Cholesterol: 0mg, Sodium: 130mg, Potassium: 450mg

Ingredients

- 6 cups kale (chopped, stems removed)
- 2 medium apples (thinly sliced, any sweet variety like Fuji or Gala)
- 1/4 cup raw sunflower seeds
- 1/4 cup dried cranberries (unsweetened)
- 1/2 avocado (sliced)
- 1 tablespoon lemon juice
- 1 tablespoon apple cider vinegar
- 2 tablespoons extra virgin olive oil
- 1 teaspoon maple syrup (optional for sweetness)
- 1/4 teaspoon sea salt
- 1/4 teaspoon freshly ground black pepper

Directions:

1. Wash and dry the kale thoroughly. Remove the tough stems and chop the kale leaves into bite-sized pieces.
2. Transfer the kale to a large salad bowl. Drizzle with 1 tablespoon of lemon juice and a pinch of sea salt.
3. Massage the Kale: Use your hands to massage the kale for 2-3 minutes until it becomes softer and slightly wilted. This technique breaks down the fibers, making the kale more tender and easier to digest.
4. Wash and thinly slice the apples. You can leave the skin on for added fiber and nutrients.
5. To prevent browning, toss the apple slices in a bit of lemon juice if desired.
6. Add the sliced apples, sunflower seeds, dried cranberries, and avocado slices to the massaged kale.
7. In a small bowl, whisk together the apple cider vinegar, extra virgin olive oil, maple syrup (if using), sea salt, and black pepper until well combined.
8. Drizzle the dressing over the salad and gently toss all the ingredients together to ensure the kale, apples, and toppings are evenly coated.
9. Serve the salad immediately for the best texture and flavor. This salad can also be stored in the fridge for up to 24 hours.

Summer Vegetable Salad

 Servings: 4   **Prep. time:** 20 min   **Total time:** 20 min

Nutritional Information (Per Serving):

Calories: 130, Protein: 3g, Carbohydrates: 17g, Fats: 7g, Fiber: 4g, Cholesterol: omg, Sodium: 300mg, Potassium: 500mg

Ingredients

- 2 cups cherry tomatoes (halved)
- 1 medium cucumber (diced)
- 1 yellow bell pepper (diced)
- 1 zucchini (thinly sliced)
- 1/2 red onion (thinly sliced)
- 1 cup fresh corn kernels (from 1-2 ears of corn)
- 1/4 cup fresh basil (chopped)
- 1/4 cup fresh parsley (chopped)
- 2 tablespoons extra virgin olive oil
- 1 tablespoon red wine vinegar
- 1 tablespoon lemon juice (freshly squeezed)
- 1 clove garlic (minced)
- 1/2 teaspoon sea salt
- 1/4 teaspoon freshly ground black pepper

Directions:

1. Wash and dry all vegetables and herbs.
2. Halve the cherry tomatoes, dice the cucumber and yellow bell pepper, and thinly slice the zucchini and red onion.
3. If using fresh corn, remove the kernels from the cob with a sharp knife. If fresh corn isn't available, you can use frozen corn (thawed) but fresh is preferable for the best texture and flavor.
4. In a large salad bowl, combine the halved cherry tomatoes, diced cucumber, yellow bell pepper, sliced zucchini, red onion, and corn kernels.
5. Add the chopped fresh basil and parsley to the bowl. Fresh herbs add vibrant flavor and nutritional benefits, especially when used in generous amounts.
6. In a small bowl, whisk together the extra virgin olive oil, red wine vinegar, lemon juice, minced garlic, sea salt, and black pepper until well combined.
7. Pour the dressing over the salad and toss gently to ensure all the vegetables are evenly coated. The fresh lemon juice and vinegar add a bright acidity that enhances the freshness of the vegetables.
8. Serve immediately for the best texture and flavor. This salad is perfect as a light main dish or as a side to a larger meal. If you prefer, you can let the salad sit for 10-15 minutes to allow the flavors to meld together.

Tomato & Basil Salad

 Servings: 4   **Prep. time:** 10 min   **Total time:** 15 min

Nutritional Information (Per Serving):

Calories: 120, Protein: 2g, Carbohydrates: 8g, Fats: 9g, Fiber: 2g, Cholesterol: omg, Sodium: 300mg, Potassium: 350mg

Ingredients

- 4 large ripe tomatoes (about 2 lbs, sliced into wedges)
- 1/2 cup fresh basil leaves (loosely packed, torn or chopped)
- 1/4 red onion (thinly sliced)
- 2 tablespoons extra virgin olive oil
- 1 tablespoon balsamic vinegar
- 1/2 teaspoon sea salt (or to taste)
- 1/4 teaspoon freshly ground black pepper (or to taste)
- 1 clove garlic (minced)
- Optional: 1 tablespoon pine nuts (toasted)

Directions:

1. Slice the tomatoes into wedges or thick slices. Tear or chop the fresh basil leaves. Thinly slice the red onion.
2. In a large bowl, combine the tomato wedges, fresh basil, and sliced red onion.
3. In a small bowl, whisk together the extra virgin olive oil, balsamic vinegar, minced garlic, sea salt, and black pepper.
4. Pour the dressing over the tomato mixture. Toss gently to ensure all the ingredients are evenly coated.
5. Let the salad sit for about 5 minutes to allow the flavors to meld together.
6. If using, sprinkle toasted pine nuts over the salad for added crunch. Serve immediately.

Roasted Veggie & Quinoa Salad

Servings: 4   **Prep. time:** 20 min   **Total time:** 50 min

Nutritional Information (Per Serving):

Calories: 320, Protein: 8g, Carbohydrates: 40g, Fats: 16g, Fiber: 7g, Cholesterol: 0mg, Sodium: 180mg, Potassium: 700mg

Ingredients

- 1 cup quinoa (dry, thoroughly rinsed)
- 2 cups water
- Pinch of salt
- 1 medium zucchini, chopped
- 1 medium bell pepper (any color), chopped
- 1 red onion, chopped
- 1 cup cherry tomatoes, halved
- 1 cup broccoli florets
- 2 tablespoons olive oil
- 1 teaspoon dried oregano
- 1 teaspoon dried thyme
- Salt and pepper to taste
- 3 tablespoons extra virgin olive oil
- 2 tablespoons balsamic vinegar
- 1 tablespoon Dijon mustard
- 1 teaspoon maple syrup or agave nectar
- 1 garlic clove, minced
- Salt and pepper to taste
- 1/4 cup fresh parsley, chopped
- 1/4 cup roasted sunflower seeds or pumpkin seeds

Directions:

1. In a medium saucepan, bring 2 cups of water to a boil. Add the thoroughly rinsed quinoa and a pinch of salt.
2. Reduce the heat to low, cover, and simmer for 15 minutes, or until the quinoa is cooked and the water is absorbed.
3. Remove from heat and let it sit covered for 5 minutes. Fluff with a fork and set aside.
4. Preheat your oven to 400°F (200°C).
5. In a large mixing bowl, combine the chopped zucchini, bell pepper, red onion, cherry tomatoes, and broccoli florets. Drizzle with olive oil, and sprinkle with dried oregano, thyme, salt, and pepper. Toss to coat the vegetables evenly.
6. Spread the vegetables in a single layer on a baking sheet lined with parchment paper. Roast in the preheated oven for 25-30 minutes, or until the vegetables are tender and slightly caramelized, stirring halfway through.
7. While the veggies are roasting, prepare the dressing. In a small bowl, whisk together the extra virgin olive oil, balsamic vinegar, Dijon mustard, maple syrup, minced garlic, salt, and pepper until well combined.
8. In a large salad bowl, combine the cooked quinoa and roasted vegetables. Pour the dressing over the mixture and toss to combine. Garnish with fresh parsley and roasted sunflower or pumpkin seeds.
9. Serve the salad warm or at room temperature. It can also be refrigerated and served chilled as a refreshing dish.

Roasted Brussels Sprouts & Quinoa Salad

Servings: 4   **Prep. time:** 15 min   **Total time:** 45 min

Nutritional Information (Per Serving):

Calories: 320, Protein: 8g, Carbohydrates: 38g, Fats: 15g, Fiber: 7g, Cholesterol: 0mg, Sodium: 240mg, Potassium: 620mg

Ingredients

- 1 cup quinoa, uncooked
- 2 cups water or vegetable broth (for cooking quinoa)
- 1 lb Brussels sprouts, trimmed and halved
- 2 tablespoons olive oil
- 1/2 teaspoon sea salt, divided
- 1/4 teaspoon black pepper
- 1/2 teaspoon garlic powder
- 1/2 teaspoon smoked paprika
- 1/4 cup dried cranberries
- 1/4 cup chopped walnuts, toasted
- 2 tablespoons fresh parsley,

Directions:

1. Rinse the quinoa under cold water to remove any bitterness.
2. In a medium saucepan, combine the rinsed quinoa and 2 cups of water or vegetable broth.
3. Bring to a boil, then reduce the heat to low, cover, and simmer for 15 minutes or until the quinoa is cooked and the liquid is absorbed.
4. Once cooked, fluff the quinoa with a fork and set aside to cool.
5. Preheat your oven to 400°F (200°C).
6. On a large baking sheet, toss the halved Brussels sprouts with 1 tablespoon of olive oil, 1/4 teaspoon of sea salt, black pepper, garlic powder, and smoked paprika.
7. Spread the Brussels sprouts in a single layer and roast for 20-25 minutes, until they are golden and crispy on the edges, tossing

chopped
- 1 tablespoon balsamic vinegar
- 1 tablespoon lemon juice
- 1 teaspoon Dijon mustard
- 1 tablespoon maple syrup
- 1 clove garlic, minced

halfway through for even roasting.

8. In a dry skillet over medium heat, toast the chopped walnuts for 2-3 minutes, stirring frequently until they are fragrant and lightly browned. Set aside.
9. In a small bowl, whisk together the balsamic vinegar, lemon juice, Dijon mustard, maple syrup, minced garlic, and the remaining 1 tablespoon of olive oil and 1/4 teaspoon of sea salt.
10. Adjust the seasoning to taste.
11. In a large mixing bowl, combine the cooked quinoa, roasted Brussels sprouts, dried cranberries, toasted walnuts, and chopped parsley.
12. Drizzle the dressing over the salad and toss gently to combine.
13. Divide the salad into four portions and serve warm or at room temperature.

Roasted Beet & Walnut Salad

Servings: 4   **Prep. time:** 15 min   **Total time:** 60 min

Nutritional Information (Per Serving):

Calories: 290 kcal, Protein: 4 g, Carbohydrates: 20 g, Fats: 23 g, Fiber: 5 g, Cholesterol: 0 mg, Sodium: 320 mg, Potassium: 550 mg

Ingredients

- 4 medium beets (about 1 lb), peeled and cut into wedges
- 2 tbsp olive oil
- 1/2 tsp salt
- 1/4 tsp black pepper
- 1/2 cup walnuts, chopped and toasted
- 4 cups mixed greens (e.g., spinach, arugula, or kale)
- 1/2 red onion, thinly sliced
- 1/4 cup fresh parsley, chopped

For the Dressing:

- 3 tbsp balsamic vinegar
- 1 tbsp Dijon mustard
- 1 tbsp maple syrup
- 1/4 cup olive oil
- Salt and pepper to taste

Directions:

1. Preheat the oven to 400°F (200°C). Line a baking sheet with parchment paper.
2. Peel the beets and cut them into wedges. Place them on the prepared baking sheet.
3. Drizzle with 2 tablespoons of olive oil, then sprinkle with 1/2 teaspoon salt and 1/4 teaspoon black pepper. Toss to coat evenly.
4. Roast the beets in the preheated oven for 40-45 minutes, flipping them halfway through to ensure even cooking.
5. The beets should be tender and slightly caramelized. Remove from the oven and allow them to cool slightly.
6. While the beets are roasting, heat a dry skillet over medium heat.
7. Add the chopped walnuts and toast them for 3-5 minutes, stirring frequently to prevent burning.
8. Once golden and fragrant, remove the walnuts from the skillet and set them aside to cool.
9. In a small bowl, whisk together 3 tablespoons of balsamic vinegar, 1 tablespoon of Dijon mustard, and 1 tablespoon of maple syrup.
10. Gradually add 1/4 cup of olive oil while whisking continuously to create an emulsified dressing.
11. Season the dressing with salt and pepper to taste.
12. In a large salad bowl, combine 4 cups of mixed greens, the roasted beets, sliced red onion, and toasted walnuts.
13. Drizzle the dressing over the salad and toss gently to coat all ingredients evenly.
14. Divide the salad into four portions.
15. Garnish with freshly chopped parsley and serve immediately.

Main Dishes

Stuffed Bell Peppers

Servings: 4   **Prep. time:** 15 min   **Total time:** 45 min

Nutritional Information (Per Serving):

Calories: 250, Protein: 10g, Carbohydrates: 42g, Fats: 5g, Fiber: 8g, Cholesterol: 0mg, Sodium: 300mg, Potassium: 700mg

Ingredients

- 4 large bell peppers (any color)
- 1 cup quinoa (uncooked)
- 1 ½ cups water or vegetable broth
- 1 can (15 oz) black beans, drained and rinsed
- 1 cup corn kernels (fresh, frozen, or canned)
- 1 cup cherry tomatoes, halved
- ½ cup diced red onion
- 1 cup chopped fresh spinach
- 2 cloves garlic, minced
- 1 tsp ground cumin
- 1 tsp smoked paprika
- 1 tsp chili powder
- Salt and black pepper, to taste
- 1 tbsp olive oil
- Fresh cilantro or parsley, for garnish (optional)
- Lime wedges, for serving (optional)

Directions:

1. Preheat your oven to 375°F (190°C).
2. Slice the tops off the bell peppers and remove the seeds and membranes. If needed, trim a small slice off the bottom of each pepper to ensure they stand upright, but be careful not to create holes.
3. Rinse the quinoa under cold water.
4. In a medium saucepan, combine the quinoa and water or vegetable broth. Bring to a boil, then reduce to a simmer. Cover and cook for 15 minutes, or until the quinoa is fluffy and the liquid is absorbed. Remove from heat and let it sit for 5 minutes before fluffing with a fork.
5. While the quinoa is cooking, heat olive oil in a large skillet over medium heat.
6. Add the diced red onion and minced garlic. Sauté for 3-4 minutes, or until the onion becomes translucent.
7. Stir in the black beans, corn, cherry tomatoes, and chopped spinach. Cook for another 3 minutes until the spinach is wilted.
8. Add the cooked quinoa to the skillet. Season with cumin, smoked paprika, chili powder, salt, and black pepper. Mix well to combine.
9. Spoon the quinoa mixture into the prepared bell peppers, packing it in tightly.
10. Place the stuffed peppers upright in a baking dish. If you have extra filling, you can spread it around the peppers in the dish.
11. Cover the baking dish with aluminum foil and bake in the preheated oven for 25 minutes.
12. Remove the foil and bake for an additional 5-10 minutes, or until the peppers are tender and slightly charred on the edges.
13. Garnish with fresh cilantro or parsley, if desired.
14. Serve with lime wedges on the side for an extra burst of flavor.

Sweet Potato & Chickpea Curry

Servings: 4   **Prep. time:** 15 min   **Total time:** 45 min

Nutritional Information (Per Serving):

Calories: 340, Protein: 10g, Carbohydrates: 45g, Fats: 15g, Fiber: 8g, Cholesterol: 0mg, Sodium: 420mg, Potassium: 850mg

Ingredients

- 2 medium sweet potatoes, peeled and diced (about 2 cups)
- 1 can (15 oz) chickpeas, drained and rinsed
- 1 can (14 oz) diced tomatoes
- 1 cup coconut milk (full-fat or light)
- 1 medium onion, diced
- 2 cloves garlic, minced
- 1 tablespoon ginger, freshly grated
- 2 tablespoons curry powder
- 1 teaspoon ground cumin
- 1 teaspoon ground coriander
- 1 teaspoon turmeric powder
- 1/2 teaspoon smoked paprika
- 1/4 teaspoon cayenne pepper (optional, for heat)
- 1 tablespoon olive oil
- 1 cup spinach (fresh or frozen)
- Salt and black pepper, to taste
- 1 tablespoon lime juice (for finishing)
- Fresh cilantro, chopped (for garnish, optional)

Directions:

1. Peel and dice the sweet potatoes into bite-sized cubes.
2. Rinse and drain the chickpeas.
3. Dice the onion, mince the garlic, and grate the ginger.
4. Heat olive oil in a large pot or deep skillet over medium heat.
5. Add diced onion and sauté for 5 minutes, or until translucent.
6. Add minced garlic and grated ginger, and cook for an additional 1-2 minutes until fragrant.
7. Stir in the curry powder, ground cumin, ground coriander, turmeric powder, smoked paprika, and cayenne pepper (if using). Cook for 1-2 minutes, stirring constantly to toast the spices and release their flavors.
8. Add the sweet potatoes to the pot and stir to coat with the spices. Pour in the diced tomatoes and coconut milk. Stir well to combine.
9. Bring the mixture to a boil, then reduce heat to a simmer. Cover and cook for 15-20 minutes, or until the sweet potatoes are tender.
10. Stir in the chickpeas and cook for an additional 5 minutes.
11. Add the spinach and cook until wilted (if using fresh) or heated through (if using frozen).
12. Season with salt and black pepper. Stir in lime juice for a fresh flavor. Garnish with chopped fresh cilantro, if desired.
13. Serve the curry hot over brown rice, quinoa, or with a side of steamed vegetables.

Lentil & Vegetable Stir-Fry

Servings: 4

Prep. time: 15 min

Total time: 35 min

Nutritional Information (Per Serving):

Calories: 290, Protein: 12g, Carbohydrates: 42g, Fats: 10g, Fiber: 11g, Cholesterol: 0mg, Sodium: 550mg, Potassium: 750mg

Ingredients

- 1 cup dried green or brown lentils, rinsed and drained
- 2 cups water (for cooking lentils)
- 2 tablespoons olive oil
- 1 medium onion, diced
- 2 cloves garlic, minced
- 1 tablespoon fresh ginger, grated
- 1 medium bell pepper, diced
- 1 medium carrot, thinly sliced
- 1 cup broccoli florets
- 1 cup snap peas (or green beans)
- 1 zucchini, diced
- 1 tablespoon soy sauce (or tamari for gluten-free option)
- 1 tablespoon rice vinegar
- 1 teaspoon sesame oil
- 1 teaspoon ground cumin
- 1/2 teaspoon smoked paprika
- 1/2 teaspoon turmeric powder
- 1/4 teaspoon black pepper
- 1/2 teaspoon sea salt (adjust to taste)
- 2 green onions, chopped (for garnish)
- 1 tablespoon sesame seeds (optional)

Directions:

1. In a medium pot, combine the rinsed lentils and 2 cups of water. Bring to a boil.
2. Reduce heat to low, cover, and simmer for 15-20 minutes until lentils are tender but still firm. Drain and set aside.
3. While lentils are cooking, prepare the vegetables. Dice the bell pepper, slice the carrot, cut the broccoli into florets, trim the snap peas, and dice the zucchini.
4. Heat olive oil in a large skillet or wok over medium heat.
5. Add diced onion and sauté for 3-4 minutes until softened.
6. Add minced garlic and grated ginger, cooking for an additional 1-2 minutes until fragrant.
7. Add bell pepper, carrot, broccoli, snap peas, and zucchini to the skillet. Stir-fry for 5-7 minutes until vegetables are crisp-tender.
8. Add cooked lentils to the skillet with the vegetables.
9. Stir in soy sauce, rice vinegar, sesame oil, ground cumin, smoked paprika, turmeric powder, black pepper, and sea salt.
10. Cook for another 2-3 minutes, stirring frequently, until everything is well combined and heated through. Remove from heat and garnish with chopped green onions and sesame seeds if desired.
11. Serve hot, either on its own or over a bed of brown rice or quinoa.

Cauliflower & Chickpea Tacos

Servings: 4   **Prep. time:** 15 min   **Total time:** 40 min

Nutritional Information (Per Serving):

Calories: 320, Protein: 11g, Carbohydrates: 40g, Fats: 14g, Fiber: 11g, Cholesterol: 0mg, Sodium: 500mg, Potassium: 800mg

Ingredients

- 1 medium head of cauliflower, cut into bite-sized florets
- 1 can (15 oz) chickpeas, drained and rinsed
- 2 tablespoons olive oil
- 1 teaspoon ground cumin
- 1 teaspoon smoked paprika
- 1/2 teaspoon turmeric powder
- 1/2 teaspoon garlic powder
- 1/4 teaspoon chili powder (adjust to taste)
- 1/2 teaspoon sea salt (adjust to taste)
- 1/4 teaspoon black pepper
- 8 small corn tortillas
- 1 cup shredded red cabbage
- 1 avocado, sliced
- 1/2 cup cherry tomatoes, halved
- 1/4 cup fresh cilantro, chopped
- 1 lime, cut into wedges

Directions:

1. Preheat the oven to 425°F (220°C).
2. In a large bowl, combine the cauliflower florets and chickpeas.
3. Drizzle with olive oil and sprinkle with ground cumin, smoked paprika, turmeric powder, garlic powder, chili powder, sea salt, and black pepper. Toss until evenly coated.
4. Spread the cauliflower and chickpeas mixture in a single layer on a baking sheet.
5. Roast in the preheated oven for 20-25 minutes, or until the cauliflower is tender and slightly crispy, and the chickpeas are golden brown. Stir halfway through for even cooking.
6. While the cauliflower and chickpeas are roasting, warm the corn tortillas.
7. Heat a skillet over medium heat. Place each tortilla in the skillet for about 30 seconds on each side until warmed and pliable. Alternatively, wrap tortillas in foil and heat in the oven for about 5 minutes.
8. Once the cauliflower and chickpeas are done roasting, remove from the oven.
9. Fill each warm tortilla with a portion of the roasted cauliflower and chickpeas.
10. Top with shredded red cabbage, avocado slices, cherry tomatoes, and chopped cilantro.
11. Serve the tacos with lime wedges on the side for squeezing over the top.

Mushroom & Spinach Stuffed Portobello Mushrooms

Servings: 4   **Prep. time:** 15 min   **Total time:** 40 min

Nutritional Information (Per Serving):

Calories: 210, Protein: 8g, Carbohydrates: 22g, Fats: 13g, Fiber: 5g, Cholesterol: 0mg, Sodium: 320mg, Potassium: 550mg

Ingredients

- 4 large portobello mushrooms, stems removed and gills scraped out
- 2 tablespoons olive oil, divided
- 1 small onion, finely diced
- 3 cloves garlic, minced
- 1 cup cremini or white mushrooms, finely chopped
- 2 cups fresh spinach, chopped
- 1/4 cup sun-dried tomatoes, finely chopped
- 1/4 cup nutritional yeast

Directions:

1. Preheat your oven to 375°F (190°C).
2. Gently wipe the portobello mushrooms with a damp paper towel to clean. Remove the stems and use a spoon to carefully scrape out the gills from the underside of the caps.
3. Heat 1 tablespoon of olive oil in a large skillet over medium heat.
4. Add the diced onion and cook for about 5 minutes, or until translucent and soft.
5. Add the minced garlic and cook for an additional 1 minute until fragrant.
6. Stir in the chopped cremini or white mushrooms and cook for 5-7 minutes, until they release their moisture and start to brown.
7. Add the chopped spinach and cook for another 2 minutes until wilted.
8. Stir in the sun-dried tomatoes, nutritional yeast, pine nuts, oregano, basil, smoked paprika, sea salt, and black pepper. Cook for another 1-2 minutes to combine all flavors. Remove from heat.

- 1/4 cup pine nuts, toasted (or chopped walnuts for a different flavor)
- 1 teaspoon dried oregano
- 1/2 teaspoon dried basil
- 1/2 teaspoon smoked paprika
- 1/4 teaspoon sea salt (adjust to taste)
- 1/4 teaspoon black pepper
- 1 tablespoon lemon juice (optional, for added flavor)

9. Optionally, add 1 tablespoon of lemon juice for extra brightness.
10. Place the portobello mushroom caps on a baking sheet lined with parchment paper or lightly oiled.
11. Brush the tops of the mushroom caps with the remaining 1 tablespoon of olive oil.
12. Spoon the mushroom and spinach filling evenly into each mushroom cap, pressing down slightly to pack it in.
13. Bake in the preheated oven for 20 minutes, or until the mushrooms are tender and the filling is golden.
14. Serve warm, either as a main dish or as a hearty side.

Butternut Squash & Black Bean Chili

 Servings: 6

 Prep. time: 20 min

 Total time: 60 min

Nutritional Information (Per Serving):

Calories: 230, Protein: 6g, Carbohydrates: 45g, Fats: 3g, Fiber: 12g, Cholesterol: 0mg, Sodium: 580mg, Potassium: 900mg

Ingredients

- 1 tablespoon olive oil
- 1 large onion, diced
- 3 cloves garlic, minced
- 1 medium butternut squash, peeled and cubed (about 4 cups)
- 1 red bell pepper, diced
- 1 yellow bell pepper, diced
- 1 (15-ounce) can black beans, drained and rinsed (or 1.5 cups cooked black beans)
- 1 (15-ounce) can diced tomatoes, with juice
- 2 cups vegetable broth
- 1 tablespoon chili powder
- 1 teaspoon ground cumin
- 1/2 teaspoon smoked paprika
- 1/4 teaspoon ground cinnamon (optional for warmth)
- 1/4 teaspoon cayenne pepper (optional for heat)
- 1 teaspoon sea salt (adjust to taste)
- 1/4 teaspoon black pepper
- 1 tablespoon lime juice (optional, for brightness)
- 1/4 cup fresh cilantro, chopped (optional, for garnish)

Directions:

1. Peel the butternut squash using a vegetable peeler, cut it in half, and remove the seeds. Dice into 1/2-inch cubes.
2. In a large pot, heat the olive oil over medium heat.
3. Add the diced onion and sauté for 5-7 minutes until soft and translucent.
4. Add the minced garlic and sauté for an additional 1 minute until fragrant.
5. Add the cubed butternut squash, diced red and yellow bell peppers, chili powder, cumin, smoked paprika, cinnamon, cayenne pepper, salt, and black pepper. Stir well to coat the vegetables in the spices.
6. Pour in the diced tomatoes with their juice and the vegetable broth. Stir to combine.
7. Bring the mixture to a boil, then reduce the heat to low and cover. Let it simmer for 25-30 minutes, or until the butternut squash is tender.
8. Once the squash is tender, stir in the black beans. Simmer for an additional 5-10 minutes to allow the flavors to meld together.
9. If using, stir in the lime juice just before serving for a fresh, tangy finish.
10. Ladle the chili into bowls and garnish with fresh cilantro, if desired.

Quinoa & Roasted Veggie Bowl

 Servings: 4

 Prep. time: 15 min

 Total time: 45 min

Nutritional Information (Per Serving):

Calories: 380, Protein: 11g, Carbohydrates: 55g, Fats: 13g, Fiber: 12g, Cholesterol: 0mg, Sodium: 500mg, Potassium: 950mg

Ingredients

- 1 cup quinoa (uncooked)
- 2 cups vegetable broth (or water)
- 1 medium sweet potato, peeled and cubed (about 2 cups)
- 1 red bell pepper, diced
- 1 zucchini, sliced into half-moons
- 1 red onion, cut into wedges
- 1 tablespoon olive oil
- 1 teaspoon ground cumin
- 1 teaspoon smoked paprika
- 1/2 teaspoon garlic powder
- 1/2 teaspoon sea salt (divided)
- 1/4 teaspoon black pepper
- 1 (15-ounce) can chickpeas, drained and rinsed
- 2 cups fresh spinach, roughly chopped
- 1 tablespoon lemon juice
- 1 avocado, sliced (for topping)
- Fresh parsley or cilantro, chopped (for garnish)

Directions:

1. Rinse 1 cup of quinoa under cold water using a fine mesh strainer to remove its natural coating (saponin), which can make it taste bitter.
2. In a medium saucepan, combine the rinsed quinoa and 2 cups of vegetable broth or water. Bring to a boil, then reduce heat to low, cover, and simmer for 15 minutes, or until the liquid is absorbed and the quinoa is tender.
3. Remove from heat and let it sit, covered, for 5 minutes. Fluff with a fork.
4. Preheat your oven to 400°F (200°C).
5. In a large bowl, combine the cubed sweet potato, diced red bell pepper, zucchini slices, and red onion wedges. Drizzle with olive oil and sprinkle with cumin, smoked paprika, garlic powder, 1/4 teaspoon of sea salt, and black pepper. Toss to coat evenly.
6. Spread the vegetables in a single layer on a baking sheet lined with parchment paper. Roast for 25-30 minutes, stirring halfway through, until the vegetables are tender and slightly caramelized.
7. While the vegetables are roasting, in a small bowl, toss the drained chickpeas with the remaining 1/4 teaspoon of sea salt and set aside.
8. In a large mixing bowl, combine the cooked quinoa, roasted vegetables, chickpeas, and chopped spinach. Drizzle with lemon juice and toss gently to combine. The heat from the quinoa and vegetables will wilt the spinach slightly.
9. Divide the mixture into 4 bowls.
10. Top each bowl with sliced avocado and garnish with fresh parsley or cilantro.

Zucchini & Corn Fritters

 Servings: 4　　 **Prep. time:** 15 min　　 **Total time:** 35 min

Nutritional Information (Per Serving):

Calories: 210, Protein: 7g, Carbohydrates: 24g, Fats: 10g, Fiber: 5g, Cholesterol: 0mg, Sodium: 250mg, Potassium: 550mg,

Ingredients

- 2 medium zucchinis (about 2 cups grated)
- 1 cup fresh or frozen corn kernels (thawed if frozen)
- 1/2 small red onion, finely chopped
- 1/4 cup fresh parsley or cilantro, chopped
- 1/2 cup chickpea flour
- 1/4 cup nutritional yeast
- 1/4 teaspoon baking powder
- 1/2 teaspoon garlic powder
- 1/2 teaspoon ground cumin
- 1/4 teaspoon smoked paprika
- 1/4 teaspoon salt
- 1/4 teaspoon black pepper
- 1/4 cup water
- 2 tablespoons olive oil (for frying)

Directions:

1. Grate the zucchinis using a box grater and place them in a clean kitchen towel or cheesecloth. Squeeze out as much moisture as possible. This step is crucial to prevent the fritters from becoming soggy.
2. In a large mixing bowl, combine the grated zucchini, corn kernels, chopped red onion, and fresh parsley or cilantro.
3. In a separate bowl, whisk together the chickpea flour, nutritional yeast, baking powder, garlic powder, ground cumin, smoked paprika, salt, and black pepper.
4. Add the dry mixture to the zucchini mixture, stirring until well combined.
5. Gradually add the water, mixing until you have a thick batter. The batter should be moist but not too wet.
6. Heat 1 tablespoon of olive oil in a large non-stick skillet over medium heat.
7. Scoop about 2 tablespoons of the batter for each fritter, placing them in the skillet and flattening slightly with a spatula to form small patties.
8. Cook for 3-4 minutes on each side, or until golden brown and crispy.
9. Transfer the cooked fritters to a plate lined with paper towels to absorb excess oil.
10. Repeat with the remaining batter, adding more oil to the skillet as needed.
11. Serve the fritters warm, garnished with additional fresh herbs if desired. These fritters pair well with a simple side salad or a dipping sauce like tahini or avocado dip.

51

Curried Cauliflower & Chickpeas

Servings: 4   **Prep. time:** 15 min   **Total time:** 45 min

Nutritional Information (Per Serving):

Calories: 360, Protein: 10g, Carbohydrates: 38g, Fats: 20g, Fiber: 11g, Cholesterol: 0mg, Sodium: 620mg, Potassium: 950mg

Ingredients

- 1 medium cauliflower, cut into florets (about 4 cups)
- 1 can (15 oz) chickpeas, drained and rinsed (or 1.5 cups cooked chickpeas)
- 1 medium onion, finely chopped
- 3 cloves garlic, minced
- 1-inch piece fresh ginger, minced
- 1 can (14 oz) diced tomatoes
- 1 can (14 oz) coconut milk (full-fat or light)
- 2 tablespoons olive oil
- 2 tablespoons curry powder
- 1 teaspoon ground cumin
- 1 teaspoon ground coriander
- 1/2 teaspoon turmeric
- 1/4 teaspoon cayenne pepper (optional, for heat)
- 1 teaspoon salt, or to taste
- 1/4 teaspoon black pepper
- 1/2 cup fresh cilantro, chopped (for garnish)
- Juice of 1/2 lemon (optional, for serving)
- Cooked brown rice or quinoa, for serving

Directions:

1. Cut the cauliflower into bite-sized florets. Mince the garlic and ginger. Chop the onion finely. If using canned chickpeas, drain and rinse them.
2. Warm the olive oil in a large skillet or pan over medium heat. Add the chopped onion and sauté for roughly 5 minutes until it softens and turns translucent.
3. Add the minced garlic and ginger, and sauté for another 1-2 minutes until fragrant.
4. Mix in the curry powder, ground cumin, ground coriander, turmeric, and cayenne pepper (optional). Cook for 1-2 minutes to toast the spices, stirring constantly to avoid burning.
5. Add the cauliflower florets to the pan and stir to evenly coat them with the spices. Cook for around 5 minutes, letting the cauliflower soak up the flavors.
6. Add the diced tomatoes with their juice and pour in the coconut milk. Stir to combine, making sure the cauliflower is submerged in the liquid. Season with salt and black pepper.
7. Bring the mixture to a simmer, then lower the heat to a gentle setting. Cover the pan and cook for 15-20 minutes, or until the cauliflower is tender and the sauce has thickened.
8. Mix in the drained chickpeas and continue cooking for an additional 5 minutes until warmed through. Add more salt or pepper to taste, if needed.
9. Remove from heat and fold in the chopped cilantro. Serve the curry over a bed of cooked brown rice or quinoa, and add a squeeze of fresh lemon juice, if desired.

Spaghetti Squash with Tomato Basil Sauce

Servings: 4   **Prep. time:** 15 min   **Total time:** 60 min

Nutritional Information (Per Serving):

Calories: 200, Protein: 4g, Carbohydrates: 33g, Fats: 7g, Fiber: 7g, Cholesterol: 0mg, Sodium: 630mg, Potassium: 1050mg

Ingredients

- 1 large spaghetti squash (about 3-4 pounds)
- 2 tablespoons olive oil
- 1 medium onion, finely chopped
- 4 cloves garlic, minced
- 1 can (28 oz) crushed tomatoes
- 1/4 cup tomato paste
- 1 teaspoon dried oregano
- 1/2 teaspoon dried thyme
- 1/2 teaspoon red pepper flakes (optional, for heat)
- 1/4 teaspoon black pepper
- 1 teaspoon salt, or to taste

Directions:

1. Set your oven to preheat, 400°F (200°C).
2. Slice the spaghetti squash in half lengthwise and remove the seeds. Brush the insides with 1 tablespoon of olive oil, then sprinkle with some salt and pepper.
3. Place the squash halves, cut-side down, on a baking sheet lined with parchment paper. Roast in the oven for 35-45 minutes, or until the flesh is tender and easily shreds with a fork.
4. While the squash is roasting, warm the remaining 1 tablespoon of olive oil in a large pan over medium heat.
5. Add the chopped onion and sauté for about 5 minutes until it becomes soft and translucent.
6. Add the minced garlic and cook for an additional 1-2 minutes until it becomes aromatic.

- 1/4 cup fresh basil leaves, chopped (plus more for garnish)
- 1 tablespoon nutritional yeast (optional, for a cheesy flavor)
- 1 tablespoon balsamic vinegar
- Fresh parsley or basil, for garnish

7. Stir in the crushed tomatoes, tomato paste, dried oregano, dried thyme, red pepper flakes (if desired), black pepper, and salt. Bring the mixture to a gentle simmer.
8. Lower the heat and let the sauce simmer for around 20 minutes, stirring occasionally to blend the flavors.
9. Mix in the chopped fresh basil, nutritional yeast (if using), and balsamic vinegar. Adjust the seasoning as needed.
10. Once the spaghetti squash is done roasting, take it out of the oven and let it cool until it is safe to handle.
11. Using a fork, scrape the flesh of the squash into long, spaghetti-like strands.
12. Place the squash strands onto four plates and top each with a generous serving of the tomato basil sauce.
13. If desired, garnish with extra fresh basil or parsley.
14. Serve while hot and enjoy this delicious, plant-based dish that's both hearty and nutritious.

Sweet Potato & Black Bean Enchiladas

Nutritional Information (Per Serving):

Calories: 330, Protein: 10g, Carbohydrates: 59g, Fats: 6g, Fiber: 14g, Cholesterol: 0mg, Sodium: 720mg, Potassium: 1100mg

Servings: 4   **Prep. time:** 20 min   **Total time:** 60 min

Ingredients

For the Filling:
- 2 medium sweet potatoes (about 1 pound), peeled and diced
- 1 tablespoon olive oil
- 1 small onion, finely chopped
- 2 cloves garlic, minced
- 1 can (15 oz) black beans, drained and rinsed
- 1 teaspoon ground cumin
- 1 teaspoon chili powder
- 1/2 teaspoon smoked paprika
- 1/2 teaspoon salt, or to taste
- 1/4 teaspoon black pepper
- 1/4 cup fresh cilantro, chopped

For the Enchilada Sauce:
- 1 can (15 oz) tomato sauce
- 2 tablespoons chili powder
- 1 teaspoon ground cumin
- 1 teaspoon garlic powder
- 1 teaspoon onion powder
- 1/2 teaspoon smoked paprika
- 1/2 teaspoon salt
- 1/4 teaspoon black pepper
- 1 cup vegetable broth

For Assembly:
- 8-10 small corn tortillas (6-inch)
- 1/4 cup nutritional yeast (optional, for a cheesy flavor)
- Fresh cilantro for garnish
- Lime wedges for serving

Directions:

1. Set the oven to preheat, 375°F (190°C).
2. Steam or boil the diced sweet potatoes for 10-15 minutes or until tender. Drain and set aside.
3. In a large pan, warm the olive oil over medium heat. Add the chopped onion and sauté for roughly 5 minutes until it softens.
4. Add the minced garlic and cook for an additional 1-2 minutes until it becomes fragrant.
5. Stir in the black beans, cooked sweet potatoes, ground cumin, chili powder, smoked paprika, salt, and black pepper. Cook for 2-3 minutes, stirring occasionally, until the mixture is well combined.
6. Remove from heat, stir in the chopped cilantro. Set the filling aside.
7. Combine the tomato sauce, chili powder, ground cumin, garlic powder, onion powder, smoked paprika, salt, black pepper, and vegetable broth in a medium saucepan.
8. Bring the mixture to a simmer over medium heat, stirring occasionally. Simmer for 10 minutes, allowing the flavors to meld. Adjust the seasoning to taste.
9. Lightly grease a 9x13-inch baking dish.
10. To make the corn tortillas more pliable, warm them in the microwave for 30 seconds or in a hot skillet for a few seconds on each side.
11. Spoon 2-3 tablespoons of the sweet potato and black bean filling onto each tortilla. Roll up the tortillas and place them seam-side down in the prepared baking dish.
12. Drizzle the enchilada sauce evenly over the rolled tortillas.
13. For a cheesy flavor, sprinkle nutritional yeast on top, if desired.
14. Cover the baking dish with aluminum foil and bake in the oven for 20 minutes.
15. Take off the foil and bake for another 10 minutes, or until the edges turn slightly crispy and the sauce is bubbling.
16. Garnish with fresh cilantro and serve with lime wedges on the side. Enjoy these flavorful and nutritious enchiladas as a wholesome plant-based main dish.

Thai Peanut Sweet Potato Noodles

 Servings: 4   **Prep. time:** 15 min   **Total time:** 35 min

Nutritional Information (Per Serving):

Calories: 350, Protein: 7g, Carbohydrates: 45g, Fats: 16g, Fiber: 8g, Cholesterol: 0mg, Sodium: 550mg, Potassium: 800mg

Ingredients

- 2 large sweet potatoes (about 1.5 lbs), spiralized into noodles
- 1 tablespoon coconut oil
- 1 red bell pepper, thinly sliced
- 1 cup shredded carrots
- 1/2 cup red cabbage, thinly sliced
- 2 cloves garlic, minced
- 1-inch piece of ginger, grated
- For garnish: 1/4 cup green onions, chopped; 1/4 cup fresh cilantro, chopped; 1/4 cup roasted peanuts, chopped; 1 tablespoon sesame seeds

Thai Peanut Sauce

- 1/3 cup natural peanut butter
- 2 tablespoons soy sauce (or tamari for gluten-free)
- 1 tablespoon lime juice
- 1 tablespoon maple syrup
- 1 tablespoon rice vinegar
- 1 teaspoon sriracha (optional, for spice)
- 2-3 tablespoons water (to thin the sauce)

Directions:

1. Peel the sweet potatoes and use a spiralizer to create noodle-like strands. If you don't have a spiralizer, you can use a julienne peeler or a sharp knife to make thin strips. Set aside.
2. In a small bowl, whisk together the peanut butter, soy sauce, lime juice, maple syrup, rice vinegar, and sriracha until smooth.
3. Gradually add 2-3 tablespoons of water, one tablespoon at a time, until the sauce is thin enough to pour. Set aside.
4. Heat coconut oil in a large skillet or wok over medium heat.
5. Add minced garlic and grated ginger, sautéing for 1-2 minutes until fragrant.
6. Add the red bell pepper, shredded carrots, and red cabbage. Stir frequently and cook for 5-7 minutes, until the vegetables are tender yet still crisp.
7. Add the spiralized sweet potato noodles to the skillet. Mix them with the vegetables and cook for another 5-7 minutes until the noodles are tender but not too soft. Be careful not to overcook, as sweet potato noodles can become mushy quickly.
8. Pour the Thai peanut sauce over the noodles and vegetables, tossing well to ensure everything is evenly coated. Cook for an additional 1-2 minutes to warm the sauce through.
9. Divide the noodles among bowls and top with chopped green onions, cilantro, roasted peanuts, and sesame seeds if desired.
10. Serve immediately while hot.

Stuffed Acorn Squash

 Servings: 4   **Prep. time:** 15 min   **Total time:** 60 min

Nutritional Information (Per Serving):

Calories: 380, Protein: 10g, Carbohydrates: 56g, Fats: 13g, Fiber: 11g, Cholesterol: 0mg, Sodium: 160mg, Potassium: 1100mg

Ingredients

- 2 acorn squashes (medium-sized)
- 1 tablespoon olive oil
- 1 small onion, finely chopped
- 2 cloves garlic, minced
- 1 cup cooked quinoa
- 1 cup cooked chickpeas (canned or freshly cooked)
- 1/2 cup dried cranberries (unsweetened)
- 1/4 cup chopped walnuts
- 1/2 teaspoon ground cinnamon
- 1/2 teaspoon ground cumin

Directions:

1. Preheat the oven to 400°F (200°C).
2. Slice the acorn squashes in half lengthwise and remove the seeds.
3. Brush the cut sides with olive oil and season with salt and pepper.
4. Place the squash halves face down on a parchment-lined baking sheet.
5. Roast in the oven for 30-35 minutes, or until the flesh is tender when pierced with a fork.
6. While the squash is roasting, warm 1 tablespoon of olive oil in a large skillet over medium heat.
7. Add the chopped onion and sauté for 3-4 minutes until softened.
8. Add minced garlic and cook for another 1-2 minutes until fragrant.
9. Stir in the cooked quinoa, chickpeas, dried cranberries, chopped walnuts, cinnamon, cumin, and nutmeg. Cook for 3-4 minutes, stirring occasionally, until everything is heated through.
10. Season the mixture with salt and pepper to taste.

- 1/4 teaspoon ground nutmeg
- Salt and pepper to taste
- 2 tablespoons fresh parsley, chopped (for garnish)
- 1 tablespoon tahini (optional, for drizzling)

11. When the squashes are done, take them out of the oven and let them cool slightly.
12. Turn the squash halves cut-side up.
13. Fill each squash half with the quinoa and chickpea stuffing, pressing it in to fill the cavity completely.
14. Place the stuffed squashes back in the oven and bake for another 10 minutes to warm through.
15. Once heated, remove them from the oven and allow them to cool slightly.
16. Top with chopped fresh parsley and, if you like, drizzle with a little tahini for added creaminess and flavor.
17. Serve warm.

Mango & Black Bean Quesadillas

Servings: 4   **Prep. time:** 15 min   **Total time:** 25 min

Nutritional Information (Per Serving):

Calories: 380, Protein: 10g, Carbohydrates: 55g, Fats: 12g, Fiber: 12g, Cholesterol: 0mg, Sodium: 400mg, Potassium: 650mg

Ingredients

- 8 small whole-grain tortillas (or gluten-free tortillas if preferred)
- 1 ripe mango, peeled, pitted, and diced (about 1 cup)
- 1 1/2 cups cooked black beans (or 1 can, drained and rinsed)
- 1 small red bell pepper, diced
- 1/4 cup red onion, finely chopped
- 1/2 cup fresh cilantro, chopped
- 1/2 teaspoon ground cumin
- 1/2 teaspoon chili powder
- 1 tablespoon lime juice
- 1 avocado, sliced
- 1/2 cup vegan cheese (optional, shredded)
- Salt and pepper to taste
- 1 tablespoon olive oil or avocado oil for cooking

Directions:

1. In a medium bowl, mix together the diced mango, cooked black beans, red bell pepper, red onion, and fresh cilantro.
2. Add the ground cumin, chili powder, lime juice, salt, and pepper to the bowl.
3. Stir well to coat all the ingredients evenly with the spices and lime juice, then set the mixture aside.
4. Place 4 tortillas on a clean surface.
5. Spread the mango and black bean mixture evenly over each tortilla.
6. If desired, sprinkle a bit of vegan cheese over the filling.
7. Add avocado slices on top for extra creaminess and healthy fats.
8. Cover each with another tortilla, pressing down gently to hold everything in place.
9. Heat a large skillet or griddle over medium heat and add a little olive oil or avocado oil.
10. When the oil is hot, put one quesadilla in the skillet.
11. Cook for 2-3 minutes on each side, until the tortilla is golden and crispy and the filling is warmed through.
12. Repeat with the remaining quesadillas, adding more oil to the skillet as necessary.
13. Once all the quesadillas are done, cut them into quarters or halves and serve immediately.
14. Optional: Garnish with extra fresh cilantro, a squeeze of lime juice, or a side of salsa for added flavor.

Baked Falafel with Tahini Sauce

Servings: 4   **Prep. time:** 20 min   **Total time:** 1 h 50 min (excluding soaking time)

Nutritional Information (Per Serving):

Calories: 380, Protein: 14g, Carbohydrates: 45g, Fats: 18g, Fiber: 10g, Cholesterol: 0mg, Sodium: 480mg, Potassium: 650mg

Ingredients

- 1 cup dried chickpeas (soaked overnight, about 2 ½ cups after soaking)
- 1 small onion, finely chopped
- 3 cloves garlic, minced
- 1/2 cup fresh parsley, chopped
- 1/2 cup fresh cilantro, chopped
- 1 tablespoon ground cumin
- 1 tablespoon ground coriander
- 1/2 teaspoon ground cayenne pepper (optional for spice)
- 1 teaspoon baking powder
- 1/2 teaspoon salt
- 1/4 teaspoon black pepper
- 2 tablespoons olive oil (for brushing)

  For the Tahini Sauce:
- 1/2 cup tahini
- 1/4 cup lemon juice (freshly squeezed)
- 2 tablespoons water (more if needed to thin the sauce)
- 1 clove garlic, minced
- 1 tablespoon maple syrup or agave syrup
- 1/4 teaspoon salt

Directions:

1. Soak the chickpeas: Place the dried chickpeas in a large bowl and cover with water. Soak them for 8-12 hours or overnight. This helps soften the chickpeas and makes them easier to blend while improving digestibility.
2. Drain and rinse the soaked chickpeas. Transfer them to a food processor.
3. Add the chopped onion, minced garlic, parsley, cilantro, cumin, coriander, cayenne pepper (if using), baking powder, salt, and black pepper.
4. Pulse the mixture in the food processor until it is well combined but still slightly coarse in texture. Avoid over-processing; you want a dough-like consistency that can hold together when formed into balls.
5. Refrigerate the mixture: Cover and refrigerate the falafel mixture for about 30 minutes to help it firm up.
6. Preheat the oven to 375°F (190°C) and line a baking sheet with parchment paper.
7. Form the falafel balls: Scoop about 2 tablespoons of the mixture and shape it into small balls or patties.
8. Place the falafel balls on the prepared baking sheet.
9. Brush the tops of the falafel with olive oil to help them crisp up in the oven.
10. Bake the falafel: Bake in the preheated oven for 25-30 minutes, flipping halfway through, until the falafel are golden brown and crispy on the outside.
11. While the falafel is baking, prepare the tahini sauce.
12. In a small bowl, whisk together the tahini, lemon juice, water, minced garlic, maple syrup (or agave), and salt until smooth and creamy.
13. Adjust the consistency by adding more water, one teaspoon at a time, until the sauce reaches your desired thickness.
14. Once the falafel are done baking, remove them from the oven and allow them to cool slightly.
15. Serve the falafel warm, drizzled with tahini sauce. You can also serve them with a side of whole-grain pita, fresh veggies, or over a bed of greens.

Vegetable & Tofu Stir-Fry

 Servings: 4

 Prep. time: 15 min

 Total time: 55 min (including marinating time)

Nutritional Information (Per Serving):

Calories: 260, Protein: 13g, Carbohydrates: 20g, Fats: 14g, Fiber: 5g, Cholesterol: 0mg, Sodium: 600mg, Potassium: 700mg

Ingredients

- 1 block (14 oz) firm tofu, drained and pressed
- 1 tablespoon soy sauce or tamari (for a gluten-free option)
- 1 tablespoon rice vinegar
- 1 tablespoon sesame oil
- 1 tablespoon cornstarch
- 2 tablespoons olive oil (for frying tofu)
- 1 red bell pepper, sliced thinly
- 1 yellow bell pepper, sliced

Directions:

1. Drain the tofu and wrap it in a clean kitchen towel. Place a heavy object (like a cast-iron skillet) on top to press out excess moisture for at least 15 minutes. This step ensures the tofu becomes crispier when cooked.
2. After pressing, cut the tofu into 1-inch cubes. In a bowl, mix together 1 tablespoon soy sauce, rice vinegar, and sesame oil. Add the tofu cubes, tossing gently to coat. Allow the tofu to marinate for at least 20 minutes for better flavor absorption.
3. After marinating, sprinkle the tofu with cornstarch and toss gently to evenly coat. This will help achieve a crispy texture when frying.
4. In a large non-stick skillet or wok, heat 2 tablespoons of olive oil over medium heat.
5. Add the tofu cubes to the skillet and cook for about 3-4 minutes on each side, until golden brown and crispy. Remove the tofu from the skillet

thinly
- 1 medium carrot, julienned or sliced thinly
- 1 small broccoli head, cut into small florets
- 1 zucchini, sliced into thin rounds
- 1 cup snap peas, ends trimmed
- 3 cloves garlic, minced
- 1 tablespoon ginger, minced
- 3 tablespoons low-sodium soy sauce or tamari
- 1 tablespoon hoisin sauce (optional for a sweeter flavor)
- 2 tablespoons water
- 1 tablespoon sesame seeds (optional for garnish)
- 2 green onions, sliced (optional for garnish)
- Cooked brown rice or quinoa (optional)

and set it aside.
6. In the same skillet, add a bit more olive oil if needed and heat over medium-high heat.
7. Add the minced garlic and ginger, sautéing for about 1 minute until fragrant.
8. Add the carrots, bell peppers, and broccoli. Stir-fry for 5-6 minutes until the vegetables start to soften but are still crisp.
9. Add the zucchini and snap peas, and continue to stir-fry for an additional 3-4 minutes.
10. Return the cooked tofu to the skillet with the vegetables.
11. In a small bowl, mix together the soy sauce, hoisin sauce (if using), and 2 tablespoons of water. Pour this sauce over the stir-fry and toss everything to coat evenly.
12. Cook for another 2 minutes to heat through and allow the flavors to meld.
13. Remove from heat and garnish with sesame seeds and sliced green onions if desired.
14. Serve the vegetable and tofu stir-fry over cooked brown rice or quinoa for a complete meal.

Spicy Lentil & Spinach Stuffed Sweet Potatoes

Servings: 4   **Prep. time:** 15 min   **Total time:** 1 h 5 min

Nutritional Information (Per Serving):

Calories: 340, Protein: 12g, Carbohydrates: 62g, Fats: 5g, Fiber: 15g, Cholesterol: 0mg, Sodium: 180mg, Potassium: 1200mg

Ingredients

- 4 medium sweet potatoes, scrubbed and washed
- 1 cup dry green or brown lentils, rinsed
- 2 ½ cups water or vegetable broth
- 1 tablespoon olive oil
- 1 medium onion, finely chopped
- 2 cloves garlic, minced
- 1 teaspoon ground cumin
- 1 teaspoon smoked paprika
- 1 teaspoon ground coriander
- ½ teaspoon ground cayenne pepper (adjust to taste)
- Salt and pepper to taste
- 3 cups fresh spinach, chopped
- 1 tablespoon tomato paste
- 1 teaspoon lemon juice
- 2 tablespoons chopped fresh cilantro (optional for garnish)

Directions:

1. Set the oven to preheat, 400°F (200°C).
2. Pierce the sweet potatoes with a fork and place them on a parchment-lined baking sheet.
3. Bake for 45-50 minutes, until tender.
4. Meanwhile, cook the lentils in 2 ½ cups of water or broth. Bring to a boil, reduce heat, cover, and simmer for 20-25 minutes until tender. Drain and set aside.
5. Heat olive oil in a skillet over medium heat. Sauté the onion for 5-7 minutes until soft.
6. Add garlic, cumin, smoked paprika, coriander, and cayenne pepper; cook for 1-2 minutes.
7. Stir in the tomato paste, then add lentils and mix well. Cook for 2-3 minutes.
8. Add spinach and cook until wilted, about 3-4 minutes.
9. Season with lemon juice, salt, and pepper.
10. Remove the sweet potatoes from the oven, let cool slightly, and cut them open.
11. Fill with the lentil-spinach mixture.
12. Garnish with cilantro if desired and serve warm.

Roasted Beet & Lentil Patties

Servings: 4   **Prep. time:** 10 min   **Total time:** 1 h 10 min

Nutritional Information (Per Serving):

Calories: 220, Protein: 10g, Carbohydrates: 30g, Fats: 8g, Fiber: 8g, Cholesterol: 0mg, Sodium: 220mg, Potassium: 530mg

Ingredients

- 1 cup cooked green or brown lentils (½ cup dry lentils, cooked)
- 1 medium beet (about 1 cup), roasted and grated
- 1 small onion, finely chopped
- 2 cloves garlic, minced
- 1 tablespoon olive oil
- ½ cup rolled oats, ground into a coarse flour
- ¼ cup sunflower seeds, ground into a coarse meal
- 2 tablespoons ground flaxseeds
- 2 tablespoons water
- 1 tablespoon soy sauce or tamari
- 1 teaspoon ground cumin
- 1 teaspoon smoked paprika
- ½ teaspoon ground coriander
- Salt and pepper to taste
- Whole grain buns, lettuce, tomato slices, avocado, or your choice of toppings

Directions:

1. Set the oven to preheat, 400°F (200°C).
2. Wash the beet, wrap it in foil, and roast for 40-45 minutes, until tender. Cool, peel, and grate finely.
3. While roasting, rinse ½ cup of dry lentils under cold water. Cook lentils in a saucepan with 1 ½ cups water. Bring to a boil, then simmer for 20-25 minutes until tender. Drain and let cool.
4. Mix ground flaxseeds with 2 tablespoons of water in a small bowl and let sit for 5-10 minutes to thicken.
5. In a skillet, heat olive oil over medium heat. Sauté chopped onion for 5-7 minutes until soft. Add garlic, cumin, smoked paprika, and coriander; cook for 1-2 minutes.
6. Combine cooked lentils, grated beet, sautéed onion, ground oats, sunflower seeds, and flaxseed mixture in a bowl.
7. Add soy sauce or tamari, season with salt and pepper, and mix until combined and firm enough to form patties.
8. Line a baking sheet with parchment paper. Shape the mixture into 8 patties and place them on the sheet.
9. Bake at 400°F (200°C) for 20-25 minutes, flipping halfway through, until firm and slightly crispy.
10. Serve the patties on whole grain buns with lettuce, tomato, and avocado.

Vegetable Paella

Servings: 4   **Prep. time:** 15 min   **Total time:** 55 min

Nutritional Information (Per Serving):

Calories: 400, Protein: 10g, Carbohydrates: 65g, Fats: 10g, Fiber: 8g, Cholesterol: 0mg, Sodium: 400mg, Potassium: 800mg

Ingredients

- 1 ½ cups short-grain rice (such as Arborio or Bomba)
- 3 cups vegetable broth
- 1 medium onion, finely chopped
- 3 cloves garlic, minced
- 1 red bell pepper, sliced into thin strips
- 1 yellow bell pepper, sliced into thin strips
- 1 medium zucchini, sliced into half-moons
- 1 cup green beans, trimmed and cut into 1-inch pieces
- 1 cup cherry tomatoes, halved

Directions:

1. Soak saffron threads in 2 tablespoons of warm water for at least 10 minutes to enhance their flavor and color.
2. In a large skillet or paella pan, heat 2 tablespoons of olive oil over medium heat.
3. Add the chopped onion and sauté for about 5 minutes until it softens.
4. Add minced garlic, red and yellow bell peppers, zucchini, and green beans, cooking for 5-7 minutes until slightly tender.
5. Stir in smoked paprika, ground turmeric, salt, and pepper. Cook for 1 minute until the spices release their aroma.
6. Add the rice, stirring to coat with the oil and spices.
7. Pour in the vegetable broth and saffron water (with threads). Stir to combine.
8. Bring to a boil, then lower the heat to a simmer. Cover and cook

- 1 cup artichoke hearts, quartered (canned or cooked)
- 1 cup frozen peas, thawed
- 1 teaspoon smoked paprika
- 1 teaspoon ground turmeric
- ½ teaspoon saffron threads, soaked in 2 tablespoons warm water
- 2 tablespoons olive oil
- Salt and pepper to taste
- Fresh parsley, chopped (for garnish)
- Lemon wedges (for serving)

for 15 minutes without stirring.

9. After 15 minutes, scatter cherry tomatoes, artichoke hearts, and peas over the rice without stirring.
10. Cover and continue cooking for another 10-15 minutes until the rice is tender and liquid is absorbed.
11. Remove from heat and let the paella sit, covered, for 5 minutes to meld the flavors.
12. Garnish with chopped parsley and serve with lemon wedges.

Chickpea & Avocado Wraps

 Servings: 4   **Prep. time:** 15 min   **Total time:** 15 min

Nutritional Information (Per Serving):

Calories: 360, Protein: 10g, Carbohydrates: 48g, Fats: 16g, Fiber: 12g, Cholesterol: 0mg, Sodium: 450mg, Potassium: 800mg

Ingredients

- 1 can (15 oz) chickpeas, drained and rinsed
- 1 large avocado, peeled, pitted, and diced
- 1 small red onion, finely chopped
- 1 medium cucumber, diced
- 1 cup cherry tomatoes, halved
- 1/4 cup fresh cilantro, chopped
- Juice of 1 lime
- 2 tablespoons tahini
- 1 teaspoon ground cumin
- 1/2 teaspoon smoked paprika
- Salt and pepper to taste
- 4 large whole wheat or gluten-free wraps
- 2 cups fresh spinach or mixed greens

Directions:

1. In a medium bowl, mash the drained chickpeas with a fork or potato masher until roughly mashed but still chunky.
2. Add the diced avocado to the mashed chickpeas and continue mashing until the avocado is fully incorporated.
3. Stir in the finely chopped red onion, diced cucumber, cherry tomatoes, and chopped cilantro.
4. Add the lime juice, tahini, ground cumin, smoked paprika, salt, and pepper. Mix everything together until well combined.
5. Lay out the wraps on a clean surface. Spread 1/4 of the chickpea and avocado mixture onto each wrap, leaving some space at the edges.
6. Top each wrap with 1/2 cup of fresh spinach or mixed greens.
7. Fold the sides of the wrap inward and then roll it up tightly from the bottom to the top.
8. Slice the wraps in half if desired, and serve immediately.

Sweet Potato & Lentil Shepherd's Pie

 Servings: 6   **Prep. time:** 25 min   **Total time:** 1 h 5 min

Nutritional Information (Per Serving):

Calories: 320, Protein: 10g, Carbohydrates: 54g, Fats: 9g, Fiber: 12g, Cholesterol: 0mg, Sodium: 480mg, Potassium: 970mg

Ingredients

- 4 large sweet potatoes (about 2 lbs), peeled and diced
- 1/4 cup unsweetened almond milk (or any plant-based milk)
- 2 tablespoons olive oil
- Salt and pepper to taste
- 1 cup dry green or brown lentils, rinsed and soaked in water for 1 hour
- 2 tablespoons olive oil
- 1 large onion, finely chopped
- 2 garlic cloves, minced
- 2 medium carrots, diced
- 2 celery stalks, diced
- 1 cup mushrooms, chopped
- 1 can (15 oz) diced tomatoes
- 2 tablespoons tomato paste
- 1 tablespoon soy sauce or tamari
- 1 teaspoon dried thyme
- 1 teaspoon dried rosemary
- 1 teaspoon smoked paprika
- Salt and pepper to taste
- 2 cups vegetable broth
- 1 cup frozen peas

Directions:

1. Put the diced sweet potatoes in a large pot and fill with water until covered. Bring the water to a boil, then cook for 15-20 minutes, or until the sweet potatoes are tender. Drain the water and place the sweet potatoes back in the pot. Mash them with almond milk, olive oil, salt, and pepper until the mixture is smooth. Set aside.
2. While the sweet potatoes are cooked, drain and rinse the lentils. Warm olive oil in a large skillet over medium heat. Sauté chopped onion for 3-4 minutes until translucent. Add minced garlic, carrots, celery, and mushrooms, and cook for 5 minutes until softened.
3. Stir in lentils, diced tomatoes, tomato paste, soy sauce, thyme, rosemary, smoked paprika, salt, and pepper. Cook for 2 minutes, then add vegetable broth. Bring to a boil, then lower the heat, cover the skillet, and let it simmer for 25 minutes until the lentils are tender and most of the liquid has been absorbed. Add the frozen peas and continue cooking for an additional 5 minutes.
4. Preheat the oven to 375°F (190°C). Spread the lentil mixture in a 9x13-inch baking dish. Top with mashed sweet potato, spreading evenly. If desired, create a pattern on the top with a fork..
5. Bake for 20 minutes until the top is lightly golden and the filling is bubbling. Let cool slightly before serving.

Spaghetti Squash with Roasted Tomato Sauce

Servings: 4   **Prep. time:** 20 min   **Total time:** 1 h 10 min

Nutritional Information (Per Serving):

Calories: 220, Protein: 4g, Carbohydrates: 28g, Fats: 10g, Fiber: 6g, Cholesterol: 0mg, Sodium: 320mg, Potassium: 900mg

Ingredients

- 1 large spaghetti squash (about 4 lbs)
- 1 tablespoon olive oil
- 1/2 teaspoon salt (divided)
- 1/4 teaspoon black pepper (divided)
- 1.5 lbs ripe tomatoes (Roma or cherry), halved
- 1 medium onion, roughly chopped
- 4 garlic cloves, peeled
- 1 tablespoon olive oil
- 1/2 teaspoon dried oregano
- 1/2 teaspoon dried basil
- 1/4 teaspoon red pepper flakes (optional, for heat)
- 1/4 teaspoon salt
- Freshly ground black pepper, to taste
- 1 tablespoon balsamic vinegar
- 1/4 cup fresh basil, chopped (for garnish)

Directions:

1. Preheat the oven to 400°F (200°C).
2. Cut the spaghetti squash in half lengthwise and scoop out the seeds.
3. Brush the inside of each half with 1/2 tablespoon olive oil, and sprinkle with 1/4 teaspoon salt and 1/8 teaspoon black pepper.
4. Place cut-side down on a parchment-lined baking sheet and roast for 40-45 minutes, until tender and easy to shred. Let it cool, then use a fork to create spaghetti-like strands. Set aside.
5.
6. While the squash cooks, prepare the tomato sauce.
7. Place halved tomatoes, chopped onions, and garlic on another baking sheet.
8. Drizzle with 1 tablespoon olive oil and sprinkle with dried oregano, dried basil, red pepper flakes, 1/4 teaspoon salt, and pepper.
9. Roast in the oven for 25-30 minutes, until the tomatoes are soft and caramelized.
10. Blend the roasted vegetables with balsamic vinegar until smooth, adjusting seasoning as needed.
11.
12. Serve the shredded spaghetti squash on 4 plates, topped with the roasted tomato sauce.
13. Garnish with fresh basil and extra pepper, if desired.
14. Enjoy warm as a main dish, paired with a side salad or steamed vegetables.

Green Bean & Tofu Stir-Fry

 Servings: 4

 Prep. time: 15 min

 Total time: 35 min

Nutritional Information (Per Serving):

Calories: 240, Protein: 12g, Carbohydrates: 16g, Fats: 14g, Fiber: 5g, Cholesterol: 0mg, Sodium: 510mg, Potassium: 510mg

Ingredients

- 14 oz (400g) firm tofu
- 1 tablespoon tamari or soy sauce (for marinating the tofu)
- 1 tablespoon cornstarch
- 2 tablespoons sesame oil (divided)
- 1 lb (450g) green beans, trimmed
- 1 red bell pepper, thinly sliced
- 1 yellow bell pepper, thinly sliced
- 3 cloves garlic, minced
- 1-inch piece of ginger, minced
- 2 tablespoons low-sodium soy sauce or tamari
- 1 tablespoon rice vinegar
- 1 tablespoon maple syrup
- 1 tablespoon sesame seeds (optional, for garnish)
- 1/4 cup fresh cilantro, chopped (optional, for garnish)
- Cooked brown rice or quinoa, for serving (optional)

Directions:

1. Drain the tofu and press it with a tofu press, or wrap it in a clean towel and place a heavy object on top for 10-15 minutes to eliminate excess moisture.
2. After pressing, slice the tofu into 1-inch cubes.
3. Toss the tofu cubes with one tablespoon of tamari or soy sauce in a bowl and let them marinate for 5 minutes.
4. After marinating, sprinkle the tofu with cornstarch and toss to coat evenly. This will help the tofu crisp up during cooking.
5. Warm 1 tablespoon of sesame oil in a large skillet or wok on medium-high heat.
6. Add the tofu cubes and cook for 5-7 minutes, turning them occasionally, until they are crispy and golden on all sides.
7. Take the tofu out and place it on a plate.
8. In the same skillet, pour the remaining 1 tablespoon of sesame oil.
9. Add the minced garlic and ginger, sautéing for 30 seconds until fragrant.
10. Add the green beans to the skillet and stir-fry for 3-4 minutes until they are tender but still slightly crisp.
11. After that, toss in the red and yellow bell peppers and stir-fry for 2-3 minutes more.
12. Add the cooked tofu back to the skillet with the vegetables.
13. In a small bowl, combine two tablespoons of soy sauce, rice vinegar, and maple syrup, whisking them together.
14. Pour the sauce over the tofu and vegetables, stirring well to coat evenly.
15. Continue cooking for 2-3 minutes to let the flavors blend, and the sauce thickens slightly.
16. Take the skillet off the heat and, if desired, sprinkle with sesame seeds and fresh cilantro.
17. Serve hot over a bed of cooked brown rice or quinoa for a complete meal.

Cabbage & Mushroom Stir-Fry

 Servings: 4

 Prep. time: 10 min

 Total time: 25 min

Nutritional Information (Per Serving):

Calories: 160, Protein: 5g, Carbohydrates: 20g, Fats: 7g, Fiber: 6g, Cholesterol: 0mg, Sodium: 370mg, Potassium: 520mg

Ingredients

- 1 tablespoon sesame oil
- 1 medium onion, thinly sliced
- 3 cloves garlic, minced
- 1-inch piece of ginger, minced
- 8 oz (225g) cremini mushrooms, sliced
- 1/2 medium head of cabbage, thinly sliced (about 4 cups)
- 1 medium carrot, julienned
- 2 tablespoons low-sodium soy sauce or tamari
- 1 tablespoon rice vinegar
- 1 tablespoon maple syrup
- 1/2 teaspoon crushed red pepper flakes (optional, for heat)
- 1 tablespoon sesame seeds (optional, for garnish)
- 2 green onions, sliced (optional, for garnish)
- Cooked brown rice or quinoa, for serving (optional)

Directions:

1. Thinly slice the onion and cabbage, and julienne the carrot. Clean and slice the mushrooms.
2. Mince the garlic and ginger, keeping them aside for later use.
3. Warm the sesame oil in a large skillet or wok on medium-high heat.
4. Add the sliced onions and sauté for 2-3 minutes until they start to soften and become translucent.
5. Add the minced garlic and ginger, and sauté for another 30 seconds until fragrant.
6. Place mushrooms in the skillet and cook them for 3-4 minutes, stirring often, until they start to brown and have released their moisture.
7. Add the sliced cabbage and julienned carrot to the skillet.
8. Stir-fry for 5-6 minutes until the cabbage is tender but still slightly crisp, and the carrots are softened.
9. Combine the rice vinegar, soy sauce and maple syrup in a small bowl.
10. Scatter the sauce over the vegetables and stir well, cooking for an additional 2 minutes to let the flavors blend.
11. Remove the stir-fry from the heat and, if you wish, sprinkle with sesame seeds and sliced green onions.
12. Serve hot over a bed of cooked brown rice or quinoa for a complete meal.

Stuffed Zucchini Boats

Servings: 4   **Prep. time:** 15 min   **Total time:** 45 min

Nutritional Information (Per Serving):

Calories: 230, Protein: 8g, Carbohydrates: 36g, Fats: 8g, Fiber: 7g, Cholesterol: 0mg, Sodium: 290mg, Potassium: 780mg

Ingredients

- 4 medium zucchini
- 1 tablespoon olive oil
- 1 medium onion, finely chopped
- 2 cloves garlic, minced
- 1 cup cherry tomatoes, diced
- 1 cup cooked quinoa (about 1/3 cup uncooked)
- 1/2 cup canned black beans, drained and rinsed
- 1/2 cup corn kernels (fresh or frozen)
- 1/2 cup fresh spinach, chopped
- 1/2 teaspoon ground cumin
- 1/2 teaspoon smoked paprika
- 1/4 teaspoon chili powder (optional, for heat)
- Salt and black pepper, to taste
- 2 tablespoons nutritional yeast (for a cheesy flavor)
- 1/4 cup fresh basil or parsley, chopped (for garnish)
- 1 tablespoon lemon juice (optional, for added brightness)

Directions:

1. Set your oven to preheat at 375°F (190°C).
2. Wash the zucchini and cut them in half (lengthwise). Remove the seeds as well as a bit of the flesh to create boats. You can use a spoon for this.
3. In a large skillet over medium heat, heat the olive oil.
4. Add the onion (chopped) and cook for 5 minutes, until softened.
5. Add the minced garlic and sauté for another minute.
6. Add the cherry tomatoes (diced) and cook for about 3 minutes until they start to break down.
7. Mix in the black beans, cooked quinoa, corn, and chopped spinach.
8. Stir in ground cumin, smoked paprika, chili powder (if using), salt, and black pepper. Cook for another 3-4 minutes until everything is heated through and the spinach is wilted.
9. Take off the heat and mix in the nutritional yeast.
10. In a baking dish place the zucchini halves , cut side up.
11. Spoon the filling mixture evenly into each zucchini boat.
12. If desired, sprinkle with a little extra nutritional yeast on top for added flavor.
13. Bake the stuffed zucchini boats in the preheated oven for about 20-25 minutes, or until the zucchini is tender and the tops are slightly golden.
14. Remove from the oven and let cool for a few minutes.
15. Use fresh parsley or basil for garnish and a squeeze of lemon juice if desired.
16. Serve warm.

Cauliflower Rice & Veggie Bowl

Servings: 4   **Prep. time:** 15 min   **Total time:** 35 min

Nutritional Information (Per Serving):

Calories: 230, Protein: 8g, Carbohydrates: 36g, Fats: 7g, Fiber: 7g, Cholesterol: 0mg, Sodium: 350mg, Potassium: 650mg

Ingredients

- 1 large head of cauliflower, cut into florets
- 1 tablespoon olive oil
- 1 medium onion, finely chopped
- 2 cloves garlic, minced
- 1 cup bell peppers, diced (any color)
- 1 cup carrots, diced
- 1 cup broccoli florets
- 1 cup cherry tomatoes, halved
- 1/2 cup frozen peas
- 1/2 cup corn kernels (fresh or frozen)
- 2 tablespoons tamari or low-sodium soy sauce
- 1 teaspoon ground cumin
- 1 teaspoon smoked paprika
- 1/2 teaspoon turmeric
- Salt and black pepper, to taste
- 2 tablespoons fresh parsley or cilantro, chopped (for garnish)
- 1 tablespoon lemon juice (optional, for added brightness)

Directions:

1. Pulse the cauliflower florets in batches in a food processor until they resemble rice grains. Alternatively, you can use a box grater.
2. Squeeze out excess moisture by transferring the cauliflower rice to a clean kitchen towel. This helps to avoid a soggy texture.
3. Heat olive oil in a large skillet over medium heat.
4. Add the onion (chopped) and cook for about 5 minutes until softened.
5. Stir in the garlic (minced) and cook for an additional 1 minute until fragrant.
6. Add the diced bell peppers, carrots, and broccoli. Cook for about 5-7 minutes, stirring occasionally, until the vegetables are tender but still crisp.
7. Mix in the cherry tomatoes, frozen peas, and corn. Cook for an additional 2-3 minutes until the tomatoes start to soften and the peas and corn are heated through.
8. Stir in the tamari or soy sauce, ground cumin, smoked paprika, turmeric, salt, and black pepper. Adjust seasoning to taste.
9. In a separate skillet, add a little olive oil and heat over medium heat.
10. Add the prepared cauliflower rice and cook for about 5-7 minutes, stirring occasionally, until it is tender and starts to brown slightly. You can add a pinch of salt or spices to flavor the rice.
11. Divide the cauliflower rice among four bowls.
12. Top each bowl with the vegetable mixture.
13. Use fresh parsley or cilantro for garnish and a squeeze of lemon juice if desired.
14. Serve warm.

Roasted Carrot & Chickpea Bowl

Servings: 4   **Prep. time:** 15 min   **Total time:** 45 min

Nutritional Information (Per Serving):

Calories: 320, Protein: 11g, Carbohydrates: 47g, Fats: 12g, Fiber: 10g, Cholesterol: 0mg, Sodium: 300mg, Potassium: 750mg

Ingredients

- 4 medium carrots, peeled and cut into 1-inch pieces
- 1 can (15 oz) chickpeas, drained and rinsed
- 2 tablespoons olive oil
- 1 teaspoon ground cumin
- 1 teaspoon smoked paprika
- 1/2 teaspoon turmeric
- 1/2 teaspoon garlic powder
- 1/2 teaspoon onion powder
- Salt and black pepper, to taste
- 2 cups cooked quinoa (or brown rice, as an alternative)
- 1 cup fresh spinach leaves
- 1/2 cup red cabbage, shredded
- 1/2 cup cherry tomatoes, halved
- 1/4 cup fresh parsley or cilantro, chopped (for garnish)
- 1 tablespoon tahini (optional, for drizzling)
- 1 tablespoon lemon juice (optional, for added brightness)

Directions:

1. Preheat the oven to 425°F (220°C).
2. On a large baking sheet, toss the carrots and chickpeas with olive oil, cumin, smoked paprika, turmeric, garlic powder, onion powder, salt, and pepper until well coated.
3. Spread everything out in a single layer on the sheet.
4. Roast for 25-30 minutes, stirring halfway through, until the carrots are tender and slightly caramelized and the chickpeas are crispy.
5. While the carrots and chickpeas are roasting, cook the quinoa according to package instructions, or reheat leftover quinoa or brown rice.
6. Divide the quinoa or brown rice into four bowls.
7. Top each bowl with roasted carrots and chickpeas, fresh spinach, shredded red cabbage, and cherry tomatoes.
8. Garnish with parsley or cilantro.
9. Drizzle with tahini and a squeeze of lemon juice for extra flavor and creaminess.
10. Serve warm or at room temperature.

Red Bean & Corn Chili

 Servings: 4

 Prep. time: 15 min

 Total time: 45 min

Nutritional Information (Per Serving):

Calories: 280, Protein: 11g, Carbohydrates: 46g, Fats: 5g, Fiber: 11g, Cholesterol: 0mg, Sodium: 470mg, Potassium: 780mg

Ingredients

- 1 tablespoon olive oil
- 1 large onion, finely chopped
- 3 cloves garlic, minced
- 1 bell pepper, diced (any color)
- 2 medium carrots, diced
- 1 cup corn kernels (fresh, frozen, or canned, drained)
- 1 can (15 oz) red beans, drained and rinsed
- 1 can (15 oz) diced tomatoes
- 1 cup vegetable broth
- 1 tablespoon tomato paste
- 1 tablespoon chili powder
- 1 teaspoon ground cumin
- 1 teaspoon smoked paprika
- 1/2 teaspoon dried oregano
- 1/4 teaspoon cayenne pepper (optional, for extra heat)
- Salt and black pepper, to taste
- Fresh cilantro or parsley, for garnish (optional)

Directions:

1. Warm olive oil in a large pot over medium heat.
2. Add the chopped onion and sauté for 5 minutes until it becomes soft and translucent.
3. Mix in the minced garlic and cook for another 1-2 minutes until aromatic.
4. Add the diced bell pepper and carrots, cooking for 5 minutes to let them soften.
5. Stir in the corn kernels, red beans, diced tomatoes, vegetable broth, and tomato paste. Mix well.
6. Season with chili powder, ground cumin, smoked paprika, dried oregano, cayenne pepper (optional), salt, and black pepper.
7. Bring the chili to a boil, then reduce the heat to a simmer and cook for 20-25 minutes, or until the vegetables are tender and the chili thickens.
8. Taste and adjust seasoning as needed, adding more salt, pepper, or chili powder to your preference.
9. Ladle the chili into bowls and, if desired, garnish with fresh cilantro or parsley.
10. Optional: Serve with whole-grain bread or over cooked quinoa for added nutrition.

Green Lentil & Kale Stuffed Peppers

Servings: 4   **Prep. time:** 15 min   **Total time:** 55 min

Nutritional Information (Per Serving):

Calories: 295, Protein: 13g, Carbohydrates: 45g, Fats: 8g, Fiber: 14g, Cholesterol: 0mg, Sodium: 440mg, Potassium: 980mg

Ingredients

- 4 large bell peppers (any color)
- 1 cup green lentils, rinsed
- 2 cups vegetable broth
- 1 tablespoon olive oil
- 1 medium onion, finely chopped
- 2 cloves garlic, minced
- 1 cup kale, chopped (stems removed)
- 1 cup diced tomatoes (canned or fresh)
- 1 teaspoon dried oregano
- 1/2 teaspoon ground cumin
- 1/2 teaspoon smoked paprika
- Salt and black pepper, to taste
- 1/4 cup nutritional yeast (optional, for a cheesy flavor)
- Fresh parsley or cilantro, for garnish (optional)

Directions:

1. Combine green lentils and vegetable broth in a medium pot.
2. Bring to a boil, then reduce to a simmer, cover, and cook for 25-30 minutes until lentils are tender but firm. Drain any extra liquid and set aside.
3. Preheat the oven to 375°F (190°C).
4. Remove the tops, seeds, and membranes from the bell peppers, then arrange them upright in a baking dish.
5. Heat olive oil in a skillet over medium heat.
6. Cook the chopped onion for 5 minutes until soft, then add minced garlic and sauté for another 1-2 minutes until fragrant.
7. Add chopped kale and cook for about 3 minutes until it wilts.
8. Mix in diced tomatoes, oregano, cumin, smoked paprika, salt, and pepper, and cook for an additional 5 minutes to blend the flavors.
9. Add the cooked lentils to the skillet and stir in nutritional yeast, if desired.
10. Taste and adjust the seasoning if necessary.
11. Stuff each bell pepper with the lentil mixture, pressing down to pack it in firmly.
12. Bake in the preheated oven for 25-30 minutes, or until the peppers are tender and starting to char at the edges.
13. Optionally, top with fresh parsley or cilantro.
14. Serve warm, either on its own or with a simple side salad.

Butternut Squash & Black Bean Burritos

Servings: 4   **Prep. time:** 15 min   **Total time:** 45 min

Nutritional Information (Per Serving):

Calories: 340, Protein: 13g, Carbohydrates: 55g, Fats: 8g, Fiber: 12g, Cholesterol: 0mg, Sodium: 620mg, Potassium: 980mg

Ingredients

- 1 medium butternut squash (about 3 cups diced)
- 1 tablespoon olive oil
- 1 teaspoon ground cumin
- 1/2 teaspoon smoked paprika
- 1/2 teaspoon chili powder
- 1/2 teaspoon garlic powder
- Salt and black pepper, to taste
- 1 can (15 oz) black beans, drained and rinsed
- 1/2 cup diced red onion
- 2 cloves garlic, minced
- 1/2 cup diced red bell pepper
- 1 cup fresh spinach, chopped
- 1/2 cup salsa (store-bought or homemade)

Directions:

1. Set the oven to preheat, 400°F (200°C).
2. Peel, remove seeds, and cut the butternut squash into 1/2-inch cubes.
3. Toss the squash with olive oil, cumin, chili powder, smoked paprika, garlic powder, salt, and pepper.
4. Arrange the squash in a single layer on a baking sheet.
5. Roast for 20-25 minutes, stirring halfway, until tender and slightly caramelized. Set aside.
6.
7. While the squash roasts, heat a large skillet over medium heat.
8. Add a little olive oil (or water for oil-free) and sauté the diced red onion for 3-4 minutes until softened.
9. Add diced red bell pepper and minced garlic, cook for 2 more minutes until the pepper is tender.
10. Stir in black beans and chopped spinach, cooking until the spinach wilts and the beans are heated through, about 3-4 minutes.

- 1/4 cup chopped fresh cilantro (optional)
- 4 large whole wheat tortillas (8-inch or larger)

Optional Toppings
- 1 avocado, sliced
- 1/4 cup vegan sour cream or cashew cream
- Lime wedges for serving
- Sliced jalapeños for extra heat

11. Add the roasted squash and salsa, heating through. Adjust seasoning with salt and pepper to taste.
12. If desired, mix in chopped cilantro.
13.
14. Warm the whole wheat tortillas in a dry skillet over medium heat for about 30 seconds per side until soft and pliable.
15. Spoon the squash and black bean mixture into the center of each tortilla.
16. Add optional toppings like avocado slices or vegan sour cream. Fold in the sides and roll up from the bottom to secure the filling.
17. Cut the burritos in half and serve warm with lime wedges and extra salsa, if desired.

Tomato & Basil Stuffed Eggplant

Servings: 4   **Prep. time:** 20 min   **Total time:** 60 min

Nutritional Information (Per Serving):

Calories: 180, Protein: 5g, Carbohydrates: 24g, Fats: 8g, Fiber: 8g, Cholesterol: 0mg, Sodium: 200mg, Potassium: 750mg

Ingredients

- 2 medium eggplants
- 1 tablespoon olive oil
- 1 medium onion, finely chopped
- 3 cloves garlic, minced
- 2 cups diced tomatoes (fresh or canned, with juices)
- 1/4 cup tomato paste
- 1 teaspoon dried oregano
- 1 teaspoon dried thyme
- Salt and black pepper, to taste
- 1/4 cup fresh basil leaves, chopped
- 1/4 cup nutritional yeast (optional, for a cheesy flavor)
- optional, for topping: 2 tablespoons pine nuts, 1/4 cup breadcrumbs

Directions:

1. Set your oven to preheat, 375°F (190°C).
2. Cut the eggplants in half lengthwise. Scoop out the flesh, leaving about a 1/2-inch thick shell. Be careful not to pierce the skin.
3. Finely chop the eggplant flesh and set it aside. Lightly salt the inside of the eggplant shells and set them aside, cut side down, on a paper towel to drain any excess moisture while you prepare the filling.
4. In a large skillet, heat the olive oil over medium heat. Add the chopped onion and sauté for about 5 minutes, until softened. Add the minced garlic and sauté for an additional minute. Stir in the chopped eggplant flesh, and cook for 5-7 min., until it becomes tender and begins to brown slightly.
5. Add the diced tomatoes, tomato paste, dried oregano, thyme, salt, and black pepper. Simmer the mixture for 10-12 minutes, stirring occasionally, until it thickens slightly and the flavors meld together.
6. Remove the skillet from heat and stir in the chopped fresh basil. Pat the eggplant shells dry with a paper towel, place them in a baking dish, and cut side up. Spoon the tomato and basil mixture evenly into each eggplant shell, pressing the filling down gently to ensure it is well-packed. Sprinkle the tops with nutritional yeast and breadcrumbs for added flavor and texture.
7. Cover the baking dish with foil and bake in the oven for 25 minutes. After 25 minutes, remove the foil and continue baking for 10-15 minutes, or until the eggplant shells are tender and the topping is golden brown. Remove the stuffed eggplants from the oven and let them cool for a few minutes. Garnish with pine nuts and additional fresh basil if desired.
8. Serve warm.

Sweet Potato & Kale Skillet

Servings: 4   **Prep. time:** 10 min   **Total time:** 30 min

Nutritional Information (Per Serving):

Calories: 230, Protein: 6g, Carbohydrates: 37g, Fats: 7g, Fiber: 9g, Cholesterol: 0mg, Sodium: 350mg, Potassium: 900mg

Ingredients

- 2 tablespoons olive oil
- 1 medium onion, diced
- 2 cloves garlic, minced
- 1 large sweet potato, peeled and diced into 1/2-inch cubes
- 1 teaspoon smoked paprika
- 1/2 teaspoon ground cumin
- 1/2 teaspoon ground black pepper
- 1/4 teaspoon red pepper flakes (optional, for heat)
- 1/4 cup vegetable broth (low sodium)
- 4 cups kale, chopped and tough stems removed
- 1 can (15 oz) black beans, drained and rinsed
- 1/2 teaspoon salt, or to taste
- 1 tablespoon fresh lemon juice
- 1 tablespoon fresh parsley or cilantro, chopped, for garnish

Directions:

1. Heat olive oil in a large skillet over medium heat.
2. Add the diced onion and sauté for 3-4 minutes until it becomes soft and translucent.
3. Stir in the minced garlic and cook for 1-2 minutes, stirring often to avoid burning.
4. Add the diced sweet potato and mix well with the onion and garlic.
5. Season with smoked paprika, ground cumin, black pepper, and red pepper flakes (if using).
6. Cook the sweet potatoes for 5-7 minutes, stirring occasionally until they start to soften.
7. Pour vegetable broth into the skillet and cover with a lid.
8. Let the sweet potatoes steam for about 5 minutes or until they are tender but still firm.
9. Uncover and add the chopped kale, stirring to combine.
10. Cook for 3-4 minutes until the kale wilts.
11. Add the drained black beans and stir, cooking until everything is heated through.
12. Season with salt to taste.
13. Drizzle fresh lemon juice over the mixture and stir to mix.
14. Garnish with fresh parsley or cilantro and serve hot.

Corn & Avocado Salad Wraps

Servings: 4 **Prep. time:** 15 min **Total time:** 15 min

Nutritional Information (Per Serving):

Calories: 270, Protein: 6g, Carbohydrates: 36g, Fats: 13g, Fiber: 9g, Cholesterol: 0mg, Sodium: 290mg, Potassium: 610mg

Ingredients

- 1 cup fresh or frozen corn kernels, thawed if frozen
- 1 large avocado, diced
- 1 cup cherry tomatoes, halved
- 1/4 cup red onion, finely chopped
- 1/4 cup fresh cilantro, chopped
- 1 tablespoon fresh lime juice
- 1/4 teaspoon sea salt
- 1/4 teaspoon black pepper
- 1/2 teaspoon cumin
- 4 large whole wheat or corn tortillas
- 1 cup fresh spinach or mixed greens
- 1/4 cup plant-based yogurt or hummus (optional, for spread)

Directions:

1. In a large mixing bowl, combine the corn kernels, diced avocado, cherry tomatoes, red onion, and fresh cilantro.
2. Add the lime juice, sea salt, black pepper, and cumin. Gently toss the ingredients together to evenly distribute the flavors without mashing the avocado.
3. Lay out the tortillas on a clean surface.
4. If using, spread a thin layer of plant-based yogurt or hummus on each tortilla.
5. Place a handful of fresh spinach or mixed greens in the center of each tortilla.
6. Spoon the corn and avocado salad evenly onto the center of each tortilla over the greens.
7. Fold the sides of each tortilla inward, then roll from the bottom to the top to form a wrap.
8. Slice each wrap in half diagonally for easier handling and a more attractive presentation.
9. Serve immediately, or wrap tightly in parchment paper for an on-the-go meal.

Spicy Tofu & Broccoli Stir-Fry

 Servings: 4   **Prep. time:** 15 min   **Total time:** 30 min

Nutritional Information (Per Serving):

Calories: 210, Protein: 12g, Carbohydrates: 15g, Fats: 12g, Fiber: 4g, Cholesterol: 0mg, Sodium: 450mg, Potassium: 450mg

Ingredients

- 14 oz (400g) extra-firm tofu, drained and pressed
- 2 cups broccoli florets
- 1 red bell pepper, sliced
- 1 medium carrot, julienned
- 1 small onion, thinly sliced
- 3 cloves garlic, minced
- 1 tablespoon fresh ginger, minced
- 2 tablespoons low-sodium soy sauce or tamari
- 1 tablespoon sriracha or other hot sauce
- 1 tablespoon rice vinegar
- 1 tablespoon maple syrup
- 2 tablespoons sesame oil (divided)
- 1 tablespoon cornstarch
- 1/4 cup water
- 1/4 teaspoon red pepper flakes (optional, for extra spice)
- Optional, for garnish: 2 tablespoons toasted sesame seeds, cooked brown rice or quinoa

Directions:

1. Drain the tofu and press it between paper towels to remove excess moisture, which helps it absorb flavors better and gives it a firmer texture.
2. Cut the tofu into 1-inch cubes.
3. Toss the tofu cubes with cornstarch in a bowl until they are evenly coated, which will make them crispy when cooked.
4. Heat 1 tablespoon of sesame oil in a large non-stick skillet or wok over medium-high heat. Arrange the tofu cubes in a single layer and cook for 3-4 minutes on each side until golden and crispy. Remove the tofu from the skillet and set aside.
5. In the same skillet, add the remaining 1 tablespoon of sesame oil.
6. Add the minced garlic and ginger, sautéing for 1 minute until they release their aroma.
7. Add the sliced onion, broccoli florets, red bell pepper, and julienned carrot, and stir-fry for 5-7 minutes until the vegetables are crisp-tender.
8. In a small bowl, mix together the soy sauce, sriracha, rice vinegar, maple syrup, and water.
9. Pour the sauce over the vegetables and stir to coat them evenly.
10. Return the tofu to the skillet and toss it with the vegetables and sauce. Cook for another 2-3 minutes until the sauce slightly thickens.
11. Serve the stir-fry over brown rice or quinoa, if desired.
12. Garnish with toasted sesame seeds and a pinch of red pepper flakes for added heat.

Stuffed Portobello Mushrooms

 Servings: 4   **Prep. time:** 15 min   **Total time:** 40 min

Nutritional Information (Per Serving):

Calories: 180, Protein: 7g, Carbohydrates: 23g, Fats: 7g, Fiber: 6g, Cholesterol: 0mg, Sodium: 200mg, Potassium: 680mg

Ingredients

- 4 large Portobello mushrooms, stems removed and gills scraped out
- 1 cup cooked quinoa
- 1/2 cup canned black beans, drained and rinsed
- 1/2 cup cherry tomatoes, diced
- 1 small red onion, finely chopped
- 2 cloves garlic, minced
- 1 cup fresh spinach, chopped
- 1 tablespoon olive oil
- 1 tablespoon balsamic vinegar
- 1 teaspoon dried oregano

Directions:

1. Preheat the oven to 375°F (190°C).
2. Gently clean the Portobello mushrooms with a damp cloth, remove the stems, and carefully scoop out the gills with a spoon to create room for the filling and minimize moisture.
3. Heat olive oil in a skillet over medium heat. Sauté the chopped onion and garlic for 3-4 minutes until the onion is soft and the garlic is aromatic.
4. Add the spinach and cook for another 2 minutes until it wilts down.
5. In a large bowl, mix together the cooked quinoa, black beans, diced cherry tomatoes, the spinach mixture, balsamic vinegar, oregano, smoked paprika, red pepper flakes (optional), salt, and pepper. Stir until well combined.
6. Optionally, add nutritional yeast for a cheesy flavor.
7. Place the Portobello mushrooms, gill side up, on a baking sheet lined

- 1/2 teaspoon smoked paprika
- 1/4 teaspoon red pepper flakes (optional)
- Salt and pepper, to taste
- 1/4 cup nutritional yeast (optional, for a cheesy flavor)
- Fresh parsley or basil, chopped for garnish

with parchment paper.

8. Fill each mushroom cap with the quinoa mixture, pressing it in gently to compact the filling. Drizzle a bit of olive oil over the top to help with roasting.

9. Bake in the oven for 20-25 minutes, or until the mushrooms are soft and the filling is hot and slightly crispy on top.

10. Remove from the oven and let them cool for a few minutes. Garnish with fresh parsley or basil if desired before serving.

Lentil & Vegetable Bolognese

Servings: 4   **Prep. time:** 15 min   **Total time:** 60 min

Nutritional Information (Per Serving):

Calories: 300 kcal, Protein: 14 g, Carbohydrates: 45 g, Fats: 7 g, Fiber: 14 g, Cholesterol: 0 mg, Sodium: 500 mg, Potassium: 1000 mg

Ingredients

- 1 cup soaked green or brown lentils
- 2 tbsp olive oil
- 1 large onion, finely chopped
- 3 garlic cloves, minced
- 2 carrots, diced
- 2 celery stalks, diced
- 1 red bell pepper, diced
- 1 zucchini, diced
- 1 can (28 oz) crushed tomatoes
- 2 tbsp tomato paste
- 1 tsp each dried oregano and basil
- 1/2 tsp smoked paprika
- 1/4 tsp red pepper flakes (optional)
- 2 cups vegetable broth
- Salt and pepper
- 1/4 cup chopped fresh parsley (for garnish)
- Whole grain pasta or zucchini noodles (optional)

Directions:

1. Soak the lentils in water for 1 hour, then drain and set them aside. This helps reduce the cooking time and improves digestion.

2. In a large pot over medium heat, heat the olive oil. Add the chopped onion and sauté for 5-7 minutes until it becomes translucent. Add minced garlic and cook for 1-2 minutes until fragrant.

3. Add the diced carrots, celery, bell pepper, and zucchini. Cook for 10 minutes, stirring occasionally, until the vegetables begin to soften.

4. Stir in the tomato paste, crushed tomatoes, dried oregano, dried basil, smoked paprika, and red pepper flakes (if desired). Cook for 5 minutes to allow the flavors to blend.

5. Add the drained lentils and vegetable broth, mixing well. Bring to a boil, then reduce the heat to low. Cover and simmer for 30 minutes, or until the lentils are tender and the sauce thickens, stirring occasionally.

6. Season with salt and pepper to taste. If the sauce is too thick, add more vegetable broth or water as needed. Serve the Bolognese over whole grain pasta, zucchini noodles, or enjoy it on its own, garnished with fresh parsley.

Vegetable & Chickpea Curry

Servings: 4   **Prep. time:** 15 min   **Total time:** 45 min

Nutritional Information (Per Serving):

Calories: 320 kcal, Protein: 10 g, Carbohydrates: 40 g, Fats: 15 g, Fiber: 10 g, Cholesterol: 0 mg, Sodium: 450 mg, Potassium: 980 mg

Ingredients

- 1 tbsp coconut or olive oil
- 1 medium onion, finely chopped
- 3 garlic cloves, minced
- 1-inch ginger, minced
- 1 tbsp curry powder
- 1 tsp each ground cumin and coriander
- 1/2 tsp turmeric
- 1/4 tsp cayenne (optional)
- 1 can (14 oz) diced tomatoes
- 1 can (14 oz) coconut milk
- 1 cup vegetable broth or water
- 1 can (15 oz) chickpeas, drained
- 2 cups cauliflower florets
- 1 large carrot, sliced
- 1 red bell pepper, chopped
- 2 cups spinach, chopped
- Salt and pepper
- 1 tbsp lemon juice
- 1/4 cup chopped cilantro
- Cooked brown rice or quinoa (optional)

Directions:

1. Heat the coconut oil in a large pot over medium heat. Add the chopped onion and sauté for 5-7 minutes until translucent.
2. Add the minced garlic and ginger. Sauté for another 1-2 minutes until fragrant.
3. Stir in the curry powder, cumin, coriander, turmeric, and cayenne pepper (if using). Cook for 1-2 minutes, stirring constantly, to toast the spices and release their flavors.
4. Add the diced tomatoes, coconut milk, and vegetable broth. Stir well to combine and bring the mixture to a gentle simmer.
5. Stir in the chickpeas, cauliflower florets, sliced carrots, and chopped red bell pepper. Cover the pot and simmer for 15-20 minutes, until the vegetables are tender.
6. In the last 5 minutes of cooking, stir in the spinach leaves. Allow them to wilt into the curry. Adjust the seasoning with salt, pepper, and a squeeze of fresh lemon juice.
7. Serve the curry over cooked brown rice or quinoa if desired. Garnish with fresh cilantro.

Pinto Bean & Corn Fritters

Servings: 4   **Prep. time:** 15 min   **Total time:** 35 min

Nutritional Information (Per Serving):

Calories: 250 kcal, Protein: 8 g, Carbohydrates: 38 g, Fats: 8 g, Fiber: 8 g, Cholesterol: 0 mg, Sodium: 380 mg, Potassium: 520 mg

Ingredients

- 1 can (15 oz) pinto beans, drained and rinsed
- 1 cup corn kernels (fresh or frozen, thawed)
- 1/2 cup red bell pepper, finely chopped
- 1/4 cup green onions, finely chopped
- 1/4 cup cilantro, chopped
- 1/2 cup whole wheat flour or chickpea flour
- 1/4 cup cornmeal
- 1/4 cup water or plant-based milk
- 1 tbsp ground flaxseed mixed with 3 tbsp water (flax egg)
- 1 tsp ground cumin
- 1 tsp smoked paprika
- 1/2 tsp garlic powder
- 1/4 tsp black pepper
- 1/2 tsp salt (optional)
- 2 tbsp olive oil or avocado oil for frying

For Serving (Optional):
- Sliced avocado
- Fresh salsa
- Lime wedges

Directions:

1. In a small bowl, mix 1 tablespoon of ground flaxseed with 3 tablespoons of water. Let it sit for 5-10 minutes until it thickens. This will act as a binder for the fritters.
2. In a large mixing bowl, mash the drained pinto beans with a fork or potato masher until they are mostly smooth, with a few chunks remaining for texture.
3. Add the corn kernels, chopped red bell pepper, green onions, cilantro, whole wheat flour (or chickpea flour), cornmeal, water or plant-based milk, cumin, smoked paprika, garlic powder, black pepper, and salt to the mashed beans. Stir in the prepared flax egg until everything is well combined.
4. Scoop out about 2 tablespoons of the mixture and form it into a small patty. Repeat with the remaining mixture to make about 12 fritters.
5. Heat 1 tablespoon of oil in a large non-stick skillet over medium heat. Once hot, add the fritters in batches, being careful not to overcrowd the pan. Cook for 3-4 minutes on each side, until golden brown and crispy. Add more oil as needed for subsequent batches.
6. Serve the fritters warm, optionally topped with sliced avocado, fresh salsa, and lime wedges.

Chickpea & Spinach Stuffed Pita

Servings: 4   **Prep. time:** 15 min   **Total time:** 25 min

Nutritional Information (Per Serving):

Calories: 290 kcal, Protein: 11 g, Carbohydrates: 45 g, Fats: 7 g, Fiber: 10 g, Cholesterol: 0 mg, Sodium: 460 mg, Potassium: 550 mg

Ingredients

- 1 can (15 oz) chickpeas, drained and rinsed
- 2 cups fresh spinach, chopped
- 1/2 cup red bell pepper, finely chopped
- 1/4 cup red onion, finely chopped
- 2 cloves garlic, minced
- 1 tbsp olive oil
- 1 tbsp lemon juice
- 1 tsp ground cumin
- 1/2 tsp smoked paprika
- 1/4 tsp turmeric
- 1/4 tsp black pepper
- 1/2 tsp salt (optional)
- 4 whole wheat pita pockets
- 1/2 cup hummus
- Fresh cilantro, chopped
- Lemon wedges

Directions:

1. Heat olive oil in a large skillet over medium heat. Add the minced garlic and cook for 1 minute until fragrant.
2. Add the red onion and red bell pepper. Sauté for 3-4 minutes until softened.
3. Stir in the chickpeas and cook for another 2 minutes, allowing them to warm through.
4. Add the chopped spinach and cook until wilted, about 2 minutes.
5. Season with cumin, smoked paprika, turmeric, black pepper, and salt. Stir well to combine.
6. Remove from heat and drizzle with lemon juice. Mix thoroughly.
7. Cut each whole wheat pita pocket in half if they are not already pre-split.
8. Gently open each pita pocket and spoon the chickpea and spinach mixture inside.
9. Optionally, serve with a dollop of hummus, fresh cilantro, and lemon wedges on the side.

Spicy Roasted Cauliflower & Quinoa

Servings: 4   **Prep. time:** 15 min   **Total time:** 45 min

Nutritional Information (Per Serving):

Calories: 330 kcal, Protein: 10 g, Carbohydrates: 50 g, Fats: 11 g, Fiber: 8 g, Cholesterol: 0 mg, Sodium: 520 mg, Potassium: 850 mg

Ingredients

- 1 large head cauliflower, cut into florets
- 2 tbsp olive oil
- 1 tsp smoked paprika
- 1/2 tsp ground cumin
- 1/2 tsp chili powder
- 1/4 tsp cayenne pepper (optional, for extra heat)
- 1/2 tsp garlic powder
- 1/2 tsp onion powder
- 1/2 tsp salt
- 1/4 tsp black pepper
- 1 cup quinoa, rinsed
- 2 cups vegetable broth (or water)
- 1 bay leaf (optional, for extra flavor)
- 1 cup cherry tomatoes, halved
- 1/2 cup red onion, finely chopped
- 1/2 cup fresh parsley or cilantro, chopped

Directions:

1. Preheat the oven to 425°F (220°C).
2. In a large bowl, toss cauliflower florets with olive oil, smoked paprika, ground cumin, chili powder, cayenne pepper (if using), garlic powder, onion powder, salt, and black pepper until well-coated.
3. Spread the cauliflower in a single layer on a baking sheet.
4. Roast for 25-30 minutes, flipping halfway through, until the cauliflower is tender and golden brown.
5. While the cauliflower roasts, combine rinsed quinoa and vegetable broth (or water) in a medium saucepan. Add the bay leaf if using.
6. Bring to a boil over medium-high heat. Once boiling, reduce the heat to low, cover, and simmer for 15 minutes.
7. Remove from heat and let the quinoa sit, covered, for 5 minutes. Fluff with a fork and discard the bay leaf.
8. In a large bowl, combine cherry tomatoes, red onion, and chopped parsley or cilantro.
9. Drizzle with lemon juice, olive oil, salt, and black pepper. Toss to combine.

- 2 tbsp lemon juice
- 1 tbsp olive oil
- 1/2 tsp salt
- 1/4 tsp black pepper

10. In a large serving bowl or individual plates, combine the cooked quinoa and roasted cauliflower.
11. Top with the tomato and onion salad.

Baked Stuffed Sweet Potatoes

Servings: 4

Prep. time: 15 min

Total time: 60 min

Nutritional Information (Per Serving):

Calories: 360 kcal, Protein: 11 g, Carbohydrates: 65 g, Fats: 11 g, Fiber: 12 g, Cholesterol: 0 mg, Sodium: 500 mg, Potassium: 1,000 mg

Ingredients

- 4 medium sweet potatoes
- 1 tbsp olive oil
- 1/2 tsp salt
- 1/4 tsp black pepper
- 1 cup cooked black beans (or 1 can, drained and rinsed)
- 1 cup corn kernels (fresh, frozen, or canned)
- 1/2 cup diced red bell pepper
- 1/2 cup diced red onion
- 1 cup chopped fresh spinach
- 1 tsp ground cumin
- 1/2 tsp smoked paprika
- 1/2 tsp garlic powder
- 1/4 tsp cayenne pepper (optional, for extra heat)
- 1/4 cup salsa (or diced tomatoes)
- 1/2 cup avocado, diced
- 1/4 cup fresh cilantro, chopped (for garnish)
- Lime wedges (for serving)

Directions:

1. Preheat the oven to 400°F (200°C).
2. Wash and scrub the sweet potatoes. Pat dry with a paper towel.
3. Prick each sweet potato several times with a fork. Rub with olive oil, salt, and black pepper.
4. Place the sweet potatoes on a baking sheet and bake for 40-45 minutes, or until tender when pierced with a fork.
5. While the sweet potatoes bake, heat a large skillet over medium heat.
6. Add a splash of water or vegetable broth to the skillet (or a small amount of oil if preferred) and sauté the diced red onion until translucent, about 3-4 minutes.
7. Add the diced red bell pepper, corn kernels, and black beans. Cook for another 5 minutes, stirring occasionally.
8. Stir in the chopped spinach, ground cumin, smoked paprika, garlic powder, and cayenne pepper (if using). Cook until the spinach is wilted, about 2 minutes.
9. Mix in the salsa (or diced tomatoes) and heat through. Remove from heat.
10. Once the sweet potatoes are done, let them cool slightly. Cut each sweet potato lengthwise down the center, without cutting all the way through.
11. Gently fluff the flesh with a fork to create space for the filling.
12. Spoon the vegetable and bean mixture into each sweet potato.
13. Top with diced avocado and garnish with fresh cilantro.
14. Serve warm with lime wedges on the side for an extra burst of flavor.

Lentil & Mushroom Shepherd's Pie

Servings: 6

Prep. time: 20 min

Total time: 60 min

Nutritional Information (Per Serving):

Calories: 290 kcal, Protein: 12 g, Carbohydrates: 47 g, Fats: 8 g, Fiber: 9 g, Cholesterol: 0 mg, Sodium: 450 mg, Potassium: 800 mg

Ingredients

- 4 large russet potatoes, peeled and cubed (about 2 pounds)
- 1/4 cup unsweetened almond milk (or other plant-based milk)
- 2 tbsp olive oil
- 1/2 tsp garlic powder
- Salt and pepper to taste
- For the Lentil & Mushroom
- 1 cup dried green or brown lentils, rinsed (or 1 can cooked lentils, drained and rinsed)
- 2 tbsp olive oil
- 1 large onion, diced
- 3 cloves garlic, minced
- 2 cups cremini mushrooms, diced
- 1 large carrot, diced
- 1 cup celery, diced
- 1 cup frozen peas
- 2 tbsp tomato paste
- 1 cup vegetable broth
- 1 tsp dried thyme
- 1 tsp dried rosemary
- 1/2 tsp smoked paprika
- 1/2 tsp ground cumin
- Salt and pepper to taste

Directions:

1. If using dried lentils, cook them according to the package directions until they are tender, about 20-25 minutes, then drain and set aside.
2. Heat olive oil in a large skillet over medium heat. Add the diced onion and cook until it turns translucent, about 5 minutes.
3. Add minced garlic and sauté for another minute until fragrant.
4. Add the diced mushrooms, carrots, and celery, cooking for 5-7 minutes until the vegetables begin to soften.
5. Mix in the tomato paste, coating the vegetables evenly.
6. Pour in the vegetable broth and bring the mixture to a simmer.
7. Add the cooked lentils, frozen peas, dried thyme, dried rosemary, smoked paprika, and ground cumin to the skillet.
8. Simmer for 10 minutes, allowing the broth to reduce slightly and the filling to thicken. Season with salt and pepper as needed.
9. Preheat the oven to 400°F (200°C).
10. Transfer the lentil and vegetable mixture into a 9x13 inch baking dish or any suitable oven-safe dish.
11. Spread the mashed potatoes evenly over the top, smoothing them with a spatula or spoon.
12. Use a fork to create ridges on the mashed potatoes to help them crisp up.
13. Bake in the oven for 20-25 minutes, or until the top is golden and the edges are bubbling.
14. Let it rest for a few minutes before serving.
15. Garnish with fresh parsley, if desired, and serve warm.

Green Bean & Almond Stir-Fry

 Servings: 4   **Prep. time:** 15 min   **Total time:** 25 min

Nutritional Information (Per Serving):

Calories: 250 kcal, Protein: 7 g, Carbohydrates: 20 g, Fats: 16 g, Fiber: 6 g, Cholesterol: 0 mg, Sodium: 650 mg, Potassium: 400 mg

Ingredients

- 1 lb (450 g) fresh green beans, trimmed and cut into bite-sized pieces
- 1 tbsp sesame oil (or another high-heat oil like avocado oil)
- 1 medium red bell pepper, sliced
- 1 medium yellow onion, thinly sliced
- 2 cloves garlic, minced
- 1 tbsp fresh ginger, minced
- 1/2 cup raw almonds, chopped
- 1/4 cup low-sodium soy sauce or tamari
- 1 tbsp maple syrup or agave nectar
- 1 tbsp rice vinegar or apple cider vinegar
- 1/2 tsp red pepper flakes

Directions:

1. Boil a pot of water and add the green beans, cooking for 2-3 minutes until they are bright green and slightly tender. Drain and transfer them immediately to a bowl of ice water to stop the cooking. Drain again and set aside.
2. Warm sesame oil in a large skillet or wok over medium heat. Add the chopped almonds and toast, stirring frequently, for about 2-3 minutes until they turn golden brown and release a fragrant aroma. Remove the almonds from the skillet and set them aside.
3. If needed, add a little more sesame oil to the skillet. Add the sliced onion and cook for 3-4 minutes until it becomes translucent.
4. Stir in the minced garlic and ginger, sautéing for about 1 minute until they become fragrant.
5. Add the sliced red bell pepper and cook for 2-3 minutes until it starts to soften slightly.
6. Add the green beans, stirring them in to combine with the other vegetables.
7. In a small bowl, mix together the soy sauce (or tamari), maple syrup, rice vinegar, and red pepper flakes (if using). Pour the sauce over the vegetables and stir well to coat everything evenly.
8. Continue to cook for another 2-3 minutes, until the green beans are

(optional, for extra spice)
- 1 tbsp sesame seeds (for garnish)
- 2 green onions, sliced (for garnish)

heated through and the sauce is fully incorporated.
9. Stir in the toasted almonds just before serving.
10. Top with sesame seeds and sliced green onions.
11. Serve warm as a main or side dish. Enjoy!

Moroccan Spiced Vegetable Tagine

 Servings: 4

 Prep. time: 15 min

 **Total time:** 55 min

Nutritional Information (Per Serving):

Calories: 320 kcal, Protein: 9 g, Carbohydrates: 55 g, Fats: 8 g, Fiber: 11 g, Cholesterol: 0 mg, Sodium: 560 mg, Potassium: 850 mg

Ingredients

- 2 tbsp olive oil
- 1 large onion, chopped
- 3 cloves garlic, minced
- 1 tbsp fresh ginger, minced
- 1 medium carrot, peeled and sliced
- 1 medium sweet potato, peeled and cubed
- 1 zucchini, sliced
- 1 red bell pepper, chopped
- 1 cup butternut squash, peeled and cubed
- 1 cup cauliflower florets
- 1 cup chickpeas, cooked (or 1 can, drained and rinsed)
- 1 cup vegetable broth (low sodium)
- 1 can (14.5 oz) diced tomatoes, with juices
- 1/2 cup dried apricots, chopped
- 1/4 cup raisins
- 2 tbsp tomato paste
- 1 tsp ground cumin
- 1 tsp ground coriander
- 1 tsp paprika
- 1/2 tsp ground cinnamon
- 1/4 tsp ground turmeric
- 1/4 tsp cayenne pepper (optional, for heat)
- 1/2 tsp salt (adjust to taste)
- 1/4 tsp black pepper
- 2 tbsp fresh cilantro or parsley, chopped (for garnish)
- 1 tbsp lemon juice

Directions:

1. Heat olive oil in a large pot or tagine over medium heat.
2. Add the chopped onion and cook until translucent, about 5 minutes.
3. Stir in the minced garlic and ginger, and cook for an additional minute until fragrant.
4. Stir in the ground cumin, coriander, paprika, cinnamon, turmeric, cayenne pepper (if using), salt, and black pepper. Cook for 1 minute to toast the spices.
5. Add the carrot, sweet potato, zucchini, red bell pepper, butternut squash, and cauliflower. Stir well to coat with the spices.
6. Add the diced tomatoes with their juices, vegetable broth, tomato paste, dried apricots, and raisins. Stir to combine.
7. Bring the mixture to a boil, then reduce the heat to low. Cover and let it simmer for 25-30 minutes, or until the vegetables are tender and the flavors have melded together.
8. Stir in the cooked chickpeas and cook for an additional 5 minutes to heat through.
9. Adjust seasoning if needed, and stir in the lemon juice for a fresh, tangy flavor.
10. Garnish with chopped fresh cilantro or parsley.
11. Serve hot over couscous, quinoa, or with crusty bread.

Soups and Stews

Creamy Butternut Squash Soup

 Servings: 4   **Prep. time:** 10 min   **Total time:** 40 min

Nutritional Information (Per Serving):

Calories: 220 , Protein: 3g, Carbohydrates: 35g, Fats: 9g, Fiber: 6g, Cholesterol: 0mg, Sodium: 290 mg (depending on the vegetable broth used) Potassium: 800mg

Ingredients

- 1 medium butternut squash (about 2 pounds, peeled, seeded, and diced)
- 1 medium onion (chopped)
- 2 cloves garlic (minced)
- 1 medium carrot (peeled and chopped)
- 1 medium apple (peeled, cored, and chopped)
- 4 cups vegetable broth (low sodium)
- 1 cup coconut milk (unsweetened, from a can)
- 1 tbsp olive oil
- 1 tsp ground cumin
- 1/2 tsp ground nutmeg
- 1/2 tsp ground cinnamon
- Salt and pepper (to taste)
- For garnish, optional: Pumpkin seeds, Fresh thyme

Directions:

1. Peel, seed, and dice the butternut squash. Chop the onion, carrot, and apple, and mince the garlic.
2. In a large pot, heat the olive oil over medium heat. Add the chopped onion and garlic, and sauté for 3-5 minutes until the onion becomes translucent. Add the diced butternut squash, carrot, and apple to the pot. Stir well, and cook for an additional 5 minutes.
3. Stir in the ground cumin, nutmeg, and cinnamon. Pour in the vegetable broth and bring the mixture to a boil.
4. Reduce the heat to low, cover the pot, and let the soup simmer for about 20 minutes, or until the vegetables are soft and fully cooked.
5. Remove the pot from heat. Use an immersion blender to puree the soup until smooth. Alternatively, transfer the soup in batches to a blender and blend until creamy. Be careful with hot liquids.
6. Stir in the coconut milk, and return the pot to low heat. Allow the soup to warm through, adjusting the consistency with more broth or coconut milk if desired.
7. Taste the soup and adjust seasoning with salt and pepper.
8. Ladle the soup into bowls. Garnish with pumpkin seeds and fresh thyme if desired. Serve hot.

Carrot & Ginger Soup

 Servings: 4   **Prep. time:** 10 min   **Total time:** 30 min

Nutritional Information (Per Serving):

Calories: 190, Protein: 3g, Carbohydrates: 23g, Fats: 11g, Fiber: 4g, Cholesterol: 0mg, Sodium: 350mg, Potassium: 650mg

Ingredients

- 1 lb carrots (about 5 medium carrots, peeled and chopped)
- 1 medium onion (chopped)
- 2 cloves garlic (minced)
- 1 tbsp fresh ginger (peeled and grated)
- 2 tbsp olive oil (or any plant-based oil)
- 4 cups vegetable broth (low sodium)
- 1 cup coconut milk (unsweetened, full-fat or light)
- 1 tsp ground cumin

Directions:

1. Peel and chop the carrots into small pieces. Finely chop the onion, mince the garlic, and grate the ginger.
2. Warm olive oil in a large pot over medium heat. Add the onion and garlic, cooking for 3-4 minutes until the onion turns translucent and the garlic is aromatic.
3. Stir in the chopped carrots and grated ginger. Add the cumin and turmeric, mixing well to coat the vegetables. Cook for about 5 minutes, letting the spices blend and the carrots start to soften.
4. Pour in the vegetable broth and bring the mixture to a boil. Reduce the heat to low, cover, and let the soup simmer for about 15 minutes, or until the carrots are soft.
5. Remove the pot from the heat. Use an immersion blender to puree the soup until smooth, or carefully transfer it in batches to a blender and blend until smooth.

- 1/2 tsp ground turmeric
- Salt and pepper (to taste)
- Juice of 1 orange (optional, for extra sweetness and depth)
- Fresh cilantro (chopped, for garnish)

6. If using a blender, return the pureed soup to the pot. Stir in the coconut milk and optional orange juice. Season with salt and pepper to taste, and heat over low for another 2-3 minutes until warmed through.
7. Serve the soup in bowls, garnished with fresh cilantro. Enjoy it hot!

Red Lentil & Carrot Soup

Servings: 4   **Prep. time:** 10 min   **Total time:** 40 min

Nutritional Information (Per Serving):

Calories: 220, Protein: 11g, Carbohydrates: 35g, Fats: 4g, Fiber: 10g, Cholesterol: 0mg, Sodium: 650mg, Potassium: 700mg

Ingredients

- 1 cup red lentils, rinsed and drained
- 4 medium carrots (about 2 cups), peeled and diced
- 1 small onion, finely chopped
- 2 cloves garlic, minced
- 1 tablespoon olive oil
- 1 teaspoon ground cumin
- 1/2 teaspoon ground coriander
- 1/2 teaspoon turmeric
- 1/4 teaspoon smoked paprika
- 1/4 teaspoon black pepper
- 1/4 teaspoon salt
- 4 cups vegetable broth
- 1 cup water (optional, for adjusting consistency)
- 1 tablespoon lemon juice (optional, for added brightness)
- Fresh cilantro or parsley, chopped (for garnish)

Directions:

1. Rinse the red lentils under cold water until the water is clear. This step removes excess starch and improves the soup's texture.
2. Peel and dice the carrots into small, even pieces to ensure consistent cooking.
3. Heat olive oil in a large pot over medium heat.
4. Add the chopped onion and sauté for 4-5 minutes until it softens.
5. Add minced garlic and cook for another 1-2 minutes until it becomes fragrant.
6. Stir in the ground cumin, coriander, turmeric, smoked paprika, black pepper, and salt, cooking for about 1 minute to release their aromas.
7. Add the diced carrots and rinsed red lentils, mixing well with the spices and aromatics.
8. Pour in the vegetable broth and bring the mixture to a boil.
9. Once boiling, reduce the heat to low, cover the pot, and let it simmer for 20-25 minutes until the lentils and carrots are tender.
10. For a smooth soup, use an immersion blender to blend directly in the pot to your preferred consistency, or transfer to a blender in batches and return to the pot. If you prefer a chunkier texture, blend only part of the soup.
11. If the soup is too thick, add up to 1 cup of water to adjust the consistency.
12. Stir in the lemon juice to enhance the flavors. Taste and adjust the seasoning with more salt, pepper, or lemon juice as needed.
13. Serve the soup hot in bowls, garnished with chopped fresh cilantro or parsley. Pair with crusty bread or a side salad for a complete meal..

Spinach & Lentil Soup

Servings: 4   **Prep. time:** 10 min   **Total time:** 40 min

Nutritional Information (Per Serving):

Calories: 230, Protein: 12g, Carbohydrates: 37g, Fats: 5g, Fiber: 11g, Cholesterol: 0mg, Sodium: 450mg (varies with broth), Potassium: 800mg

Ingredients

- 1 tbsp olive oil
- 1 large onion (diced)
- 3 cloves garlic (minced)
- 1 large carrot (diced)
- 1 celery stalk (diced)
- 1 cup dried green or brown lentils (rinsed and drained)
- 1 large potato (peeled and diced)
- 6 cups vegetable broth (low sodium)
- 2 cups water
- 2 cups fresh spinach (chopped)
- 1 tsp ground cumin
- 1/2 tsp smoked paprika
- 1/4 tsp turmeric
- 1/4 tsp black pepper
- 1/2 tsp sea salt (or to taste)
- 1 tbsp lemon juice (optional, for added brightness)

Directions:

1. Rinse and drain the lentils. Dice the onion, carrot, celery, and potato. Mince the garlic and chop the spinach.
2. Heat the olive oil in a large pot over medium heat. Add the diced onion and cook for 5 minutes, or until softened. Add the minced garlic and cook for another 1 minute, stirring frequently.
3. Add the diced carrot, celery, and potato to the pot. Stir well and cook for about 5 minutes. Add the rinsed lentils and cook for an additional 2 minutes, stirring frequently.
4. Stir in the ground cumin, smoked paprika, turmeric, black pepper, and sea salt. Mix to coat the vegetables and lentils with the spices. Pour in the vegetable broth and water. Stir to combine.
5. Bring the mixture to a boil. Reduce heat to low, cover, and simmer for 25 minutes, or until the lentils and vegetables are tender.
6. Stir in the chopped spinach and cook for an additional 5 minutes, until the spinach is wilted and tender. Remove the pot from heat and stir in the lemon juice, if using.
7. For a creamier texture, use an immersion blender to partially blend the soup, or blend in batches using a countertop blender, leaving some chunks for texture.

Carrot & Coriander Soup

Servings: 4   **Prep. time:** 10 min   **Total time:** 35 min

Nutritional Information (Per Serving):

Calories: 180, Protein: 4g, Carbohydrates: 32g, Fats: 5g, Fiber: 7g, Cholesterol: 0mg, Sodium: 400mg (varies with broth), Potassium: 700mg

Ingredients

- 1 tbsp olive oil
- 1 large onion (diced)
- 3 cloves garlic (minced)
- 6 medium carrots (peeled and sliced)
- 1 large potato (peeled and diced)
- 4 cups vegetable broth (low sodium)
- 1 cup water
- 1 tsp ground coriander
- 1/2 tsp ground cumin
- 1/4 tsp turmeric
- 1/4 tsp black pepper
- 1/2 tsp sea salt (or to taste)
- 1/2 cup fresh cilantro (chopped, plus extra for garnish)
- 1 tbsp lemon juice (optional, for added brightness)

Directions:

1. Peel and slice the carrots, then peel and chop the potato into small cubes. Dice the onion, mince the garlic, and chop the cilantro.
2. Heat olive oil in a large pot over medium heat. Add the diced onion and cook for about 5 minutes until it softens. Add the garlic and sauté for another minute, stirring frequently to prevent burning.
3. Add the sliced carrots and chopped potato to the pot, stirring to mix well. Cook for about 5 minutes to begin softening the vegetables.
4. Sprinkle in the ground coriander, cumin, turmeric, black pepper, and salt, stirring to coat the vegetables with the spices. Pour in the vegetable broth and water, mixing everything together.
5. Bring to a boil, then reduce the heat, cover, and let it simmer for 20 minutes, or until the carrots and potatoes are soft.
6. Remove the pot from the heat and use an immersion blender to blend the soup until smooth, or carefully blend in batches using a blender, then return it to the pot. Stir in the cilantro and add lemon juice if desired. Taste and adjust seasoning if necessary. Serve hot, garnished with more cilantro if you like.

Roasted Red Pepper & Tomato Soup

Servings: 4   **Prep. time:** 15 min   **Total time:** 45 min

Nutritional Information (Per Serving):

Calories: 130, Protein: 3g, Carbohydrates: 25g, Fats: 4g, Fiber: 6g, Cholesterol: 0mg, Sodium: 450mg (varies with broth), Potassium: 650mg

Ingredients

- 4 large red bell peppers (halved, seeded, and cored)
- 6 medium tomatoes (quartered)
- 1 large onion (diced)
- 3 cloves garlic (minced)
- 1 tbsp olive oil
- 3 cups vegetable broth (low sodium)
- 1 cup water
- 1 tsp dried basil
- 1/2 tsp dried oregano
- 1/4 tsp smoked paprika
- 1/4 tsp black pepper
- 1/2 tsp sea salt (or to taste)
- 1 tbsp balsamic vinegar (optional, for added depth)
- Fresh basil leaves (for garnish, optional)

Directions:

1. Set your oven to preheat, 425°F (220°C). Line a baking sheet with parchment paper.
2. Place the halved red bell peppers and quartered tomatoes on a baking sheet. Drizzle with about 1 teaspoon of olive oil and roast for 25 minutes, until the peppers are charred and the tomatoes are softened.
3. While the vegetables are roasting, heat 1 tablespoon of olive oil in a large pot over medium heat. Add the diced onion and sauté for 5-7 minutes until translucent. Add the minced garlic and cook for 1 more minute.
4. After roasting, remove the peppers and tomatoes from the oven and let them cool slightly. Peel off the skins from the peppers, which should come off easily.
5. Add the roasted peppers and tomatoes to the pot with the onions and garlic, stirring to mix.
6. Pour in the vegetable broth and water, then stir in the dried basil, oregano, smoked paprika, black pepper, and sea salt. Bring the soup to a boil.
7. Reduce the heat and let it simmer for 15 minutes to allow the flavors to develop.
8. Blend the soup with an immersion blender until smooth, or carefully blend in batches in a countertop blender. Be cautious with hot liquids; let the soup cool slightly if necessary.
9. Stir in the balsamic vinegar, if desired, and adjust the seasoning as needed. Serve hot, garnished with fresh basil leaves if you like.

Ginger & Turmeric Carrot Soup

Servings: 4   **Prep. time:** 10 min   **Total time:** 40 min

Nutritional Information (Per Serving):

Calories: 140, Protein: 3g, Carbohydrates: 30g, Fats: 4g, Fiber: 7g, Cholesterol: 0mg, Sodium: 450mg (varies with broth), Potassium: 750mg

Ingredients

- 1 tbsp olive oil
- 1 large onion (diced)
- 3 cloves garlic (minced)
- 2 tbsp fresh ginger (grated)
- 1 tbsp fresh turmeric (grated) or 1 tsp ground turmeric
- 6 large carrots (peeled and chopped)
- 4 cups vegetable broth (low sodium)
- 1 cup water
- 1/2 tsp ground cumin
- 1/2 tsp ground coriander
- 1/4 tsp cayenne pepper (optional, for heat)
- 1/2 tsp sea salt (or to taste)
- 1/4 tsp black pepper
- 1 tbsp lemon juice (for added brightness, optional)
- Fresh cilantro (for garnish, optional)

Directions:

1. Warm 1 tablespoon of olive oil in a large pot over medium heat. Add the diced onion and sauté for 5-7 minutes until it turns translucent. Add the minced garlic, grated ginger, and grated or ground turmeric, and cook for another 2 minutes until the mixture becomes aromatic.
2. Add the chopped carrots to the pot. Sprinkle in the ground cumin, ground coriander, and cayenne pepper (if using), stirring well. Cook for 2-3 minutes to allow the spices to coat the carrots and release their fragrance.
3. Pour in the vegetable broth and water, stirring to combine. Bring the mixture to a boil.
4. Lower the heat and let the soup simmer for 20-25 minutes, or until the carrots are soft.
5. Blend the soup with an immersion blender until smooth, or carefully transfer in batches to a countertop blender. Let the soup cool slightly before blending to prevent splattering.
6. Add the lemon juice, if desired. Taste and adjust the seasoning with sea salt and black pepper as needed. Serve hot, garnished with fresh cilantro, if you like.

Roasted Tomato & Garlic Soup

 Servings: 4   **Prep. time:** 15 min   **Total time:** 60 min

Nutritional Information (Per Serving):

Calories: 130, Protein: 3g, Carbohydrates: 22g, Fats: 4g, Fiber: 5g, Cholesterol: 0mg, Sodium: 350mg (varies with broth), Potassium: 670mg

Ingredients

- 2 lbs (900g) ripe tomatoes (about 6-8 medium-sized, cut in half)
- 1 head garlic (top sliced off to expose cloves)
- 2 tbsp olive oil
- 1 medium onion (diced)
- 2 cups vegetable broth (low sodium)
- 1 tsp dried basil
- 1 tsp dried oregano
- 1/2 tsp smoked paprika
- Salt and black pepper (to taste)
- 1 tbsp balsamic vinegar
- 1/4 cup fresh basil leaves (for garnish, optional)

Directions:

1. Set the oven to preheat, 400°F (200°C).
2. Arrange the halved tomatoes and garlic cloves (cut side up) on a baking sheet. Drizzle 1 tablespoon of olive oil over the tomatoes and garlic, then season with salt and black pepper.
3. Roast for 30-35 minutes until the tomatoes are caramelized and the garlic is soft. Once done, remove from the oven and let them cool slightly.
4. While the tomatoes and garlic are roasting, heat 1 tablespoon of olive oil in a large pot over medium heat. Add the diced onion and sauté for 5-7 minutes until it becomes translucent.
5. When the roasted tomatoes and garlic are cool enough to handle, squeeze the garlic cloves out of their skins. Blend the roasted tomatoes and garlic in a blender or food processor until smooth, or use an immersion blender directly in the pot.
6. Combine the tomato-garlic puree with the sautéed onions in the pot, stirring until well mixed.
7. Pour in the vegetable broth, and add dried basil, oregano, and smoked paprika. Stir and bring the mixture to a simmer.
8. Allow the soup to simmer for 10-15 minutes to develop the flavors. Taste and adjust with more salt, black pepper, and a bit of balsamic vinegar if desired.
9. Serve hot, garnished with fresh basil leaves if you wish.

Roasted Cauliflower Soup

 Servings: 4   **Prep. time:** 15 min   **Total time:** 55 min

Nutritional Information (Per Serving):

Calories: 190, Protein: 4g, Carbohydrates: 28g, Fats: 8g, Fiber: 6g, Cholesterol: 0mg, Sodium: 400mg (varies with broth), Potassium: 760mg

Ingredients

- 1 large head of cauliflower (about 2 lbs or 900g, cut into florets)
- 2 tbsp olive oil
- 1 large onion (diced)
- 3 cloves garlic (minced)
- 4 cups vegetable broth (low sodium)
- 1 medium potato (peeled and diced, about 1 cup)
- 1 tsp ground cumin
- 1/2 tsp smoked paprika
- 1/4 tsp ground turmeric
- 1/2 cup unsweetened

Directions:

1. Preheat the oven to 425°F (220°C).
2. On a baking sheet, toss cauliflower florets with 1 tbsp olive oil, salt, and black pepper. Spread out in a single layer.
3. Roast in the oven for 25-30 minutes, or until the cauliflower is golden brown and tender. Stir halfway through for even roasting.
4. While the cauliflower is roasting, heat the remaining 1 tbsp olive oil in a large pot over medium heat.
5. Add the diced onion and cook for about 5 minutes until translucent.
6. Add minced garlic and cook for an additional 1-2 minutes until fragrant.
7. Once the cauliflower is roasted, add it to the pot with the onions and garlic.
8. Stir in the diced potato, ground cumin, smoked paprika, and ground turmeric.
9. Pour in the vegetable broth and bring the mixture to a boil.
10. Reduce the heat and let the soup simmer for 15 minutes, or until the potato

almond milk (or any plant-based milk)
- Salt and black pepper (to taste)
- 1 tbsp fresh lemon juice (optional, for brightness)
- 2 tbsp fresh parsley (chopped, for garnish)

is tender.

11. Using an immersion blender, carefully blend the soup until smooth. If you don't have an immersion blender, transfer the soup in batches to a countertop blender.
12. Stir in the unsweetened almond milk and let the soup heat through for a couple more minutes.
13. Adjust seasoning with salt, black pepper, and lemon juice (if using) to taste.
14. Ladle into bowls and garnish with chopped fresh parsley.

Moroccan Lentil Soup

 Servings: 4   **Prep. time:** 15 min   **Total time:** 45 min

Nutritional Information (Per Serving):

Calories: 220, Protein: 11g, Carbohydrates: 33g, Fats: 6g, Fiber: 11g, Cholesterol: 0mg, Sodium: 380mg (varies with broth), Potassium: 850mg

Ingredients

- 1 cup dried green or brown lentils
- 1 tbsp olive oil
- 1 large onion (diced)
- 3 cloves garlic (minced)
- 1 large carrot (diced)
- 1 celery stalk (diced)
- 1 red bell pepper (diced)
- 1 can (14.5 oz) diced tomatoes (with juice)
- 4 cups vegetable broth
- 1 tbsp ground cumin
- 1 tsp ground coriander
- 1 tsp ground paprika
- 1/2 tsp ground turmeric
- 1/4 tsp ground cinnamon
- 1/4 tsp cayenne pepper (adjust to taste for heat)
- 1 bay leaf
- 1 cup fresh spinach (chopped)
- Salt and black pepper (to taste)
- 1 tbsp fresh lemon juice (for added brightness, optional)
- 2 tbsp fresh cilantro (chopped, for garnish)

Directions:

1. Drizzle 1 tablespoon of olive oil over the tomatoes and garlic, then season with salt and black pepper.
2. Roast for 30-35 minutes until the tomatoes are caramelized and the garlic is soft. Once done, remove from the oven and let them cool slightly.
3. While the tomatoes and garlic are roasting, heat 1 tablespoon of olive oil in a large pot over medium heat. Add the diced onion and sauté for 5-7 minutes until it becomes translucent.
4. When the roasted tomatoes and garlic are cool enough to handle, squeeze the garlic cloves out of their skins. Blend the roasted tomatoes and garlic in a blender or food processor until smooth, or use an immersion blender directly in the pot.
5. Combine the tomato-garlic puree with the sautéed onions in the pot, stirring until well mixed.
6. Pour in the vegetable broth, and add dried basil, oregano, and smoked paprika. Stir and bring the mixture to a simmer.
7. Allow the soup to simmer for 10-15 minutes to develop the flavors. Taste and adjust with more salt, black pepper, and a bit of balsamic vinegar if desired.
8. Serve hot, garnished with fresh basil leaves if you wish.

Minestrone Soup

 Servings: 6   **Prep. time:** 15 min   **Total time:** 45 min

Nutritional Information (Per Serving):

Calories: 220, Protein: 10g, Carbohydrates: 35g, Fats: 5g, Fiber: 8g, Cholesterol: 0mg, Sodium: 380mg (varies with broth), Potassium: 850mg

Ingredients

- 1 tbsp olive oil
- 1 large onion (diced)
- 3 cloves garlic (minced)
- 2 large carrots (diced)
- 2 celery stalks (diced)
- 1 large zucchini (diced)
- 1 cup green beans (trimmed and cut into 1-inch pieces)
- 1 red bell pepper (diced)
- 1 can (14.5 oz) diced tomatoes (with juice)
- 1 can (15 oz) kidney beans (rinsed and drained)
- 1 cup cooked or canned chickpeas (rinsed and drained)
- 4 cups vegetable broth (low sodium)
- 1 cup small pasta (such as elbow macaroni or ditalini)
- 1 cup fresh spinach (chopped, or kale)
- 1 tsp dried oregano
- 1 tsp dried basil
- 1/2 tsp dried thyme
- 1 bay leaf
- Salt and black pepper (to taste)
- 1 tbsp fresh lemon juice (optional, for added brightness)
- 2 tbsp fresh parsley (chopped, for garnish)

Directions:

1. Warm olive oil in a large pot over medium heat.
2. Add diced onion and cook for 5 minutes until it becomes translucent.
3. Add minced garlic and sauté for 1 minute until aromatic.
4. Add diced carrots, celery, zucchini, green beans, and red bell pepper.
5. Cook for 5-7 minutes, stirring occasionally, until the vegetables begin to soften.
6. Mix in diced tomatoes with their juices, along with kidney beans and chickpeas, and cook for 2 more minutes.
7. Pour in vegetable broth, then add dried oregano, basil, thyme, and a bay leaf.
8. Bring the pot to a boil, then reduce the heat and let it simmer for 15 minutes.
9. Add pasta and continue to simmer for 10 minutes, or until the pasta and vegetables are tender.
10. Stir in fresh spinach and cook for 2 minutes until wilted.
11. Remove the bay leaf.
12. Season with salt and black pepper, and add a squeeze of lemon juice for extra brightness if desired.
13. Ladle the soup into bowls and top with fresh parsley before serving.

Spicy Sweet Potato & Black Bean Soup

Servings: 6   **Prep. time:** 15 min   **Total time:** 45 min

Nutritional Information (Per Serving):

Calories: 235, Protein: 10g, Carbohydrates: 39g, Fats: 6g, Fiber: 10g, Cholesterol: 0mg, Sodium: 360mg (varies with broth), Potassium: 850mg

Ingredients

- 2 tbsp olive oil
- 1 large onion (diced)
- 3 cloves garlic (minced)
- 1 tbsp fresh ginger (minced)
- 1 large sweet potato (peeled and diced into 1-inch cubes)
- 1 red bell pepper (diced)
- 1 can (15 oz) black beans (rinsed and drained)
- 1 can (14.5 oz) diced tomatoes (with juice)
- 4 cups vegetable broth (low sodium)
- 1-2 tsp chili powder (adjust to taste)
- 1/2 tsp smoked paprika

Directions:

1. Warm olive oil in a large pot over medium heat.
2. Add diced onion and cook for around 5 minutes until it becomes translucent.
3. Add minced garlic and ginger, cooking for another minute until aromatic.
4. Add diced sweet potato and red bell pepper to the pot.
5. Sauté for 5 minutes, stirring occasionally.
6. Sprinkle in the chili powder, smoked paprika, ground cumin, cayenne (if using), and turmeric. Stir to evenly coat the vegetables with the spices.
7. Mix in the black beans, diced tomatoes (with their juice), and vegetable broth.
8. Bring the mixture to a boil, then lower the heat to a simmer. Let it cook for 20 minutes, or until the sweet potatoes are soft.
9. Add corn and chopped kale or spinach, cooking for an additional 5 minutes until the greens are wilted and the corn is warmed through.
10. Season with salt and black pepper to taste.

- 1/2 tsp ground cumin
- 1/4 tsp cayenne pepper (optional, for extra heat)
- 1/2 tsp turmeric powder (for added color and health benefits)
- 1 cup corn kernels (fresh or frozen)
- 1 cup chopped kale or spinach (for added greens)
- Salt and black pepper (to taste)
- 1 tbsp lime juice (for brightness, optional)
- 2 tbsp fresh cilantro (chopped, for garnish)

11. For a tangy finish, stir in lime juice if desired.
12. Serve the soup in bowls, garnished with fresh cilantro.

Coconut & Red Lentil Soup

 Servings: 6

 Prep. time: 15 min

 Total time: 45 min

Nutritional Information (Per Serving):

Calories: 260, Protein: 10g, Carbohydrates: 35g, Fats: 12g, Fiber: 8g, Cholesterol: 0mg, Sodium: 300mg (varies with broth), Potassium: 800mg

Ingredients

- tbsp coconut oil (or olive oil)
- 1 large onion (diced)
- 3 cloves garlic (minced)
- 1 tbsp fresh ginger (minced)
- 1 large carrot (peeled and diced)
- 1 celery stalk (diced)
- 1 red bell pepper (diced)
- 1 cup red lentils (rinsed)
- 1 can (14 oz) coconut milk
- 4 cups vegetable broth
- 1 tsp ground turmeric
- 1 tsp ground cumin
- 1/2 tsp smoked paprika
- 1/2 tsp ground coriander
- 1/4 tsp cayenne pepper (optional, for extra heat)
- 1 cup baby spinach or kale (chopped)
- Juice of 1 lime (for brightness, optional)
- Salt and black pepper (to taste)
- 2 tbsp fresh cilantro (chopped, for garnish)

Directions:

1. Warm coconut oil in a large pot over medium heat.
2. Add the diced onion and cook for about 5 minutes until it turns translucent.
3. Mix in the minced garlic and ginger, cooking for 1 minute until they release their aroma.
4. Add the diced carrots, celery, and red bell pepper. Sauté for around 5 minutes, stirring occasionally, until the vegetables start to soften.
5. Add the rinsed red lentils and season with ground turmeric, cumin, smoked paprika, ground coriander, and cayenne pepper (if using).
6. Stir well to ensure the lentils and vegetables are evenly coated with the spices.
7. Pour in the coconut milk and vegetable broth.
8. Bring the mixture to a boil, then lower the heat to maintain a gentle simmer. Cook for 20-25 minutes, or until the lentils are tender and the vegetables are fully cooked.
9. Add the chopped spinach or kale, and cook for another 5 minutes until the greens are wilted.
10. Adjust seasoning with salt and black pepper according to taste.
11. For a fresh, tangy flavor, add lime juice if desired.
12. Serve the soup hot, ladled into bowls, and garnish with fresh cilantro.

Carrot, Sweet Potato & Coconut Soup

 Servings: 6

Prep. time: 15 min

 Total time: 45 min

Nutritional Information (Per Serving):

Calories: 230, Protein: 3g, Carbohydrates: 34g, Fats: 10g, Fiber: 7g, Cholesterol: 0mg, Sodium: 310mg (varies with broth), Potassium: 800mg

Ingredients

- 1 tbsp coconut oil (or other plant-based oil)
- 1 large onion (diced)
- 3 cloves garlic (minced)
- 4 large carrots (peeled and chopped)
- 2 medium sweet potatoes (peeled and diced)
- 1 can (14 oz) full-fat coconut milk (unsweetened)
- 4 cups vegetable broth (low sodium)
- 1 tbsp fresh ginger (grated)
- 1 tsp ground cumin
- 1/2 tsp ground turmeric
- 1/2 tsp paprika
- 1/4 tsp ground cinnamon
- Salt and black pepper (to taste)
- 1 tbsp fresh lime juice (for added brightness)
- 2 tbsp fresh cilantro (chopped, for garnish)

Directions:

1. Warm coconut oil in a large pot over medium heat.
2. Add the diced onion and sauté for about 5 minutes until it becomes translucent.
3. Add the minced garlic and grated ginger, cooking for 1 minute until they become aromatic.
4. Add the chopped carrots and diced sweet potatoes, stirring occasionally, and cook for 5 minutes.
5. Sprinkle in the ground cumin, turmeric, paprika, and cinnamon, stirring well to coat the vegetables evenly with the spices.
6. Pour in the vegetable broth and bring the mixture to a boil.
7. Lower the heat to a simmer and cook for about 20 minutes, or until the carrots and sweet potatoes are soft.
8. Blend the soup using an immersion blender until it reaches a smooth consistency. If you don't have an immersion blender, carefully blend the soup in batches using a countertop blender.
9. If using a countertop blender, return the blended soup to the pot.
10. Stir in the coconut milk and cook for an additional 5 minutes to heat through.
11. Add lime juice and adjust the seasoning with salt and black pepper as needed.
12. Serve the soup hot, ladled into bowls, and garnish with fresh cilantro.

Lentil, Kale & Quinoa Soup

 Servings: 6

 Prep. time: 15 min

 Total time: 45 min

Nutritional Information (Per Serving):

Calories: 290, Protein: 12g, Carbohydrates: 49g, Fats: 6g, Fiber: 12g, Cholesterol: 0mg, Sodium: 550mg (varies with broth and added salt), Potassium: 850mg

Ingredients

- 1 tbsp olive oil
- 1 large onion, diced
- 3 cloves garlic, minced
- 1 large carrot, diced
- 2 celery stalks, diced
- 1 cup dried lentils (green or brown)
- 1/2 cup quinoa, rinsed
- 1 can (15 oz) diced tomatoes
- 6 cups vegetable broth
- 1 tsp ground cumin
- 1/2 tsp paprika
- 1/2 tsp dried thyme
- 1/4 tsp turmeric
- 1 bay leaf
- 4 cups chopped kale
- 2 tbsp lemon juice
- Salt and black pepper, to taste

Directions:

1. Cook the diced onion in a large pot over medium heat for about 5 minutes until soft and translucent.
2. Add minced garlic and sauté for 1 minute until fragrant.
3. Add diced carrots and celery, cooking for another 5 minutes, stirring occasionally.
4. Mix in rinsed lentils, ground cumin, paprika, dried thyme, turmeric, and a bay leaf, coating the vegetables.
5. Pour in diced tomatoes and vegetable broth, stirring well.
6. Bring to a boil, then reduce to a simmer.
7. Cover and cook for 20 minutes, or until lentils are tender.
8. Add rinsed quinoa and cook for another 10 minutes, until quinoa is done and kale is tender.
9. Remove the bay leaf.
10. Add lemon juice for freshness.
11. Season with salt and pepper to taste.
12. Garnish with fresh parsley before serving (optional).

Broccoli, Leek & Potato Soup

 Servings: 6 **Prep. time:** 15 min **Total time:** 45 min

Nutritional Information (Per Serving):

Calories: 185, Protein: 5g, Carbohydrates: 34g, Fats: 4g, Fiber: 7g, Cholesterol: 0mg, Sodium: 440mg (varies with broth and added salt), Potassium: 830mg

Ingredients

- 1 tbsp olive oil (or other plant-based oil)
- 1 large leek (white and light green parts only, sliced thinly)
- 3 cloves garlic (minced)
- 1 large potato (peeled and diced)
- 4 cups broccoli florets (about 1 large head of broccoli)
- 1 large carrot (diced)
- 1 cup celery (diced)
- 4 cups vegetable broth (low sodium)
- 1 cup unsweetened almond milk (or other plant-based milk)
- 1 tsp dried thyme
- 1/2 tsp dried rosemary
- 1/4 tsp ground nutmeg
- Salt and black pepper (to taste)
- 2 tbsp nutritional yeast (optional, for added flavor)
- 1 tbsp lemon juice (for brightness)

Directions:

1. Warm olive oil in a large pot over medium heat.
2. Add the sliced leek and cook for about 5 minutes until it softens.
3. Mix in the minced garlic and cook for another minute until it becomes fragrant.
4. Add diced potato, broccoli florets, carrot, and celery, stirring occasionally for about 5 minutes.
5. Pour in the vegetable broth and bring to a boil.
6. Lower the heat to a simmer, then add dried thyme, rosemary, ground nutmeg, salt, and black pepper.
7. Cover and cook for 20 minutes, or until the vegetables are soft.
8. Blend the soup with an immersion blender until smooth, or carefully transfer it in batches to a blender, blend until smooth, and return to the pot.
9. For a chunkier soup, blend only half and leave the rest with texture.
10. Mix in almond milk and nutritional yeast (if using) and simmer for another 5 minutes to warm through.
11. Add lemon juice, then taste and adjust the seasoning with salt and pepper.
12. Serve the soup hot, ladled into bowls.

Tomato & Cucumber Gazpacho

 Servings: 4 **Prep. time:** 15 min **Total time:** 60 min (chilling)

Nutritional Information (Per Serving):

Calories: 130, Protein: 3g, Carbohydrates: 14g, Fats: 8g, Fiber: 4g, Cholesterol: 0mg, Sodium: 250mg, Potassium: 600mg

Ingredients

- 4 large ripe tomatoes (2 lbs), chopped
- 1 large cucumber, peeled and diced
- 1 small red bell pepper, diced
- 1 small green bell pepper, diced
- 1 small red onion, diced
- 2 garlic cloves, minced
- 1/4 cup extra-virgin olive oil
- 2 tbsp red wine or apple cider vinegar
- 1 tsp ground cumin
- 1/2 tsp smoked paprika
- 1/2 tsp dried oregano
- Salt and black pepper
- 1/4 cup chopped fresh basil (plus extra for garnish)
- 1 cup low-sodium vegetable broth (chilled)

Directions:

1. Dice the tomatoes, cucumber, bell peppers, and red onion into small pieces.
2. Mince the garlic finely.
3. In a large bowl, combine the diced tomatoes, cucumber, bell peppers, red onion, and minced garlic.
4. Add the olive oil, red wine vinegar, ground cumin, smoked paprika, dried oregano, salt, and black pepper, stirring to mix well. Mix in the chopped basil and vegetable broth.
5. Blend the mixture using an immersion blender until smooth, or blend in batches using a standard blender if needed.
6. For a thicker texture, blend only part of the soup, leaving some chunks for added texture.
7. Pour the blended gazpacho into a container, cover, and refrigerate for at least an hour to chill and let the flavors meld together.
8. Before serving, taste the gazpacho and adjust the seasoning with more salt, pepper, or a splash of lemon juice if needed.
9. Serve the chilled gazpacho in bowls, garnished with extra chopped basil.

Red Kidney Bean & Spinach Soup

Servings: 4   **Prep. time:** 15 min   **Total time:** 45 min

Nutritional Information (Per Serving):

Calories: 220, Protein: 12g, Carbohydrates: 34g, Fats: 5g, Fiber: 10g, Cholesterol: 0mg, Sodium: 450mg, Potassium: 700mg

Ingredients

- 1 cup dried red kidney beans (or 2 cups canned, drained, and rinsed)
- 4 cups vegetable broth (low-sodium)
- 1 tablespoon extra-virgin olive oil
- 1 large onion (diced)
- 3 cloves garlic (minced)
- 2 medium carrots (diced)
- 2 celery stalks (diced)
- 1 red bell pepper (diced)
- 1 teaspoon ground cumin
- 1/2 teaspoon smoked paprika
- 1/2 teaspoon dried thyme
- 1/4 teaspoon black pepper
- 1/2 teaspoon salt (or to taste)
- 1 bay leaf
- 2 cups fresh spinach (chopped)
- 1 tablespoon lemon juice (optional, for added brightness)
- 2 tablespoons fresh parsley (chopped, for garnish)

Directions:

1. If using dried beans, soak them in water overnight, then drain and rinse.
2. For canned beans, just drain and rinse.
3. To cook dried beans, place them in a large pot with enough water to cover by 2 inches. Bring to a boil, then simmer for 45-60 minutes until tender. Drain and set aside.
4. For canned beans, you can skip this step.
5. Warm olive oil in a large pot over medium heat.
6. Add diced onion and sauté for 5 minutes until soft.
7. Add minced garlic and cook for 1 minute until aromatic.
8. Add diced carrots, celery, and red bell pepper, cooking for another 5 minutes with occasional stirring.
9. Sprinkle in ground cumin, smoked paprika, dried thyme, black pepper, and salt. Stir and cook for 1 minute to release the spices' aroma.
10. Pour in vegetable broth, then add the cooked beans (or canned beans) and a bay leaf, stirring to mix well.
11. Bring to a boil, then reduce heat to a simmer for 20 minutes, or until the vegetables are tender and flavors are blended.
12. Mix in chopped spinach and cook for 2-3 minutes until wilted.
13. Add a splash of lemon juice for a fresh flavor, if desired.
14. Adjust seasoning with salt and pepper to taste.
15. Serve in bowls, topped with fresh parsley..

Hearty Lentil & Vegetable Stew

Servings: 4   **Prep. time:** 15 min   **Total time:** 45 min

Nutritional Information (Per Serving):

Calories: 285, Protein: 12g, Carbohydrates: 45g, Fats: 7g, Fiber: 14g, Cholesterol: 0mg, Sodium: 360mg (depending on the vegetable broth used) Potassium: 960mg

Ingredients

- 1 cup dried green or brown lentils (soaked for 1-2 hours and rinsed)
- 1 large carrot (diced)
- 2 medium potatoes (diced)
- 1 zucchini (diced)
- 1 cup spinach (chopped)
- 1 can (14.5 oz) diced tomatoes (no salt added)
- 1 small onion (finely chopped)
- 3 cloves garlic (minced)
- 4 cups vegetable broth (low sodium)
- 1 tsp dried thyme
- 1 tsp ground cumin

Directions:

1. Soak lentils in water for 1-2 hours to reduce cooking time and improve digestibility. After soaking, rinse under cold water and set aside.
2. Warm olive oil in a large pot over medium heat. Add chopped onion and garlic, sautéing for about 5 minutes until the onion turns translucent.
3. Add diced carrots and potatoes to the pot. Cook for another 5 minutes, stirring occasionally, until they soften.
4. Stir in cumin, smoked paprika, and thyme. Cook for 1 minute to release the aroma of the spices.
5. Add the soaked lentils, diced tomatoes (with juice), and vegetable broth. Add the bay leaf. Stir and bring to a boil.
6. Lower the heat, cover, and let it simmer for 20-25 minutes until lentils and vegetables are tender.

- 1 tsp smoked paprika
- 1 bay leaf
- 2 tbsp olive oil
- Salt and pepper (to taste)
- Fresh parsley (for garnish, optional)

7. In the last 5 minutes, add diced zucchini and chopped spinach. Stir and cook until zucchini is soft and spinach is wilted.
8. Taste and add salt and pepper as needed. Remove the bay leaf before serving.
9. Spoon the stew into bowls, garnish with fresh parsley if desired, and serve warm.

Sweet Potato & Black Bean Stew

Servings: 4   **Prep. time:** 10 min   **Total time:** 35 min

Nutritional Information (Per Serving):

Calories: 270, Protein: 7g, Carbohydrates: 52g, Fats: 5g, Fiber: 12g, Cholesterol: 0mg, Sodium: 320mg (depending on the vegetable broth and tomatoes used), Potassium: 950mg

Ingredients

- 2 medium sweet potatoes, peeled and diced (1/2-inch cubes)
- 1 can black beans (15 oz), drained and rinsed
- 1 medium onion, chopped
- 2 cloves garlic, minced
- 1 red bell pepper, chopped
- 1 can diced tomatoes (14.5 oz, no salt added)
- 2 cups low-sodium vegetable broth
- 1 tbsp olive oil
- 1 tsp ground cumin
- 1 tsp smoked paprika
- 1/2 tsp ground cinnamon
- 1/4 tsp cayenne pepper (optional)
- Salt and pepper, to taste
- Juice of 1 lime
- Fresh cilantro, chopped (for garnish)

Directions:

1. Cut the sweet potatoes into 1/2-inch pieces. Dice the bell pepper and onion, finely chop the garlic.
2. In a large pot, warm olive oil over medium heat. Add the garlic and onion, cook for 3-4 minutes until the onion is soft and fragrant.
3. Add the sweet potatoes and bell pepper. Sprinkle in the ground cumin, smoked paprika, ground cinnamon, and cayenne pepper (if desired). Cook for 3-4 minutes, allowing the spices to toast and the vegetables to soften.
4. Pour in the diced tomatoes, including their juices and the vegetable broth. Stir everything together.
5. Bring to a boil, then reduce to a simmer. Cover the pot and cook for about 15 minutes or until the sweet potatoes are tender.
6. After draining and rinsing, add the black beans and continue to simmer for another 5 minutes to combine the flavors.
7. Taste and adjust the seasoning with salt and pepper, and stir in lime juice for a fresh touch.
8. Serve in bowls, garnished with chopped cilantro. Enjoy it while hot!

White Bean & Kale Stew

Servings: 4   **Prep. time:** 10 min   **Total time:** 35 min

Nutritional Information (Per Serving):

Calories: 210, Protein: 8g, Carbohydrates: 35g, Fats: 5g, Fiber: 8g, Cholesterol: 0mg, Sodium: 420mg (depending on the vegetable broth used) Potassium: 750mg

Ingredients

- 1 tbsp olive oil (or plant-based oil)
- 1 medium onion, chopped
- 3 cloves garlic, minced
- 2 medium carrots, peeled and diced
- 2 celery stalks, diced
- 1 medium potato, peeled and diced
- 1 tsp dried thyme
- 1/2 tsp dried rosemary
- 1/2 tsp smoked paprika
- 4 cups low-sodium vegetable broth
- 2 cups cooked white beans (or 1 can, drained and rinsed)
- 4 cups kale, roughly chopped (stems removed)
- Salt and pepper, to taste
- Juice of 1/2 lemon (optional)
- Fresh parsley, chopped (for garnish)

Directions:

1. Dice the onion, mince the garlic, and cut the carrots, celery, and potato into small pieces. Roughly chop the kale, removing any thick stems.
2. Warm olive oil in a large pot over medium heat. Cook the onion for 3-4 minutes until it softens. Add garlic and sauté for 1 minute until it becomes aromatic.
3. Add the carrots, celery, and potato to the pot. Sprinkle with thyme, rosemary, and smoked paprika. Stir occasionally and cook for about 5 minutes, allowing the vegetables to soften slightly and absorb the flavors.
4. Pour in the vegetable broth and bring to a gentle boil. Lower the heat, cover, and let it simmer for 15 minutes, or until the vegetables are tender. Add the white beans and kale, stirring to combine. Simmer for another 5 minutes until the kale wilts and the beans are warmed through.
5. Adjust seasoning with salt, pepper, and a splash of lemon juice for a bright flavor if desired.
6. Serve hot, spooned into bowls and topped with fresh parsley.

Cabbage & White Bean Stew

Servings: 4   **Prep. time:** 15 min   **Total time:** 45 min

Nutritional Information (Per Serving):

Calories: 210, Protein: 10g, Carbohydrates: 36g, Fats: 4g, Fiber: 9g, Cholesterol: 0mg, Sodium: 450mg (varies with broth), Potassium: 800mg

Ingredients

- 1 tbsp olive oil
- 1 large onion (diced)
- 3 cloves garlic (minced)
- 2 medium carrots (diced)
- 1 celery stalk (diced)
- 4 cups cabbage (shredded)
- 1 can (15 oz) white beans (such as cannellini or great northern, drained and rinsed)
- 1 can (14.5 oz) diced tomatoes (no salt added)
- 4 cups vegetable broth (low sodium)
- 1 cup water
- 1 tsp dried thyme
- 1/2 tsp dried rosemary
- 1/2 tsp paprika
- 1/4 tsp black pepper
- 1/2 tsp sea salt (or to taste)
- 1 tbsp lemon juice (optional, for extra flavor)

Directions:

1. Chop the celery, carrots and onion into small pieces. Mince the garlic and shred the cabbage.
2. Warm olive oil in a large pot over medium heat. Add the onion and sauté for 5 minutes until softened. Add the garlic and cook for another minute, stirring constantly.
3. Add the carrots and celery to the pot, stirring to combine. Cook for about 5 minutes until they soft.
4. Add the shredded cabbage and continue to cook for another 5 minutes, stirring occasionally, until the cabbage starts to wilt.
5. Mix in the white beans, diced tomatoes, thyme, rosemary, paprika, black pepper, and salt.
6. Pour in the vegetable broth and water, stirring well to combine, and bring to a boil.
7. Lower the heat, cover the pot, and let it simmer for 20 minutes, or until the vegetables are tender and flavors are blended.
8. Add lemon juice if desired. Taste and adjust seasoning as needed. Serve hot, ladled into bowls.

Eggplant & Tomato Stew

 Servings: 4   **Prep. time:** 15 min   **Total time:** 45 min

Nutritional Information (Per Serving):

Calories: 210, Protein: 4g, Carbohydrates: 24g, Fats: 12g, Fiber: 8g, Cholesterol: 0mg, Sodium: 400mg, Potassium: 740mg

Ingredients

- 1 large eggplant, peeled and cut into 1-inch cubes
- 2 tablespoons olive oil
- 1 large onion, diced
- 3 cloves garlic, minced
- 1 red bell pepper, diced
- 2 cups cherry tomatoes, halved (or 1 can (14.5 oz) diced tomatoes)
- 1 cup vegetable broth
- 1 tablespoon tomato paste
- 1 teaspoon dried basil
- 1 teaspoon dried oregano
- 1/2 teaspoon smoked paprika
- 1/2 teaspoon ground cumin
- 1/4 teaspoon chili flakes (optional, for heat)
- 1/2 teaspoon sea salt (adjust to taste)
- 1/4 teaspoon black pepper
- 1 cup fresh spinach, chopped
- 1 tablespoon balsamic vinegar (optional, for extra flavor)

Directions:

1. Place the eggplant cubes in a colander, sprinkle with sea salt, and let them sit for 15 minutes to remove excess moisture and bitterness. Rinse the eggplant and pat dry with a paper towel.
2. In a large pot, heat olive oil over medium heat.
3. Add the diced onion and cook for about 5 minutes until it becomes translucent and soft.
4. Add the minced garlic and sauté for another minute until aromatic.
5. Add the eggplant cubes and diced red bell pepper, cooking for 5-7 minutes, stirring occasionally, until the eggplant begins to soften and turn golden.
6. Add cherry tomatoes (or canned diced tomatoes) and tomato paste, stirring to mix well.
7. Pour in the vegetable broth and add dried basil, oregano, smoked paprika, cumin, chili flakes (if desired), sea salt, and black pepper. Stir to combine.
8. Bring to a boil, then lower the heat and let it simmer uncovered for 20 minutes, stirring occasionally, until the eggplant is tender and the stew has thickened.
9. Mix in the chopped spinach and cook for 2 more minutes, just until the spinach wilts.
10. Add balsamic vinegar, if desired, for added depth of flavor.
11. Serve hot, with a side of quinoa, brown rice, or whole grain bread, if you like.

Pumpkin & Chickpea Stew

 Servings: 4   **Prep. time:** 15 min   **Total time:** 45 min

Nutritional Information (Per Serving):

Calories: 350, Protein: 9g, Carbohydrates: 45g, Fats: 15g, Fiber: 11g, Cholesterol: 0mg, Sodium: 550mg, Potassium: 950mg

Ingredients

- 1 tablespoon olive oil
- 1 medium onion, chopped
- 3 garlic cloves, minced
- 1-inch piece fresh ginger, peeled and grated
- 1 medium pumpkin (about 2 lbs), peeled, seeded, and cut into 1-inch cubes (or use 4 cups canned pumpkin puree)
- 1 can (15 oz) chickpeas, drained and rinsed (or 1 1/2 cups cooked chickpeas)
- 1 can (14.5 oz) diced tomatoes, with juices

Directions:

1. If using fresh pumpkin, peel, remove the seeds, and cut into 1-inch cubes. Rinse and drain the chickpeas if using canned. Set aside.
2. In a large pot, warm olive oil over medium heat. Add chopped onion and sauté for about 5 minutes until soft and translucent.
3. Add minced garlic and grated ginger, cooking for another 1-2 minutes until aromatic.
4. Add pumpkin cubes to the pot, stirring to combine with the onion, garlic, and ginger.
5. Sprinkle in ground cumin, coriander, turmeric, smoked paprika, and cinnamon, stirring to coat the pumpkin evenly with the spices.
6. Pour in vegetable broth, diced tomatoes with their juices, and coconut milk. Mix well.
7. Bring to a boil, then lower the heat and cover. Simmer for 20 minutes, or until the pumpkin is tender and easily pierced with a fork.

- 1 can (14 oz) coconut milk
- 2 cups vegetable broth
- 1 teaspoon ground cumin
- 1 teaspoon ground coriander
- 1/2 teaspoon ground turmeric
- 1/2 teaspoon smoked paprika
- 1/4 teaspoon ground cinnamon
- Salt and pepper to taste
- 2 cups fresh spinach or kale
- Optional for garnish: 1/4 cup fresh cilantro, chopped; 1 tablespoon lime juice

8. Stir in chickpeas and simmer for an additional 5 minutes to blend the flavors.
9. Add chopped spinach or kale and cook for 2-3 minutes until wilted.
10. Taste and adjust seasoning with salt and pepper.
11. For a fresh finish, stir in lime juice if desired and garnish with fresh cilantro. Serve hot in bowls, and enjoy as is or with quinoa, brown rice, or whole-grain bread for a heartier meal.

Spicy Chickpea & Spinach Stew

 Servings: 4   **Prep. time:** 10 min   **Total time:** 35 min

Nutritional Information (Per Serving):

Calories: 210, Protein: 8g, Carbohydrates: 30g, Fats: 7g, Fiber: 8g, Cholesterol: 0mg, Sodium: 600mg, Potassium: 800mg

Ingredients

- 1 tablespoon olive oil
- 1 medium onion, finely chopped
- 3 cloves garlic, minced
- 1-inch piece fresh ginger, minced
- 1 teaspoon cumin seeds
- 1 teaspoon ground coriander
- 1 teaspoon smoked paprika
- 1/2 teaspoon ground turmeric
- 1/2 teaspoon cayenne pepper (adjust to taste)
- 1 can (15 oz) chickpeas, drained and rinsed
- 1 can (14.5 oz) diced tomatoes (with juices)
- 1 cup vegetable broth (low sodium)
- 1 teaspoon salt, or to taste
- 4 cups fresh spinach leaves
- 1 tablespoon fresh lemon juice
- Fresh cilantro, chopped, for garnish

Directions:

1. Warm olive oil in a large pot over medium heat.
2. Add chopped onion and sauté for 5 minutes until soft and translucent.
3. Mix in minced garlic and ginger, sautéing for 1-2 minutes while stirring frequently to avoid burning.
4. Add cumin seeds, ground coriander, smoked paprika, turmeric, and cayenne pepper. Stir continuously and cook for 1 minute to enhance their flavors.
5. Add the drained chickpeas, stirring well to coat them with the spices.
6. Pour in diced tomatoes with their juices and vegetable broth, stirring to mix everything together.
7. Season with salt as needed.
8. Bring the mixture to a gentle boil, then reduce heat to low and let it simmer uncovered for 15 minutes to allow flavors to blend and the stew to thicken slightly.
9. Mix in fresh spinach leaves and cook for an additional 2-3 minutes until wilted and well combined.
10. Remove from heat and add fresh lemon juice for a bright finish.
11. Serve hot, ladling the stew into bowls and garnishing with chopped cilantro. Enjoy with whole grain bread or brown rice, if desired.

Coconut & Butternut Squash Stew

 Servings: 4   **Prep. time:** 15 min   **Total time:** 45 min

Nutritional Information (Per Serving):

Calories: 280, Protein: 4g, Carbohydrates: 32g, Fats: 16g, Fiber: 6g, Cholesterol: 0mg, Sodium: 400mg (varies with broth), Potassium: 850mg

Ingredients

- 1 tbsp coconut oil
- 1 large onion (diced)
- 3 cloves garlic (minced)
- 1 tbsp fresh ginger (grated)
- 1 medium butternut squash (peeled, seeded, and cubed, about 4 cups)
- 1 large carrot (peeled and diced)
- 1 bell pepper (diced, any color)
- 1 can (14 oz) coconut milk (full-fat or light)
- 2 cups vegetable broth (low sodium)
- 1 cup water
- 1 tbsp curry powder (mild or to taste)
- 1/2 tsp ground cumin
- 1/2 tsp ground turmeric
- 1/4 tsp red pepper flakes (optional, for heat)
- 1/2 tsp sea salt (or to taste)
- 1/4 tsp black pepper
- 1 cup spinach (chopped)
- 1 tbsp lime juice (optional, for added brightness)
- Fresh cilantro (for garnish, optional)

Directions:

1. Warm 1 tbsp of coconut oil in a large pot over medium heat. Sauté the diced onion for 5-7 minutes until soft and translucent. Add the minced garlic and grated ginger, cooking for an additional 2 minutes until fragrant.
2. Add the cubed butternut squash, diced carrot, and bell pepper. Sprinkle it with curry powder, cumin, turmeric, and red pepper flakes if you want some heat. Stir and cook for 2-3 minutes to evenly coat the vegetables with the spices.
3. Pour in the coconut milk, vegetable broth, and water. Stir everything together and bring to a boil.
4. Reduce the heat to a simmer and cook for 25-30 minutes, or until the squash and carrots are tender.
5. Add the chopped spinach, stirring until it wilts, about 2 minutes. For a tangy flavor, add a squeeze of lime juice if you like. Taste and adjust seasoning with sea salt and black pepper.
6. Serve hot, with a garnish of fresh cilantro if desired.

Moroccan Spiced Chickpea Stew

Servings: 4   **Prep. time:** 15 min   **Total time:** 45 min

Nutritional Information (Per Serving):

Calories: 270, Protein: 8g. Carbohydrates: 46g, Fats: 7g, Fiber: 8g, Cholesterol: 0mg, Sodium: 400mg (varies with broth), Potassium: 850mg

Ingredients

- 1 tbsp olive oil
- 1 large onion, diced
- 3 cloves garlic, minced
- 1 tbsp fresh ginger, grated
- 2 tsp ground cumin
- 1 tsp ground coriander
- 1 tsp paprika
- 1/2 tsp turmeric
- 1/2 tsp cinnamon
- 1/4 tsp cayenne pepper (optional)
- 1 can diced tomatoes (14 oz, no salt added)
- 1 can chickpeas (14 oz, rinsed and drained)
- 1 medium carrot, diced
- 1 medium sweet potato, diced
- 1 cup low-sodium vegetable broth
- 1/2 cup dried apricots, chopped
- 1/2 cup raisins (optional)
- 1 cup spinach, chopped
- 1 tbsp lemon juice
- Salt and black pepper, to taste
- Fresh cilantro, for garnish (optional)

Directions:

1. Warm 1 tbsp of olive oil in a large pot over medium heat. Cook the diced onion for 5-7 minutes until it softens and becomes translucent. Add minced garlic and grated ginger, sautéing for another 2 minutes until fragrant.
2. Mix in the ground cumin, coriander, paprika, turmeric, cinnamon, and cayenne pepper (if using). Cook for 1-2 minutes to enhance the spices' aroma.
3. Add diced carrots, sweet potatoes, and chopped dried apricots, stirring to evenly coat with the spices. Pour in the diced tomatoes and vegetable broth, mixing well.
4. Bring the stew to a boil, then reduce heat to low. Cover and simmer for 20-25 minutes, or until the vegetables are soft.
5. Add chickpeas and chopped spinach, stirring to combine. Simmer for another 5 minutes until the spinach wilts and chickpeas are warmed through.
6. Stir in lemon juice, and season with salt and black pepper to taste. Serve hot, with fresh cilantro on top if desired.

Green Bean & Potato Stew

Servings: 4   **Prep. time:** 15 min   **Total time:** 45 min

Nutritional Information (Per Serving):

Calories: 190, Protein: 5g, Carbohydrates: 34g, Fats: 6g, Fiber: 7g, Cholesterol: 0mg, Sodium: 350mg (varies with broth), Potassium: 830mg

Ingredients

- 1 lb (450g) green beans (trimmed and cut into 1-inch pieces)
- 4 medium potatoes (about 1.5 lbs or 675g, peeled and diced)
- 1 large onion (diced)
- 2 cloves garlic (minced)
- 2 cups vegetable broth (low sodium)
- 1 can (14.5 oz or 410g) diced tomatoes (no added salt)
- 1 cup carrots (sliced)
- 1 tsp dried thyme
- 1/2 tsp dried rosemary
- 1/2 tsp smoked paprika
- 2 tbsp olive oil
- Salt and black pepper (to taste)
- 2 tbsp fresh parsley (chopped, for garnish)

Directions:

1. Trim and cut the green beans. Dice the potatoes, slice the carrots, mince the garlic, and dice the onion.
2. Heat 2 tbsp olive oil in a large pot over medium heat. Sauté the onion for 5 minutes until translucent.
3. Add the garlic and cook for 1-2 minutes until fragrant.
4. Stir in the potatoes and carrots, cooking for 5 minutes while stirring occasionally.
5. Add vegetable broth, diced tomatoes with their juice, and green beans.
6. Mix in dried thyme, rosemary, smoked paprika, salt, and pepper.
7. Bring to a boil, then lower the heat. Cover and simmer for 20-25 minutes until the potatoes and carrots are tender.
8. Adjust seasoning to taste. For a thicker stew, mash some potatoes.
9. Serve hot, garnished with fresh parsley.

Chard & Cannellini Bean Stew

  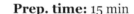

Servings: 6   **Prep. time:** 15 min   **Total time:** 40 min

Nutritional Information (Per Serving):

Calories: 220, Protein: 11g, Carbohydrates: 35g, Fats: 6g, Fiber: 10g, Cholesterol: 0mg, Sodium: 320mg (varies with broth), Potassium: 800mg

Ingredients

- 1 tbsp olive or plant-based oil
- 1 large onion, diced
- 3 garlic cloves, minced
- 2 carrots, peeled and diced
- 2 celery stalks, diced
- 1 red bell pepper, diced
- 1 zucchini, diced
- 1 can (15 oz) cannellini beans, rinsed and drained (or 1.5 cups cooked)
- 1 bunch Swiss chard, chopped (stems removed)
- 1 can (14.5 oz) diced tomatoes (no added salt)
- 4 cups low-sodium vegetable broth
- 1 tsp dried thyme
- 1 tsp dried basil
- 1/2 tsp smoked paprika
- 1/4 tsp red pepper flakes (optional)
- 1 bay leaf
- 1 tbsp balsamic vinegar
- Salt and black pepper
- 1 tbsp chopped fresh parsley (for garnish)

Directions:

1. Warm olive oil in a large pot over medium heat.
2. Add diced onion and sauté for about 5 minutes until it becomes translucent.
3. Mix in minced garlic and cook for another minute until it releases its aroma.
4. Add the diced carrots, celery, red bell pepper, and zucchini.
5. Cook for around 5 minutes, stirring occasionally, until the vegetables begin to soften.
6. Stir in the rinsed cannellini beans, dried thyme, dried basil, smoked paprika, and red pepper flakes (if using).
7. Mix well to coat the vegetables and beans with the spices.
8. Pour in the diced tomatoes and vegetable broth.
9. Add the bay leaf and bring the pot to a boil.
10. Lower the heat to a simmer and cook for 15 minutes, letting the flavors blend and the vegetables soften.
11. Mix in the chopped Swiss chard and cook for another 5 minutes until the chard has wilted.
12. Stir in the balsamic vinegar for added depth of flavor.
13. Adjust seasoning with salt and black pepper to taste.
14. Ladle the stew into bowls and garnish with fresh parsley.

Peanut & Sweet Potato Stew

 Servings: 6 **Prep. time:** 15 min **Total time:** 45 min

Nutritional Information (Per Serving):

Calories: 350, Protein: 12g, Carbohydrates: 46g, Fats: 15g, Fiber: 8g, Cholesterol: omg, Sodium: 400mg (varies with broth and soy sauce), Potassium: 800mg

Ingredients

- 1 tbsp olive oil (or other plant-based oil)
- 1 large onion (diced)
- 3 cloves garlic (minced)
- 1 tbsp fresh ginger (grated)
- 2 large sweet potatoes (peeled and diced)
- 1 red bell pepper (diced)
- 1 cup natural peanut butter (smooth, no added sugar)
- 1 can (14 oz) diced tomatoes (no salt added)
- 4 cups vegetable broth (low sodium)
- 1 cup frozen peas (or fresh)
- 1 tbsp soy sauce (or tamari for gluten-free)
- 1 tsp ground cumin
- 1/2 tsp smoked paprika
- 1/2 tsp ground turmeric
- 1/4 tsp cayenne pepper (adjust to taste)
- Salt and black pepper (to taste)
- 1 tbsp lime juice (for added brightness)
- 2 tbsp chopped fresh cilantro (for garnish)

Directions:

1. Heat the olive oil in a large pot over medium heat.
2. Add the diced onion and cook for about 5 minutes, until softened.
3. Stir in the minced garlic and grated ginger, cooking for an additional 1 minute until fragrant.
4. Add the diced sweet potatoes and red bell pepper to the pot.
5. Cook for about 5 minutes, stirring occasionally.
6. Stir in the ground cumin, smoked paprika, ground turmeric, and cayenne pepper.
7. Mix well to coat the vegetables with the spices.
8. Add the natural peanut butter and stir until well combined with the vegetables.
9. Pour in the diced tomatoes and vegetable broth.
10. Stir well to combine all ingredients.
11. Bring the mixture to a boil, then reduce the heat to a simmer.
12. Cover and cook for 20-25 minutes, or until the sweet potatoes are tender.
13. Stir in the frozen peas and soy sauce.
14. Cook for an additional 5 minutes until peas are heated through.
15. Adjust seasoning with salt and black pepper to taste.
16. Stir in lime juice for added brightness.
17. Ladle the stew into bowls and garnish with chopped fresh cilantro.

Cauliflower & Chickpea Stew

 Servings: 6 **Prep. time:** 15 min **Total time:** 40 min

Nutritional Information (Per Serving):

Calories: 320, Protein: 10g, Carbohydrates: 39g, Fats: 14g, Fiber: 8g, Cholesterol: omg, Sodium: 500mg (varies with broth and added salt), Potassium: 800mg

Ingredients

- 2 tbsp olive oil (or other plant-based oil)
- 1 large onion (diced)
- 3 cloves garlic (minced)
- 1 tbsp fresh ginger (grated)
- 1 medium head cauliflower (cut into florets)
- 1 can (15 oz) chickpeas (rinsed and drained)
- 1 large carrot (diced)
- 1 cup diced tomatoes (canned, no salt added)
- 4 cups vegetable broth (low sodium)
- 1 tsp ground cumin
- 1/2 tsp smoked paprika

Directions:

1. Warm olive oil in a large pot over medium heat.
2. Add diced onion and sauté for about 5 minutes until softened and translucent.
3. Add minced garlic and grated ginger, cooking for 1 minute until fragrant.
4. Add cauliflower florets and diced carrot, sautéing for about 5 minutes and stirring occasionally.
5. Mix in ground cumin, smoked paprika, ground turmeric, and cayenne pepper, stirring well to coat the vegetables with the spices.
6. Pour in diced tomatoes and vegetable broth, stirring to combine.
7. Bring to a boil, then reduce to a simmer.
8. Cover and cook for 15 minutes, or until the cauliflower and

- 1/2 tsp ground turmeric
- 1/4 tsp cayenne pepper (adjust to taste)
- 1/2 cup coconut milk (canned, full-fat or light)
- 1 tbsp lemon juice
- Salt and black pepper (to taste)
- 2 tbsp chopped fresh cilantro (for garnish)

carrots are tender.

9. Add chickpeas and coconut milk, simmering for another 5 minutes until heated through and slightly thickened.
10. Stir in lemon juice and season with salt and black pepper.
11. Garnish with fresh cilantro before serving.

Winter Squash & Lentil Stew

Servings: 6   **Prep. time:** 15 min   **Total time:** 55 min

Nutritional Information (Per Serving):

Calories: 230, Protein: 10g, Carbohydrates: 39g, Fats: 5g, Fiber: 11g, Cholesterol: 0mg, Sodium: 340mg (varies with broth and added salt), Potassium: 800mg

Ingredients

- 1 tbsp olive oil (or other plant-based oil)
- 1 large onion (diced)
- 3 cloves garlic (minced)
- 1 large winter squash (such as butternut or acorn, peeled and cubed, about 4 cups)
- 1 cup dried green or brown lentils (rinsed, no soaking needed)
- 2 carrots (diced)
- 2 celery stalks (diced)
- 1 red bell pepper (diced)
- 1 can (14.5 oz) diced tomatoes (no added salt)
- 4 cups vegetable broth (low sodium)
- 1 tsp ground cumin
- 1 tsp smoked paprika
- 1/2 tsp ground turmeric
- 1/2 tsp dried thyme
- Salt and black pepper (to taste)
- 2 cups fresh spinach (or kale, chopped)
- 2 tbsp lemon juice (for brightness)
- 2 tbsp chopped fresh parsley (for garnish)

Directions:

1. Warm olive oil in a large pot over medium heat.
2. Add diced onion and cook for about 5 minutes until softened.
3. Mix in minced garlic and cook for 1 minute until fragrant.
4. Add cubed winter squash, carrots, celery, and red bell pepper. Cook for 5 minutes, stirring occasionally.
5. Add rinsed lentils, diced tomatoes with their juice, and vegetable broth.
6. Sprinkle in ground cumin, smoked paprika, ground turmeric, dried thyme, salt, and black pepper. Stir well.
7. Bring the mixture to a boil, then reduce heat to low and cover the pot.
8. Simmer for 30-35 minutes, stirring occasionally, until lentils and squash are tender.
9. Add fresh spinach or kale, cooking for another 5 minutes until wilted.
10. Season with more salt and pepper if needed, and stir in lemon juice for brightness.
11. Serve hot in bowls, garnished with fresh parsley..

Sauces, Dips & Dressings

Creamy Avocado Lime Dressing

Servings: 4   **Prep. time:** 10 min   **Total time:** 10 min

Nutritional Information (Per Serving):

Calories: 130 kcal, Protein: 1.2g, Carbohydrates: 6g, Fats: 12g, Fiber: 4.5g, Cholesterol: 0mg, Sodium: 75mg, Potassium: 350mg

Ingredients

- 1 large ripe avocado (about 200g flesh)
- 2 tablespoons fresh lime juice (about 1 lime)
- 1 clove garlic, minced
- 2 tablespoons extra virgin olive oil
- 2 tablespoons fresh cilantro leaves
- 1/4 teaspoon ground cumin
- 1/4 teaspoon sea salt (adjust to taste)
- 1/8 teaspoon black pepper
- 2-4 tablespoons water (to achieve desired consistency)

Directions:

1. Cut the avocado in half, remove the pit, and scoop the flesh into a blender or food processor.
2. Mince the garlic to enhance its flavor.
3. Add the avocado, lime juice, minced garlic, olive oil, cilantro leaves, cumin, sea salt, and black pepper to the blender.
4. Blend on medium until smooth and creamy.
5. Add water gradually, 1 tablespoon at a time, blending until you reach the desired consistency. Use less water for a thicker dressing, more for a thinner one.
6. Taste and adjust the seasoning with more salt, lime juice, or cumin as needed.
7. Transfer the dressing to a dish or jar. Use right away or chill for a cooler flavor.
8. Store any leftovers in an airtight container in the fridge for up to 3 days. If it thickens, stir in a bit of water or lime juice before using again.

Tahini Lemon Sauce

Servings: 6   **Prep. time:** 5 min   **Total time:** 5 min

Nutritional Information (Per Serving):

Calories: 160 kcal, Protein: 4.5g, Carbohydrates: 5g, Fats: 14g, Fiber: 3g, Cholesterol: 0mg, Sodium: 105mg, Potassium: 130mg

Ingredients

- 1/2 cup tahini (sesame seed paste)
- 1/4 cup fresh lemon juice (about 2 lemons)
- 2 tablespoons extra virgin olive oil
- 1 clove garlic, minced
- 1/4 teaspoon ground cumin
- 1/4 teaspoon sea salt (adjust to taste)
- 1/8 teaspoon ground black pepper
- 1/4 cup water (adjust for desired consistency)
- 1 tablespoon fresh parsley, finely chopped (optional for garnish)

Directions:

1. Juice the lemons to get fresh lemon juice. Mince the garlic to boost its flavor and ensure it's evenly distributed in the sauce.
2. In a medium bowl, combine tahini, fresh lemon juice, and olive oil. Stir until the mixture thickens.
3. Add minced garlic, ground cumin, sea salt, and black pepper, mixing well to blend the flavors.
4. Slowly add water, stirring continuously, until the sauce reaches your preferred consistency. Use less water for a thicker sauce, more for a thinner one.
5. Taste and adjust seasoning with extra salt, lemon juice, or cumin, as needed.
6. Pour the tahini lemon sauce into a serving dish. Optionally, garnish with finely chopped parsley for a pop of color and added flavor.
7. Store leftovers in an airtight container in the fridge for up to 5 days. Stir before using, as the sauce may thicken when chilled.

Roasted Red Pepper Hummus

 Servings: 8   **Prep. time:** 10 min   **Total time:** 40 min

Nutritional Information (Per Serving):

Calories: 110 kcal, Protein: 3g, Carbohydrates: 10g, Fats: 6g, Fiber: 3g, Cholesterol: 0mg, Sodium: 120mg, Potassium: 180mg

Ingredients

- 2 large red bell peppers
- 1 1/2 cups cooked chickpeas (or one 15-ounce can, drained and rinsed)
- 1/4 cup tahini (sesame seed paste)
- 2 tablespoons extra virgin olive oil
- 3 tablespoons fresh lemon juice (about 1 lemon)
- 2 cloves garlic, minced
- 1/2 teaspoon ground cumin
- 1/4 teaspoon smoked paprika
- 1/2 teaspoon sea salt (adjust to taste)
- 2-3 tablespoons water (adjust for desired consistency)
- Fresh parsley, chopped

Directions:

1. Preheat the oven to 400°F (200°C) and line a baking sheet with parchment paper. Place red bell peppers on the sheet.
2. Roast for 25-30 minutes, turning occasionally, until the skins are charred and blistered.
3. Once done, transfer the peppers to a bowl and cover with a plate or plastic wrap to steam for 10 minutes—this helps with peeling.
4. Peel off the skins, remove seeds and stems, and set the roasted pepper flesh aside.
5. In a food processor, blend the roasted peppers with chickpeas, tahini, minced garlic, lemon juice, cumin, smoked paprika, and sea salt.
6. Blend until smooth, adding water gradually, a tablespoon at a time, until you reach your preferred consistency. For a creamier texture, add a bit more olive oil.
7. Taste and adjust seasoning with additional salt, lemon juice, or smoked paprika if needed.
8. Spoon the hummus into a bowl, drizzle with olive oil, and garnish with fresh parsley, if desired.
9. Store any leftovers in the fridge in an airtight container for up to 5 days. Stir before serving.

Cashew Cream Sauce

 Servings: 8   **Prep. time:** 10 min   **Total time:** 4 h 20 min (including soaking time)

Nutritional Information (Per Serving):

Calories: 90 kcal, Protein: 3g, Carbohydrates: 5g Fats: 7g, Fiber: 1g, Cholesterol: 0mg, Sodium: 75mg, Potassium: 125mg

Ingredients

- 1 cup raw cashews
- 1/2 cup water (plus more for soaking)
- 2 tablespoons fresh lemon juice (about 1 lemon)
- 1 tablespoon nutritional yeast (optional, for a cheesy flavor)
- 1 clove garlic, minced
- 1/2 teaspoon sea salt (adjust to taste)
- 1/4 teaspoon ground black pepper
- 1/4 teaspoon onion powder
- 1/4 teaspoon smoked paprika (optional, for added depth of flavor)

Directions:

1. Place raw cashews in a bowl and cover with water. Soak for at least 4 hours or overnight to soften them for a smoother, creamier sauce.
2. After soaking, drain and rinse the cashews under cold water to remove any phytic acid.
3. In a high-speed blender or food processor, combine the soaked cashews, 1/2 cup fresh water, lemon juice, minced garlic, nutritional yeast, sea salt, black pepper, onion powder, and smoked paprika (if desired).
4. Blend on high until completely smooth and creamy, stopping to scrape down the sides or adding more water as needed to reach your desired consistency.
5. Taste and adjust seasoning with more salt, lemon juice, or spices to suit your preference.
6. The cashew cream sauce is ready to serve over pasta, vegetables, or as a dip.
7. Store any leftovers in an airtight container in the refrigerator for up to 5 days. The sauce may thicken as it cools; thin it with a little water if needed before using.

Spicy Mango Salsa

 Servings: 6 **Prep. time:** 15 min **Total time:** 15 min

Nutritional Information (Per Serving):

Calories: 50 kcal, Protein: 1g, Carbohydrates: 12g Fats: 0.2g, Fiber: 2g, Cholesterol: 0mg, Sodium: 50mg, Potassium: 175mg

Ingredients

- 2 ripe mangoes, peeled and diced (about 2 cups)
- 1/2 red bell pepper, finely chopped
- 1/2 red onion, finely chopped
- 1 medium jalapeño pepper, seeded and minced (use more or less depending on spice preference)
- 1/4 cup fresh cilantro, finely chopped
- Juice of 1 lime (about 2 tablespoons)
- 1 tablespoon fresh orange juice (optional, for added sweetness)
- 1/4 teaspoon sea salt (adjust to taste)
- 1/4 teaspoon ground cumin (optional, for a deeper flavor)

Directions:

1. Peel and dice the mangoes into small cubes, using ripe ones for the best taste and texture.
2. Finely chop the red bell pepper, red onion, and jalapeño pepper for even flavor distribution.
3. In a large bowl, combine the diced mangoes, red bell pepper, red onion, jalapeño, and chopped cilantro.
4. Squeeze lime juice over the mixture, and add orange juice if desired for a refreshing tang that enhances the flavors.
5. Sprinkle with sea salt and ground cumin (if using). Gently toss until everything is well mixed.
6. Taste and adjust seasoning with more lime juice, salt, or jalapeño for extra heat, if needed.
7. Serve the mango salsa right away, or let it sit for a few minutes to let the flavors meld. It goes great with tortilla chips, tacos, grilled veggies, or as a salad topping.
8. Store any leftovers in an airtight container in the fridge for up to 2 days. Stir well before serving, as it may become juicier over time.

Cilantro Lime Yogurt Dressing

 Servings: 8 **Prep. time:** 10 min **Total time:** 10 min

Nutritional Information (Per Serving):

Calories: 25 kcal, Protein: 0.5g, Carbohydrates: 2 Fats: 2g, Fiber: 0.5g, Cholesterol: 0mg, Sodium: 100mg, Potassium: 35mg

Ingredients

- 1 cup unsweetened plant-based yogurt (e.g., almond, cashew, or coconut yogurt)
- 1/2 cup fresh cilantro leaves, packed
- Juice of 1 lime (about 2 tablespoons)
- 1 tablespoon apple cider vinegar
- 1 clove garlic, minced
- 1 tablespoon extra virgin olive oil
- 1/2 teaspoon sea salt (adjust to taste)
- 1/4 teaspoon ground cumin (optional, for added depth of flavor)
- 1-2 tablespoons water (to thin, if needed)

Directions:

1. Rinse and pat dry the cilantro leaves, removing any thick stems to avoid bitterness. Measure 1/2 cup of packed cilantro leaves.
2. In a blender or food processor, combine plant-based yogurt, cilantro leaves, lime juice, apple cider vinegar, minced garlic, olive oil, sea salt, and ground cumin (if desired).
3. Blend until smooth and creamy. If the dressing is too thick, add 1-2 tablespoons of water and blend again to reach your preferred consistency.
4. Taste and adjust seasoning as needed, adding more lime juice for tanginess or a pinch of salt to enhance the flavor.
5. Transfer the dressing to a jar or serving container. Use immediately, or chill for a deeper flavor.
6. Store leftovers in an airtight container in the fridge for up to 5 days. Shake or stir well before using.

Garlic Herb Vinaigrette

Servings: 10   **Prep. time:** 10 min   **Total time:** 10 min

Nutritional Information (Per Serving):

Calories: 110 kcal, Protein: 0g, Carbohydrates: 1g Fats: 11g, Fiber: 0g, Cholesterol: 0mg, Sodium: 120mg, Potassium: 10mg

Ingredients

- /2 cup extra virgin olive oil
- 1/4 cup apple cider vinegar
- 1 tablespoon Dijon mustard
- 1 clove garlic, minced
- 1 tablespoon fresh lemon juice
- 2 tablespoons fresh parsley, finely chopped
- 1 tablespoon fresh basil, finely chopped
- 1 teaspoon fresh thyme leaves, finely chopped
- 1/2 teaspoon sea salt (adjust to taste)
- 1/4 teaspoon freshly ground black pepper
- 1 teaspoon maple syrup or agave nectar (optional, for a touch of sweetness)

Directions:

1. Wash and finely chop the fresh parsley, basil, and thyme. Remove any large stems to ensure a smooth texture in the vinaigrette.
2. Peel and mince the garlic clove finely to ensure it disperses evenly throughout the vinaigrette, providing a robust garlic flavor.
3. In a small mixing bowl or a mason jar, add the olive oil, apple cider vinegar, Dijon mustard, minced garlic, lemon juice, chopped herbs, sea salt, black pepper, and maple syrup (if using).
4. If using a bowl, whisk the ingredients together vigorously until the vinaigrette is well-emulsified and the oil and vinegar are fully combined.
5. If using a mason jar, secure the lid tightly and shake well for 30 seconds to 1 minute until the ingredients are fully mixed and emulsified.
6. Taste the vinaigrette and adjust the seasoning as desired, adding more salt, pepper, or lemon juice to suit your taste.
7. Use the vinaigrette immediately over salads, roasted vegetables, or as a marinade. If not using right away, let it sit for a few minutes to allow the flavors to meld.
8. Store any leftover vinaigrette in an airtight container in the refrigerator for up to 1 week. Before using, allow it to come to room temperature and shake or stir well to recombine the ingredients.

Basil Pesto

Servings: 8   **Prep. time:** 10 min   **Total time:** 10 min

Nutritional Information (Per Serving):

Calories: 180 kcal, Protein: 3g, Carbohydrates: 3g, Fats: 18g, Fiber: 2g, Cholesterol: 0mg, Sodium: 150mg, Potassium: 90mg

Ingredients

- 2 cups fresh basil leaves, packed
- 1/2 cup raw walnuts or pine nuts (soaked for 2 hours, then drained)
- 1/3 cup extra virgin olive oil
- 2 cloves garlic, minced
- 2 tablespoons nutritional yeast
- 2 tablespoons fresh lemon juice
- 1/2 teaspoon sea salt (adjust to taste)
- 1/4 teaspoon freshly ground black pepper

Directions:

1. If using raw walnuts or pine nuts, soak them in water for 2 hours to soften them for a smoother pesto. Drain and rinse the nuts thoroughly after soaking. Wash and dry the basil leaves.
2. Mince the garlic to ensure it blends evenly.
3. Add basil leaves, soaked nuts, minced garlic, nutritional yeast, lemon juice, sea salt, and black pepper to a food processor or blender. Pulse a few times to begin breaking down the ingredients.
4. With the machine running, slowly drizzle in the olive oil. Blend until the pesto is smooth and creamy, pausing occasionally to scrape down the sides and ensure everything is well mixed.
5. If the pesto seems too thick, gradually add water, a tablespoon at a time, until you reach your desired consistency.
6. Taste and adjust the seasoning, adding extra salt, lemon juice, or nutritional yeast as needed.
7. Enjoy the pesto immediately on pasta, as a spread, or as a dip. It's also delicious mixed into grain bowls or drizzled over roasted vegetables.
8. Keep any leftover pesto in an airtight container in the refrigerator for up to 5 days. For longer preservation, freeze it in ice cube trays, then move the cubes to a sealed container and store them in the freezer for up to 3 months.

Smoky Chipotle Sauce

Servings: 8   **Prep. time:** 10 min   **Total time:** 30 min

Nutritional Information (Per Serving):

Calories: 90, Protein: 3g, Carbohydrates: 7g, Fats: 6g, Fiber: 1g, Cholesterol: 0mg, Sodium: 110mg, Potassium: 120mg

Ingredients

- 1 cup raw cashews (soaked in water for at least 2 hours or overnight)
- 1-2 chipotle peppers in adobo sauce (adjust for spice level)
- 2 tablespoons tomato paste
- 1 tablespoon apple cider vinegar
- 2 cloves garlic, minced
- 1 tablespoon maple syrup
- 1 teaspoon smoked paprika
- 1 teaspoon cumin powder
- 1/2 teaspoon salt
- 1/4 teaspoon black pepper
- 1 cup water (adjust for desired consistency)
- Juice of 1 lime

Directions:

1. Soak raw cashews in water for at least 2 hours, or overnight, to soften them and enhance the sauce's creaminess.
2. Drain and rinse the cashews.
3. In a high-speed blender, combine the soaked cashews, chipotle peppers, tomato paste, apple cider vinegar, minced garlic, maple syrup, smoked paprika, cumin, salt, black pepper, and water.
4. Blend on high until smooth and creamy. If the sauce is too thick, gradually add more water until you reach the desired consistency.
5. Taste and adjust the seasoning as needed, adding more lime juice, salt, or chipotle for extra flavor or heat.
6. Transfer the sauce to a bowl or jar. It can be used immediately or kept in the fridge.
7. Store any leftover sauce in an airtight container in the refrigerator for up to 5 days.

Sun-Dried Tomato Tapenade

Servings: 8   **Prep. time:** 15 min   **Total time:** 30 min

Nutritional Information (Per Serving):

Calories: 100, Protein: 2g, Carbohydrates: 6g, Fats: 8g, Fiber: 2g, Cholesterol: 0mg, Sodium: 280mg, Potassium: 250mg

Ingredients

- 1 cup sun-dried tomatoes (not in oil)
- 1/4 cup raw almonds
- 1/4 cup pitted black olives (preferably Kalamata or other mild variety)
- 2 tablespoons capers, drained
- 2 cloves garlic, minced
- 2 tablespoons fresh lemon juice
- 1/4 cup extra-virgin olive oil
- 1 tablespoon chopped fresh basil (or 1 teaspoon dried basil)
- 1/2 teaspoon dried oregano
- 1/4 teaspoon red pepper flakes (optional, for heat)
- 1/4 teaspoon salt
- 1/4 teaspoon black pepper

Directions:

1. If the sun-dried tomatoes are very dry, soak them in warm water for about 10 minutes to soften. Drain well and pat dry with a paper towel.
2. In a dry skillet over medium heat, toast the raw almonds for 3-4 minutes, stirring frequently, until they are golden and fragrant. Let them cool before using.
3. In a food processor, combine the sun-dried tomatoes, toasted almonds, black olives, capers, minced garlic, lemon juice, olive oil, basil, oregano, red pepper flakes (if using), salt, and black pepper.
4. Pulse the ingredients until they form a coarse paste. You can process it to your desired texture—smooth or slightly chunky.
5. Taste the tapenade and adjust the seasoning as needed. You might want to add more lemon juice or salt to enhance the flavors.
6. Transfer the tapenade to a serving bowl. Let it sit for at least 15 minutes to allow the flavors to meld. Serve at room temperature.
7. Store any leftover tapenade in an airtight container in the refrigerator for up to 1 week.

Snacks

Spicy Roasted Chickpeas

Servings: 4   **Prep. time:** 10 min   **Total time:** 30 min

Nutritional Information (Per Serving):

Calories: 150, Protein: 6g, Carbohydrates: 20g, Fats: 6g, Fiber: 5g, Cholesterol: 0mg, Sodium: 300mg, Potassium: 320mg

Ingredients

- 1 can (15 oz) chickpeas (garbanzo beans), drained and rinsed
- 1 tablespoon extra-virgin olive oil
- 1 teaspoon smoked paprika
- 1/2 teaspoon ground cumin
- 1/2 teaspoon ground coriander
- 1/4 teaspoon ground cayenne pepper (adjust to taste for heat)
- 1/2 teaspoon garlic powder
- 1/2 teaspoon onion powder
- 1/2 teaspoon sea salt
- 1/4 teaspoon black pepper
- Optional: 1/2 teaspoon nutritional yeast (for a cheesy flavor)

Directions:

1. Preheat the oven to 400°F (200°C).
2. Drain and rinse the chickpeas, then pat them dry thoroughly with paper towels to help them crisp up.
3. In a large bowl, mix the chickpeas with olive oil, smoked paprika, cumin, coriander, cayenne pepper, garlic powder, onion powder, sea salt, black pepper, and nutritional yeast (if using). Toss until the chickpeas are evenly coated.
4. Spread the chickpeas in a single layer on a parchment-lined baking sheet for extra crunch.
5. Roast for 20-25 minutes, shaking the pan halfway through to ensure even cooking. Keep an eye on them near the end to prevent burning. The chickpeas should be golden and crispy.
6. Let them cool on the baking sheet for a few minutes; they'll continue to crisp as they cool. Serve as a snack or add to salads.
7. Store any leftover chickpeas in an airtight container at room temperature for up to a week. They're best enjoyed fresh but will stay crunchy for a few days.

Apple Slices with Almond Butter and Chia Seeds

Servings: 4   **Prep. time:** 10 min   **Total time:** 10 min

Nutritional Information (Per Serving):

Calories: 150, Protein: 4g, Carbohydrates: 20g, Fats: 8g, Fiber: 5g, Cholesterol: 0mg, Sodium: 2mg, Potassium: 210mg

Ingredients

- 2 large apples (e.g., Fuji or Honeycrisp)
- 1/4 cup almond butter (unsweetened and smooth)
- 2 tablespoons chia seeds
- 1 tablespoon pure maple syrup or agave syrup (optional, for extra sweetness)
- 1/4 teaspoon ground cinnamon (optional, for extra flavor)

Directions:

1. Wash and core the apples. Slice them into thin rounds, about 1/4-inch thick. You can leave the skin on for added fiber and nutrients.
2. If your almond butter is too thick, you can slightly warm it to make it easier to spread. Simply microwave it in short bursts (5-10 seconds) or stir it until smooth.
3. Arrange the apple slices on a plate or serving tray.
4. Spread a thin layer of almond butter on each apple slice. You can use a small spoon or knife to do this.
5. Sprinkle chia seeds evenly over the almond butter-coated apple slices.
6. Drizzle the apple slices with pure maple syrup or agave syrup for added sweetness, if desired.
7. Sprinkle ground cinnamon over the top for an extra touch of flavor.
8. Serve immediately or store in an airtight container for up to 1 day. The apple slices are best enjoyed fresh but can be kept in the refrigerator for a short time.

Kale Chips

 Servings: 4   **Prep. time:** 10 min   **Total time:** 30 min

Nutritional Information (Per Serving):

Calories: 90, Protein: 3g, Carbohydrates: 8g, Fats: 6g, Fiber: 2g, Cholesterol: 0mg, Sodium: 220mg, Potassium: 350mg

Ingredients

- 1 large bunch of kale (about 8-10 cups of kale leaves)
- 1 tablespoon olive oil
- 1/2 teaspoon sea salt
- 1/2 teaspoon smoked paprika (for a smoky flavor, optional)
- 1/4 teaspoon garlic powder (optional)
- 1/4 teaspoon onion powder (optional)
- 1 tablespoon nutritional yeast (optional, for a cheesy flavor)

Directions:

1. Set the oven to preheat, 300°F (150°C) to ensure the kale gets crispy without burning.
2. Wash and thoroughly dry the kale using a salad spinner or a clean kitchen towel; dry leaves make crispier chips.
3. Remove the tough stems and tear the kale into bite-sized pieces. Place in a large bowl, drizzle with olive oil, and toss to coat evenly.
4. Season with sea salt, smoked paprika, garlic powder, onion powder, and nutritional yeast if using. Toss again to evenly distribute the seasonings.
5. Arrange the kale in a single layer on a baking sheet, making sure not to overcrowd. Use a second sheet if needed for even cooking.
6. Bake for 15-20 minutes, checking after 15 minutes to ensure the chips don't burn. They should be crisp and dry, not chewy.
7. Allow the kale chips to cool on the baking sheet, where they will continue to crisp up.
8. Store any remaining chips in an airtight container at room temperature for up to one week.

Stuffed Dates with Walnuts

 Servings: 4   **Prep. time:** 10 min   **Total time:** 30 min

Nutritional Information (Per Serving):

Calories: 170, Protein: 3g, Carbohydrates: 28g, Fats: 7g, Fiber: 3g, Cholesterol: 0mg, Sodium: 1mg, Potassium: 280mg

Ingredients

- 24 Medjool dates (pitted)
- 1/2 cup raw walnuts (chopped)
- 1/4 cup almond butter or cashew butter
- 1 tablespoon maple syrup (optional, for added sweetness)
- 1/2 teaspoon ground cinnamon
- 1/4 teaspoon vanilla extract (optional)
- Pinch of sea salt

Directions:

1. If the dates are not already pitted, carefully cut a slit down one side of each date and remove the pit.
2. In a small bowl, mix the chopped walnuts with the almond or cashew butter. If desired, add maple syrup, ground cinnamon, vanilla extract, and a pinch of sea salt for extra flavor. Stir until well combined.
3. Using a small spoon or a piping bag, fill each date with the walnut mixture. Press the filling into the date gently to ensure it stays in place.
4. Arrange the stuffed dates on a plate or tray. Refrigerate for at least 10 minutes to allow the flavors to meld and the filling to firm up.
5. Serve the stuffed dates as a nutritious snack or a delightful addition to a party platter.

Energy Balls

Servings: 12   **Prep. time:** 10 min   **Total time:** 30 min

Nutritional Information (Per Serving):

Calories: 190, Protein: 4g, Carbohydrates: 26g, Fats: 8g, Fiber: 4g, Cholesterol: 0mg, Sodium: 5mg, Potassium: 350mg

Ingredients

- 1 cup pitted Medjool dates (about 12 dates)
- 1/2 cup raw almonds
- 1/2 cup rolled oats (gluten-free if needed)
- 1/4 cup unsweetened shredded coconut
- 2 tablespoons chia seeds
- 2 tablespoons raw cacao powder (or cocoa powder)
- 1 tablespoon maple syrup or agave nectar (optional, for added sweetness)
- 1/2 teaspoon vanilla extract
- Pinch of sea salt

Directions:

1. If the dates are not already pitted, carefully cut a slit down one side of each date and remove the pit.
2. Mix the chopped walnuts with the almond or cashew butter in a small bowl. Add maple syrup, ground cinnamon, vanilla extract, and a pinch of sea salt for extra flavor if desired. Stir until well combined.
3. Fill each date with the walnut mixture using a small spoon or a piping bag. Press the filling into the date gently to ensure it stays in place.
4. Arrange the stuffed dates on a plate or tray. Refrigerate for 10 minutes to allow the flavors to meld and the filling to firm up.
5. Serve the stuffed dates as a nutritious snack or a delightful addition to a party platter.

Sweet Potato Fries

Servings: 4   **Prep. time:** 10 min   **Total time:** 35 min

Nutritional Information (Per Serving):

Calories: 190, Protein: 2g, Carbohydrates: 32g, Fats: 6g, Fiber: 5g, Cholesterol: 0mg, Sodium: 290 mg (with 1/4 teaspoon sea salt), Potassium 600mg

Ingredients

- 4 medium sweet potatoes (about 1.5 lbs or 680g)
- 2 tablespoons olive oil
- 1 teaspoon smoked paprika
- 1/2 teaspoon ground cumin
- 1/2 teaspoon garlic powder
- 1/2 teaspoon onion powder
- 1/4 teaspoon ground black pepper
- 1/4 teaspoon sea salt (adjust to taste)
- Optional: 1/4 teaspoon cayenne pepper for extra heat

Directions:

1. Preheat the oven to 425°F (220°C).
2. If desired, peel the sweet potatoes and cut them into thin strips or wedges, about 1/4 to 1/2 inch thick.
3. Soak the sweet potato pieces in cold water for 30 minutes to remove excess starch, which helps them bake up crispier.
4. Drain the potatoes and pat them dry thoroughly with a clean towel.
5. In a large bowl, toss the sweet potato strips with olive oil until fully coated.
6. Season with smoked paprika, ground cumin, garlic powder, onion powder, black pepper, sea salt, and cayenne pepper (if using). Toss well to distribute the spices evenly.
7. Spread the seasoned sweet potatoes in a single layer on a parchment-lined or lightly greased baking sheet, making sure they don't overlap for even cooking.
8. Bake for 20-25 minutes, turning halfway through, until the fries are golden and crispy on the edges.
9. Let the fries cool for a few minutes before serving. They're best enjoyed fresh and warm.

Baked Plantain Chips

Servings: 4   **Prep. time:** 10 min   **Total time:** 30 min

Nutritional Information (Per Serving):

Calories: 180, Protein: 1g, Carbohydrates: 38g, Fats: 3g, Fiber: 4g, Cholesterol: 0mg, Sodium: 300mg (with 1/2 teaspoon sea salt), Potassium: 850mg

Ingredients

- 2 large green plantains (about 1 lb or 450g)
- 1 tablespoon olive oil
- 1/2 teaspoon sea salt (adjust to taste)
- 1/2 teaspoon smoked paprika (optional, for a smoky flavor)
- 1/2 teaspoon garlic powder (optional, for added flavor)
- 1/4 teaspoon ground black pepper (optional)

Directions:

1. Preheat the oven to 425°F (220°C).
2. Trim the ends of the plantains, make a slit along the length of the skin, and carefully peel them.
3. Slice the plantains into thin rounds, about 1/8 inch (3 mm) thick; use a mandoline slicer for consistent thickness if available.
4. Place the slices in a bowl, drizzle with olive oil, and toss to coat evenly.
5. Season with sea salt and any other desired spices, such as smoked paprika, garlic powder, or black pepper. Toss to distribute the seasoning uniformly.
6. Spread the plantain slices in a single layer on a parchment-lined baking sheet, ensuring they aren't overlapping for even baking.
7. Bake for 15-20 minutes, flipping halfway through, until the chips are golden brown and crispy. Watch carefully to prevent burning.
8. Let the chips cool on the baking sheet for a few minutes to crisp up further before serving.

Nutty Granola Clusters

Servings: 8   **Prep. time:** 10 min   **Total time:** 35 min

Nutritional Information (Per Serving):

Calories: 250, Protein: 7g, Carbohydrates: 30g, Fats: 14g, Fiber: 5g, Cholesterol: 0mg, Sodium: 120mg, Potassium: 300mg

Ingredients

- cups rolled oats
- 1 cup raw nuts (such as almonds, walnuts, and cashews), roughly chopped
- 1/2 cup raw seeds (such as pumpkin seeds and sunflower seeds)
- 1/2 cup unsweetened shredded coconut
- 1/4 cup chia seeds
- 1/4 cup maple syrup or agave nectar
- 1/4 cup coconut oil, melted
- 1/2 teaspoon vanilla extract
- 1/2 teaspoon ground cinnamon
- 1/4 teaspoon sea salt
- 1/2 cup dried fruit (such as raisins, cranberries, or chopped dried apricots), optional

Directions:

1. Preheat your oven to 350°F (175°C). Line a baking sheet with parchment paper.
2. In a large mixing bowl, combine the rolled oats, chopped nuts, seeds, shredded coconut, and chia seeds. Mix well to evenly distribute.
3. In a separate bowl, whisk together the melted coconut oil, maple syrup (or agave nectar), vanilla extract, ground cinnamon, and sea salt.
4. Pour the wet mixture over the dry ingredients. Stir thoroughly to ensure all the dry ingredients are well-coated with the wet mixture.
5. Spread the mixture evenly onto the prepared baking sheet. Press down with a spatula to compact the mixture slightly, which helps in forming clusters.
6. Bake in the preheated oven for 20-25 minutes, or until the granola is golden brown and crisp. Stir halfway through to ensure even baking.
7. Allow the granola to cool completely on the baking sheet. It will harden as it cools. Once cooled, break it into clusters and mix in the dried fruit if using.
8. Store the granola clusters in an airtight container at room temperature for up to 2 weeks.

Pineapple & Coconut Bites

 Servings: 12   **Prep. time:** 10 min   **Total time:** 1 h 10 min

Nutritional Information (Per Serving):

Calories: 90, Protein: 1g, Carbohydrates: 11g, Fats: 5g, Fiber: 1g, Cholesterol: 0mg, Sodium: 40mg, Potassium: 90mg

Ingredients

- 1 cup dried pineapple, chopped into small pieces
- 1 cup unsweetened shredded coconut
- 1/2 cup raw cashews, finely chopped
- 1/4 cup almond meal or finely ground almonds
- 2 tablespoons coconut oil, melted
- 2 tablespoons maple syrup or agave nectar
- 1 teaspoon vanilla extract
- 1/4 teaspoon sea salt

Directions:

1. Chop the dried pineapple into small pieces to make blending easier.
2. Finely chop the raw cashews if they aren't already finely ground.
3. In a medium bowl, mix the chopped dried pineapple, shredded coconut, chopped cashews, and almond meal thoroughly.
4. In a separate small bowl, whisk together melted coconut oil, maple syrup (or agave), vanilla extract, and sea salt until fully combined.
5. Pour the wet ingredients over the dry mixture and stir well to coat all the ingredients evenly.
6. Form the mixture into bite-sized balls using your hands or a small cookie scoop, pressing firmly to ensure they hold together. Arrange the balls on a parchment-lined tray or plate.
7. Refrigerate for at least 1 hour to let them set and firm up.
8. Serve the pineapple and coconut bites chilled. Store any leftovers in an airtight container in the fridge for up to two weeks.

Homemade Trail Mix

 Servings: 8   **Prep. time:** 10 min   **Total time:** 10 min

Nutritional Information (Per Serving):

Calories: 230, Protein: 6g, Carbohydrates: 25g, Fats: 13g, Fiber: 4g, Cholesterol: 0mg, Sodium: 60mg, Potassium: 300mg

Ingredients

- 1 cup raw almonds
- 1 cup raw cashews
- 1 cup raw pumpkin seeds (pepitas)
- 1 cup dried unsweetened cranberries
- 1/2 cup unsweetened shredded coconut
- 1/2 cup raw sunflower seeds
- 1/2 cup dark chocolate chips (optional)
- 1/2 teaspoon ground cinnamon
- 1/4 teaspoon sea salt

Directions:

1. If desired, lightly toast the raw almonds, cashews, and pumpkin seeds for enhanced flavor and crunch. To do this, preheat your oven to 350°F (175°C). Spread the nuts and seeds in a single layer on a baking sheet and toast for 5-7 minutes, stirring occasionally, until fragrant and slightly golden. Let them cool completely before mixing.
2. In a large bowl, combine the raw almonds, cashews, pumpkin seeds, dried cranberries, shredded coconut, and sunflower seeds.
3. If using, add the dark chocolate chips to the bowl. These add a touch of sweetness and richness but can be omitted for a lower-calorie option.
4. Sprinkle the ground cinnamon and sea salt over the mixture. Stir thoroughly to ensure even distribution of the seasoning.
5. Mix all the ingredients until evenly distributed. Transfer the trail mix to an airtight container or resealable bags.
6. Enjoy the trail mix as a snack on the go, a topping for yogurt, or a crunchy addition to salads.
7. Store the trail mix in an airtight container in a cool, dry place. It will keep for up to 2 weeks at room temperature or up to 1 month in the refrigerator.

Zucchini Fritters

Servings: 4   **Prep. time:** 15 min   **Total time:** 35 min

Nutritional Information (Per Serving):

Calories: 130, Protein: 5g, Carbohydrates: 15g, Fats: 6g, Fiber: 4g, Cholesterol: 0mg, Sodium: 230mg, Potassium: 350mg

Ingredients

- 2 medium zucchinis (about 2 cups grated)
- 1/2 cup chickpea flour (also known as besan or gram flour)
- 1/4 cup finely chopped fresh parsley
- 2 tablespoons nutritional yeast
- 1 small onion, finely chopped
- 2 cloves garlic, minced
- 1 tablespoon ground flaxseed mixed with 3 tablespoons water (flax egg)
- 1/2 teaspoon baking powder
- 1/2 teaspoon turmeric powder
- 1/2 teaspoon paprika
- 1/4 teaspoon black pepper
- 1/4 teaspoon sea salt
- 1 tablespoon olive oil (for cooking)

Directions:

1. Wash and grate the zucchinis. Place the grated zucchini in a clean kitchen towel or cheesecloth and squeeze out as much moisture as possible to keep the fritters from becoming soggy.
2. Mix ground flaxseed with water in a small bowl and let it sit for about 5 minutes to thicken.
3. In a large bowl, combine chickpea flour, nutritional yeast, baking powder, turmeric, paprika, black pepper, and sea salt.
4. In another bowl, mix the grated zucchini, chopped parsley, chopped onion, and minced garlic. Stir in the flax egg.
5. Add the zucchini mixture to the dry ingredients and stir until thoroughly combined. The batter should be thick and cohesive. Adjust with water if too dry or more chickpea flour if too wet.
6. Heat olive oil in a non-stick skillet over medium heat. Spoon dollops of the batter into the hot skillet and flatten them with the back of the spoon to form fritters.
7. Cook each side for about 3-4 minutes, or until golden brown and crispy. Adjust the heat as needed to avoid burning.
8. Transfer the fritters to a plate lined with paper towels to drain any excess oil. Serve warm.
9. Pair with vegan yogurt or a simple tomato salsa for dipping.

Crispy Baked Tofu Cubes

Servings: 4   **Prep. time:** 15 min   **Total time:** 40 min

Nutritional Information (Per Serving):

Calories: 150, Protein: 14g, Carbohydrates: 10g, Fats: 8g, Fiber: 2g, Cholesterol: 0mg, Sodium: 580mg, Potassium: 320mg

Ingredients

- 1 block (14 oz) extra-firm tofu
- 1 tablespoon olive oil
- 1 tablespoon soy sauce (or tamari for gluten-free)
- 1 tablespoon cornstarch
- 1 teaspoon garlic powder
- 1 teaspoon onion powder
- 1/2 teaspoon smoked paprika
- 1/2 teaspoon ground turmeric
- 1/4 teaspoon black pepper
- 1/4 teaspoon sea salt

Directions:

1. Preheat the oven to 400°F (200°C).
2. Drain the tofu and wrap it in a clean kitchen towel. Place a heavy object on top (like a can or a skillet) and let it press for 10-15 minutes to remove excess moisture. This step is crucial for achieving a crispy texture.
3. After pressing, cut the tofu into 1-inch cubes.
4. In a large bowl, mix the soy sauce and olive oil. Add the tofu cubes and gently toss to coat evenly.
5. In a separate bowl, combine the cornstarch, garlic powder, onion powder, smoked paprika, ground turmeric, black pepper, and sea salt.
6. Sprinkle the seasoning mixture over the tofu cubes and gently toss until all the pieces are evenly coated. The cornstarch helps to create a crispy exterior.
7. Line a baking sheet with parchment paper or a silicone baking mat.
8. Spread the tofu cubes in a single layer on the baking sheet, making sure they are not touching to allow for even crisping.
9. Bake in the preheated oven for 20-25 minutes, flipping the tofu halfway through, until golden brown and crispy.
10. Allow the tofu to cool slightly before serving. Enjoy as a snack, or toss into salads, grain bowls, or stir-fries.

Vegan Sushi Rolls

Servings: 4   **Prep. time:** 15 min   **Total time:** 40 min

Nutritional Information (Per Serving):

Calories: 250, Protein: 5g, Carbohydrates: 45g, Fats: 8g, Fiber: 6g, Cholesterol: 0mg, Sodium: 430mg, Potassium: 550mg

Ingredients

- 1 cup sushi rice (short-grain or medium-grain)
- 1 1/4 cups water
- 2 tablespoons rice vinegar
- 1 tablespoon maple syrup or agave syrup
- 1/2 teaspoon sea salt
- 1 medium cucumber, julienned
- 1 medium carrot, julienned
- 1/2 avocado, sliced
- 1/2 red bell pepper, julienned
- 1/4 cup red cabbage, finely shredded
- 1/2 cup baby spinach leaves
- 4 sheets nori (seaweed)
- Soy sauce or tamari, for dipping
- Pickled ginger, for serving
- Wasabi, for serving

Directions:

1. Rinse the sushi rice under cold water until the water runs clear to remove excess starch.
2. Combine the rinsed rice and water in a rice cooker or pot. Cook according to the rice cooker's instructions or bring to a boil, then cover and simmer on low heat for 20 minutes until the water is absorbed.
3. Remove from heat and let it sit, covered, for 10 minutes. Fluff with a fork.
4. In a small bowl, mix the rice vinegar, maple syrup, and sea salt.
5. Gently fold the seasoning mixture into the cooked rice. Let it cool to room temperature.
6. While the rice is cooling, prepare the vegetables. Julienne the cucumber, carrot, and red bell pepper. Slice the avocado and shred the cabbage.
7. Place a bamboo sushi mat on a flat surface and cover it with plastic wrap.
8. Lay a sheet of nori on the bamboo mat, shiny side down.
9. With wet fingers, spread a thin layer of sushi rice evenly over the nori, leaving a 1-inch border at the top edge.
10. Arrange the cucumber, carrot, avocado, red bell pepper, red cabbage, and spinach in a line along the bottom edge of the rice.
11. Using the bamboo mat, gently lift the edge of the nori over the filling and roll it tightly away from you. Press gently to ensure a tight roll.
12. Seal the edge of the nori with a little water.
13. Slice the roll into 6-8 pieces using a sharp knife, dipped in water to prevent sticking.
14. Arrange the sushi rolls on a serving platter. Serve with soy sauce, pickled ginger, and wasabi.

Pumpkin Seed Clusters

Servings: 4   **Prep. time:** 10 min   **Total time:** 25 min

Nutritional Information (Per Serving):

Calories: 150, Protein: 5g, Carbohydrates: 10g, Fats: 10g, Fiber: 2g, Cholesterol: 0mg, Sodium: 0mg, Potassium: 180mg

Ingredients

- 1 cup raw pumpkin seeds (shelled)
- 1/4 cup almond butter (unsweetened)
- 2 tablespoons pure maple syrup (or agave nectar)
- 1 tablespoon chia seeds (optional, for added texture and nutrition)
- 1/4 teaspoon ground cinnamon (optional, for flavor)
- Pinch of sea salt (optional)

Directions:

1. Preheat your oven to 350°F (175°C). Line a baking sheet with parchment paper.
2. In a medium bowl, combine the pumpkin seeds, almond butter, and maple syrup. Stir until well mixed. If using chia seeds, ground cinnamon, and a pinch of sea salt, add them to the mixture and stir until evenly distributed.
3. Scoop spoonfuls of the mixture onto the prepared baking sheet. Gently press down to form clusters. Make them as large or small as you like.
4. Bake in the preheated oven for 10-12 minutes, or until the edges are lightly golden. Keep an eye on them to avoid burning.
5. Allow the clusters to cool completely on the baking sheet. They will harden as they cool. Once cooled, gently break apart any large clusters if desired.
6. Store in an airtight container at room temperature for up to 1 week, or refrigerate for longer shelf life.

Desserts

Chocolate Avocado Pudding

 Servings: 4   **Prep. time:** 10 min   **Setting time:** 30 min (optional)

Nutritional Information (Per Serving):

Calories: 180, Protein: 3g, Carbohydrates: 21g, Fats: 10g, Fiber: 6g, Cholesterol: 0mg, Sodium: 10mg, Potassium: 485mg

Ingredients

- 2 ripe avocados (peeled and pitted)
- 1/4 cup unsweetened cocoa powder (preferably raw)
- 1/4 cup pure maple syrup (or agave nectar for a lower glycemic option)
- 1/4 cup almond milk (or any plant-based milk)
- 1 teaspoon vanilla extract
- Pinch of sea salt (optional, to enhance flavor)
- Fresh berries or mint leaves (for garnish, optional)

Directions:

1. Halve the avocados, remove the pits, and scoop the flesh into a food processor or blender.
2. Add the cocoa powder, maple syrup, almond milk, and vanilla extract to the avocados. Blend until smooth and creamy.
3. Taste and adjust the sweetness by adding more maple syrup if needed, blending again to mix thoroughly.
4. Optionally, add a pinch of sea salt and blend to incorporate.
5. For a thicker consistency and richer flavor, chill the pudding in serving bowls for at least 30 minutes before serving.
6. Garnish with fresh berries or mint leaves if desired. Serve chilled or at room temperature.

Chocolate-Dipped Coconut Bars

 Servings: 4   **Prep. time:** 10 min   **Setting time:** 30 min (optional)

Nutritional Information (Per Serving):

Calories: 180, Protein: 2g, Carbohydrates: 15g, Fats: 14g, Fiber: 3g, Cholesterol: 0mg, Sodium: 50mg, Potassium: 150mg

Ingredients

- 2 cups unsweetened shredded coconut
- 1 cup almond flour
- 1/2 cup pure maple syrup (or agave nectar)
- 1/4 cup coconut oil, melted
- 1 teaspoon vanilla extract
- 1/4 teaspoon sea salt
- 1/2 cup dairy-free dark chocolate chips (or chopped dark chocolate)
- 1 tablespoon coconut oil (to help with melting)

Directions:

1. In a large bowl, mix together the unsweetened shredded coconut, almond flour, maple syrup, melted coconut oil, vanilla extract, and sea salt.
2. Stir well until the mixture is uniformly combined and holds together when pressed.
3. Line an 8x8-inch baking dish with parchment paper, leaving extra on the sides for easy lifting.
4. Firmly press the coconut mixture into the baking dish, using a spoon or your hands to compact it tightly.
5. Refrigerate for at least 30 minutes to allow the mixture to firm up.
6. In a heatproof bowl, combine dairy-free dark chocolate chips with 1 tablespoon of coconut oil.
7. Melt the chocolate using a double boiler or microwave in 20-second intervals, stirring between each interval until smooth.
8. Take the chilled coconut mixture out of the refrigerator and lift it from the dish using the parchment overhang.
9. Cut into 12 bars. Dip each bar into the melted chocolate, letting any excess drip off, and place on a parchment-lined tray.
10. Refrigerate the tray for at least 1 hour to allow the chocolate to set.
11. Once the chocolate is fully set, the bars are ready to enjoy. Store any leftovers in an airtight container in the fridge for up to a week.

Banana Nice Cream

Servings: 2   **Prep. time:** 10 min   **Total time:** 10 min

Nutritional Information (Per Serving):

Calories: 130, Protein: 1g, Carbohydrates: 34g, Fats: 0.5g, Fiber: 4g, Cholesterol: 0mg, Sodium 5mg, Potassium: 450mg

Ingredients

- 4 ripe bananas (peeled and sliced, preferably frozen)
- 1/4 cup unsweetened almond milk (or any plant-based milk of choice)
- 1/2 teaspoon vanilla extract
- Optional add-ins:
- 1 tablespoon cocoa powder (for chocolate nice cream)
- 1 tablespoon almond butter (for extra creaminess)
- 1/4 cup frozen berries (for berry-flavored nice cream)
- 1 tablespoon maple syrup (if extra sweetness is desired)

Directions:

1. If you haven't already, peel and slice the bananas. For best results, freeze the banana slices for at least 2 hours or overnight.
2. Place the frozen banana slices in a high-speed blender or food processor.
3. Add the almond milk and vanilla extract. Blend on high until the mixture becomes smooth and creamy. This may take a few minutes, and you might need to stop occasionally to scrape down the sides of the blender.
4. If using, add cocoa powder for chocolate flavor, almond butter for creaminess, frozen berries for a fruity twist, or maple syrup for extra sweetness. Blend again until fully incorporated.
5. Spoon the nice cream into bowls or cones. For a firmer texture, you can freeze it for 10-15 minutes, but it's best enjoyed immediately for a soft-serve consistency.
6. Top with fresh fruit, nuts, or seeds if desired.

Raw Vegan Brownies

Servings: 12   **Prep. time:** 15 min   **Total time:** 1 h 15 min (1 h for chilling)

Nutritional Information (Per Serving):

Calories: 150, Protein: 3g, Carbohydrates: 16g, Fats: 9g, Fiber: 3g, Cholesterol: 0mg, Sodium: 10mg, Potassium: 250mg

Ingredients

- 1 cup medjool dates, pitted
- 1 cup raw walnuts
- 1/2 cup raw cacao powder (or unsweetened cocoa powder)
- 1/4 cup raw almond butter (or any nut/seed butter)
- 1/4 cup pure maple syrup (or agave nectar)
- 1/4 teaspoon sea salt
- 1/2 teaspoon vanilla extract
- 1/4 cup unsweetened shredded coconut (optional, for added texture)

Directions:

1. If the medjool dates are not soft, soak them in warm water for about 10 minutes to soften. Drain and pat dry with a paper towel before using.
2. In a food processor, combine the medjool dates and raw walnuts. Pulse until the mixture resembles coarse crumbs.
3. Add the raw cacao powder, raw almond butter, pure maple syrup, sea salt, and vanilla extract. Process until the mixture starts to form a sticky dough. You may need to scrape down the sides of the bowl to ensure even mixing.
4. Line an 8x8-inch baking dish with parchment paper, leaving some overhang for easy removal.
5. Press the brownie mixture firmly and evenly into the prepared dish. Use the back of a spoon or your hands to compact the mixture tightly.
6. Place the dish in the refrigerator for at least 1 hour to set. This helps the brownies firm up and makes them easier to cut into squares.
7. After chilling, lift the brownies out of the dish using the parchment paper and cut into 12 squares. Optionally, roll in shredded coconut for added texture.
8. Store the brownies in an airtight container in the refrigerator for up to 1 week or freeze for up to 3 months.

Baked Cinnamon Apples

Servings: 4   **Prep. time:** 10 min   **Total time:** 40 min

Nutritional Information (Per Serving):

Calories: 170, Protein: 2g, Carbohydrates: 34g, Fats: 5g, Fiber: 5g, Cholesterol: omg, Sodium: 15mg, Potassium: 250mg

Ingredients

- 4 medium apples (e.g., Honeycrisp, Fuji, or Gala)
- 1/4 cup chopped walnuts (optional)
- 1/4 cup raisins or dried cranberries
- 2 tablespoons pure maple syrup (or agave nectar)
- 1 tablespoon coconut oil (or melted plant-based butter)
- 1 teaspoon ground cinnamon
- 1/4 teaspoon ground nutmeg
- 1/4 teaspoon vanilla extract
- Pinch of sea salt

Directions:

1. Preheat the oven to 350°F (175°C).
2. Wash and core the apples, creating a hollow center. You can use an apple corer or a paring knife for this. Peeling the apples is optional; leaving the skin on provides extra fiber.
3. In a small bowl, mix together the chopped walnuts, raisins or dried cranberries, maple syrup, melted coconut oil, cinnamon, nutmeg, vanilla extract, and a pinch of sea salt. Stir until well combined.
4. Fill each apple with the mixture, pressing it down slightly to pack the filling tightly.
5. Arrange the stuffed apples in a baking dish. Lightly greasing the dish with coconut oil is optional.
6. Bake for 25-30 minutes, or until the apples are tender. Baking time will depend on the size and variety of the apples.
7. Let the apples cool slightly before serving. Enjoy them warm or at room temperature.
8. Store any leftovers in an airtight container in the refrigerator for up to 3 days. Reheat in the oven or microwave before serving.

Berry Coconut Popsicles

Servings: 6   **Prep. time:** 15 min   **Total time:** 4-6 hours for settings

Nutritional Information (Per Serving):

Calories: 120, Protein: 1g, Carbohydrates: 15g, Fats: 8g, Fiber: 2g, Cholesterol: omg, Sodium: 15mg, Potassium: 170mg

Ingredients

- cup fresh or frozen mixed berries (e.g., strawberries, blueberries, raspberries)
- 1 can (13.5 oz) full-fat coconut milk (or light coconut milk for a lower-fat option)
- 2 tablespoons pure maple syrup (or agave nectar)
- 1 tablespoon fresh lemon juice (about 1/2 lemon)
- 1 teaspoon vanilla extract
- Optional: 1 tablespoon chia seeds (for added texture and nutrients)

Directions:

1. If using fresh berries, rinse them thoroughly. If using frozen berries, let them thaw slightly.
2. Place the berries in a blender or food processor. Blend until smooth. If desired, you can leave some small chunks for added texture.
3. In a mixing bowl, combine the coconut milk, pure maple syrup, fresh lemon juice, and vanilla extract. Stir until well combined. If using chia seeds, add them to this mixture.
4. Pour the berry puree into the popsicle molds, filling them about halfway.
5. Gently pour the coconut mixture on top of the berry puree, leaving a small space at the top of each mold.
6. For a marble effect, use a small spoon or a skewer to gently swirl the berry puree and coconut mixture together.
7. Insert the popsicle sticks into the molds. If the sticks don't stay upright, freeze the popsicles for about 1 hour, then insert the sticks.
8. Place the molds in the freezer and freeze for at least 4-6 hours or until completely frozen. For best results, freeze overnight.
9. To release the popsicles, run warm water briefly over the outside of the molds. Gently pull on the sticks to remove the popsicles.
10. Serve immediately or store in an airtight container in the freezer for up to 2 weeks.

Vegan Chocolate Chip Cookies

 Servings: 12   **Prep. time:** 15 min   **Total time:** 35 min

Nutritional Information (Per Serving):

Calories: 140, Protein: 1.8g, Carbohydrates: 21g, Fats: 6.5g, Fiber: 2g, Cholesterol: 0mg, Sodium: 120mg, Potassium: 150mg

Ingredients

- 1 cup (200g) coconut sugar
- 1/2 cup (120ml) refined coconut oil (solid form, not melted)
- 1/4 cup (60ml) almond milk (or other plant-based milk)
- 1 tablespoon ground flaxseed
- 2 tablespoons water (for flax egg)
- 1 teaspoon vanilla extract
- 1 1/2 cups (180g) whole wheat flour (or all-purpose flour)
- 1 teaspoon baking powder
- 1/2 teaspoon baking soda
- 1/4 teaspoon sea salt
- 1/2 cup (90g) vegan chocolate chips

Directions:

1. Preheat the oven to 350°F (175°C) and line a baking sheet with parchment paper.
2. Mix 1 tablespoon flaxseed with 2 tablespoons water in a small bowl; let it rest for 5 minutes to thicken.
3. In a large bowl, beat together coconut sugar and coconut oil until smooth. Add the flax mixture, almond milk, and vanilla, mixing well.
4. Whisk together flour, baking powder, baking soda, and salt in a separate bowl, then gradually add to the wet ingredients, stirring until just combined.
5. Fold in chocolate chips.
6. Drop spoonfuls of dough onto the baking sheet, spacing them 2 inches apart. Flatten slightly with a spoon.
7. Bake for 10-12 minutes, until the edges are golden. Cool on the baking sheet for 5 minutes, then transfer to a wire rack.
8. Store in an airtight container for up to 1 week, or freeze for up to 3 months.

Peanut Butter Oat Bars

 Servings: 12   **Prep. time:** 10 min   **Total time:** 1 h 10 min

Nutritional Information (Per Serving):

Calories: 180, Protein: 5g, Carbohydrates: 22g, Fats: 9g, Fiber: 3g, Cholesterol: 0mg, Sodium: 70mg, Potassium: 250mg

Ingredients

- 1 1/2 cups (135g) rolled oats
- 1/2 cup (130g) natural peanut butter
- 1/4 cup (60ml) maple syrup (or agave nectar)
- 1/4 cup (30g) chopped nuts (such as almonds or walnuts, optional)
- 1/4 cup (20g) unsweetened shredded coconut (optional)
- 1/4 cup (30g) raisins or dried fruit (such as chopped dates or cranberries)
- 1/4 teaspoon sea salt
- 1/2 teaspoon vanilla extract

Directions:

1. Line an 8x8-inch (20x20cm) baking pan with parchment paper, leaving extra on the sides for easy removal.
2. In a small saucepan over low heat, melt the peanut butter and maple syrup, stirring until smooth.
3. In a large bowl, combine rolled oats, sea salt, and optional add-ins like nuts, shredded coconut, or dried fruit.
4. Pour the melted peanut butter mixture over the dry ingredients, add vanilla extract, and mix until everything is well-coated.
5. Press the mixture firmly and evenly into the prepared pan using a spoon or your hands.
6. Chill in the refrigerator for at least 1 hour, or until the bars are firm.
7. Lift the bars out using the parchment overhang and cut into 12 pieces.
8. Store in an airtight container in the fridge for up to 1 week, or freeze for up to 3 months.

Coconut Macaroons

Servings: 12   **Prep. time:** 15 min   **Total time:** 1 h 15 min

Nutritional Information (Per Serving):

Calories: 140, Protein: 2g, Carbohydrates: 12g, Fats: 10g, Fiber: 3g, Cholesterol: 0mg, Sodium: 70mg, Potassium: 150mg

Ingredients

- 2 1/2 cups (200g) unsweetened shredded coconut
- 1/2 cup (120g) coconut cream
- 1/4 cup (60ml) maple syrup
- 1/4 cup (60ml) almond butter
- 1/4 teaspoon sea salt
- 1/2 teaspoon vanilla extract
- Optional: 1/4 cup (50g) vegan chocolate chips for dipping (or drizzling)

Directions:

1. Preheat your oven to 350°F (175°C) and line a baking sheet with parchment paper.
2. In a large bowl, combine the shredded coconut, coconut cream, maple syrup, almond butter, sea salt, and vanilla extract. Mix well until all ingredients are fully incorporated.
3. Using a small cookie scoop or tablespoon, scoop the mixture and form small mounds on the prepared baking sheet. Press them down slightly to form compact, rounded shapes.
4. Bake in the preheated oven for 15-20 minutes, or until the edges are golden brown. Keep an eye on them to prevent burning.
5. Allow the macaroons to cool on the baking sheet for about 10 minutes. They will firm up as they cool.
6. If using chocolate, melt the vegan chocolate chips in a double boiler or microwave. Once melted, dip the bottoms of the cooled macaroons into the chocolate or drizzle over the top. Place back on the parchment paper and let the chocolate set.
7. Refrigerate the macaroons for at least 1 hour to ensure they are fully set and to enhance their flavor.
8. Store in an airtight container in the refrigerator for up to 1 week, or freeze for up to 2 months.

Lemon Cashew Energy Balls

  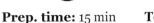

Servings: 12   **Prep. time:** 15 min   **Total time:** 45 min

Nutritional Information (Per Serving):

Calories: 130, Protein: 2g, Carbohydrates: 17g, Fats: 7g, Fiber: 2g, Cholesterol: 0mg, Sodium: 40mg, Potassium: 170mg

Ingredients

- 1 cup (130g) raw cashews
- 1 cup (160g) pitted dates
- 1/4 cup (60ml) fresh lemon juice
- 1 tablespoon lemon zest
- 1 tablespoon coconut oil
- 1/4 teaspoon vanilla extract
- 1/4 teaspoon sea salt
- Optional: 2 tablespoons desiccated coconut for rolling

Directions:

1. If the cashews are not already soaked, soak them in water for at least 2 hours or overnight. This softens them and makes them easier to blend. Drain and rinse well before use.
2. In a food processor, combine the soaked cashews and pitted dates. Pulse until they form a coarse, crumbly mixture.
3. Add the lemon juice, lemon zest, coconut oil, vanilla extract, and sea salt to the food processor. Blend until the mixture starts to clump together and forms a dough-like consistency. You may need to scrape down the sides of the bowl and blend again.
4. Scoop out tablespoon-sized portions of the mixture and roll them between your hands to form balls. If desired, roll each ball in desiccated coconut for a coating.
5. Place the rolled energy balls on a baking sheet or plate lined with parchment paper. Refrigerate for at least 30 minutes to help them firm up.
6. Store the energy balls in an airtight container in the refrigerator for up to 1 week or freeze for up to 2 months.

Stuffed Figs with Almonds

 Servings: 8　　 **Prep. time:** 15 min　　 **Total time:** 30 min

Nutritional Information (Per Serving):

Calories: 180, Protein: 4g, Carbohydrates: 24g, Fats: 8g, Fiber: 4g, Cholesterol: 0mg, Sodium: 35mg, Potassium: 320mg

Ingredients

- 8 large fresh figs (if fresh figs are unavailable, dried figs can be used; soak them in warm water for 30 minutes)
- 1/2 cup (70g) raw almonds
- 2 tablespoons maple syrup
- 1 tablespoon almond butter
- 1/4 teaspoon ground cinnamon
- 1/4 teaspoon vanilla extract
- Pinch of sea salt

Directions:

1. If using whole almonds, chop them coarsely or pulse them in a food processor to create a rough almond meal. Alternatively, you can use a pre-ground almond meal.
2. In a bowl, combine the chopped almonds, maple syrup, almond butter, ground cinnamon, vanilla extract, and a pinch of sea salt. Mix until all ingredients are well incorporated into a thick, spreadable paste.
3. Gently cut a small slit or cross on the top of each fig, creating an opening without cutting all the way through.
4. Using a small spoon or a piping bag, fill each fig with the almond mixture. Press down gently to pack the filling inside.
5. Arrange the stuffed figs on a plate or serving dish. Chill in the refrigerator for at least 15 minutes to allow the filling to set.
6. Serve chilled as a nutritious snack or a sophisticated appetizer.

Mango Sorbet

 Servings: 4　　 **Prep. time:** 15 min　　 **Setting time:** 2-4 hours (or until firm)

Nutritional Information (Per Serving):

Calories: 130, Protein: 1g, Carbohydrates: 33g, Fats: 0.5g, Fiber: 3g, Cholesterol: 0mg, Sodium: 10mg, Potassium: 350mg

Ingredients

- 3 cups (450g) fresh mango chunks (about 2 large mangoes, peeled and diced; use frozen mango if fresh is not available)
- 1/2 cup (120ml) coconut water (or any plant-based milk for a creamier texture)
- 1/4 cup (60ml) lime juice (about 2 limes)
- 1/4 cup (60ml) maple syrup (adjust to taste; can substitute with agave syrup or date syrup)
- 1 teaspoon vanilla extract (optional, for extra flavor)
- Pinch of sea salt (to enhance flavor)

Directions:

1. If using fresh mangoes, peel and dice them. For frozen mango chunks, ensure they aren't fully thawed before blending.
2. Place mango chunks, coconut water, lime juice, maple syrup, vanilla extract (if desired), and a pinch of sea salt in a high-speed blender or food processor.
3. Blend until the mixture is smooth and creamy, scraping down the sides as needed for a consistent texture.
4. Taste and adjust the flavor by adding more maple syrup or lime juice if you prefer.
5. Transfer the mango mixture to a freezer-safe container.
6. Freeze for 2-4 hours, stirring every 30 minutes during the first 2 hours to ensure even freezing and minimize ice crystals.
7. Let the sorbet soften slightly at room temperature before serving for easier scooping.
8. Serve in bowls or cones and enjoy right away.

Vegan Banana Bread

Servings: 10 **Prep. time:** 15 min **Total time:** 1 h 15 min

Nutritional Information (Per Serving):

Calories: 180, Protein: 3g, Carbohydrates: 29g, Fats: 7g, Fiber: 3g, Cholesterol: 0mg, Sodium: 150mg, Potassium: 350mg

Ingredients

- 3 ripe bananas (about 1 1/2 cups mashed; the riper, the better)
- 1/4 cup (60ml) coconut oil (melted; or use any neutral oil like avocado oil)
- 1/4 cup (60ml) maple syrup (or agave syrup)
- 1/4 cup (60ml) non-dairy milk (such as almond, soy, or oat milk)
- 1 teaspoon vanilla extract
- 1 1/2 cups (180g) whole wheat flour (or all-purpose flour for a lighter texture)
- 1 teaspoon baking powder
- 1/2 teaspoon baking soda
- 1/2 teaspoon ground cinnamon
- 1/4 teaspoon sea salt
- 1/2 cup (70g) chopped walnuts (optional; or use any nuts or seeds)
- 1/4 cup (45g) dark chocolate chips (optional; use dairy-free)

Directions:

1. Set the oven to preheat, 350°F (175°C).
2. Lightly grease a 9x5-inch loaf pan with coconut oil or line it with parchment paper.
3. Mash bananas in a large bowl until smooth, making about 1 1/2 cups of puree.
4. In a separate bowl, whisk together the melted coconut oil, maple syrup, non-dairy milk, and vanilla extract.
5. Mix the wet ingredients into the mashed bananas until thoroughly combined.
6. In another bowl, combine the flour, baking powder, baking soda, cinnamon, and salt.
7. Gently fold the dry ingredients into the banana mixture, mixing just until combined. Avoid overmixing.
8. If using, fold in chopped walnuts or chocolate chips.
9. Pour the batter into the prepared loaf pan, spreading it evenly.
10. Bake for 50-60 minutes, or until a toothpick inserted in the center comes out clean.
11. Allow the bread to cool in the pan for about 10 minutes before transferring to a wire rack to cool completely.
12. Once fully cooled, slice and enjoy plain or with a spread of your choice.

Dark Chocolate Covered Strawberries

Servings: 12 **Prep. time:** 15 min **Total time:** 45 min

Nutritional Information (Per Serving):

Calories: 90, Protein: 1g, Carbohydrates: 10g, Fats: 6g, Fiber: 2g, Cholesterol: 0mg, Sodium: 0mg, Potassium: 200mg

Ingredients

- 12 large strawberries (fresh and washed, preferably organic)
- 4 oz (115g) dark chocolate (70% cocoa or higher, ensure it's dairy-free)
- 1 tablespoon coconut oil (to help with smooth melting and coating)
- 2 tablespoons chopped nuts (such as almonds or pistachios, optional for garnish)
- 1 tablespoon shredded coconut (unsweetened, optional for garnish)

Directions:

1. Prepare Strawberries: Wash and thoroughly dry the strawberries.
2. Melt Chocolate: In a heatproof bowl, combine chopped dark chocolate and coconut oil. Melt over simmering water or in the microwave in 30-second intervals, stirring until smooth.
3. Dip Strawberries: Hold each strawberry by the stem, dip into the melted chocolate, and let excess drip off. Optionally, sprinkle with chopped nuts or shredded coconut.
4. Set: Place dipped strawberries on a parchment-lined sheet and refrigerate for 30 minutes, or until the chocolate is set.
5. Serve: Enjoy chilled.

Caramelized Pears with Walnuts

Servings: 4   **Prep. time:** 10 min   **Total time:** 25 min

Nutritional Information (Per Serving):

Calories: 210, Protein: 3g, Carbohydrates: 31g, Fats: 10g, Fiber: 4g, Cholesterol: 0mg, Sodium: 0mg, Potassium: 300mg

Ingredients

- 4 ripe pears (medium-sized, peeled, cored, and sliced)
- 2 tablespoons coconut oil (or other plant-based oil)
- 1/4 cup pure maple syrup
- 1 teaspoon vanilla extract
- 1/2 teaspoon ground cinnamon
- 1/4 teaspoon ground nutmeg
- 1/4 cup chopped walnuts (toasted, if preferred)
- 2 tablespoons shredded coconut (optional, for garnish)
- Fresh mint leaves (optional, for garnish)

Directions:

1. Peel the pears and cut them in half. Remove the cores and slice the pears into 1/2-inch thick wedges.
2. In a large skillet, heat 2 tablespoons of coconut oil over medium heat until it is melted and shimmering.
3. Add the pear slices to the skillet in a single layer. Cook for about 5 minutes, turning occasionally with a spatula, until the pears start to soften and become golden brown on the edges.
4. Pour 1/4 cup of pure maple syrup over the pears. Add 1 teaspoon of vanilla extract, 1/2 teaspoon of ground cinnamon, and 1/4 teaspoon of ground nutmeg. Stir gently to combine.
5. Reduce the heat to low and continue to cook the pears for another 5-7 minutes, stirring occasionally, until the pears are tender and the syrup has thickened into a caramel-like sauce.
6. While the pears are cooking, heat a small, dry skillet over medium heat. Add 1/4 cup of chopped walnuts and toast for 2-3 minutes, stirring frequently, until they are fragrant and lightly browned. Remove from heat and set aside.
7. Remove the skillet from the heat. Transfer the caramelized pears to serving plates or bowls. Top with the toasted walnuts. If desired, sprinkle with 2 tablespoons of shredded coconut and garnish with fresh mint leaves.
8. Enjoy the caramelized pears warm, as a delightful dessert or a sweet treat.

Raspberry Chia Jam

Servings: 12   **Prep. time:** 10 min   **Total time:** 10 min + Setting time 1-2 h

Nutritional Information (Per Serving):

Calories: 35, Protein: 1g, Carbohydrates: 9g, Fat 0g, Fiber: 2g, Cholesterol: 0mg, Sodium: 0mg, Potassium: 100mg

Ingredients

- 2 cups fresh or frozen raspberries (if using frozen, thaw before using)
- 1/4 cup pure maple syrup (or agave syrup, adjust to taste)
- 2 tablespoons chia seeds
- 1 tablespoon lemon juice
- 1/2 teaspoon vanilla extract (optional)

Directions:

1. In a saucepan, combine raspberries and maple syrup. Heat over medium until raspberries break down, about 5-7 minutes.
2. Mash the mixture with a fork or blender for a smoother texture (optional).
3. Stir in chia seeds, lemon juice, and vanilla extract (if using).
4. Simmer on low for 2-3 minutes, stirring frequently, until thickened.
5. Let the jam cool slightly, then transfer to a jar. Refrigerate for at least 1-2 hours or overnight to thicken.
6. Use on toast, yogurt, or pastries. Store in the fridge for up to 2 weeks.

Vegan Pumpkin Pie Bites

 Servings: 12   **Prep. time:** 15 min   **Total time:** 15 min + Setting time 1-2 h

Nutritional Information (Per Serving):

Calories: 130, Protein: 3g, Carbohydrates: 17g, Fats: 7g, Fiber: 3g, Cholesterol: 0mg, Sodium: 60mg, Potassium: 150mg

Ingredients

- 1 cup raw pecans
- 1/2 cup pitted dates
- 1/4 cup unsweetened shredded coconut
- 1/4 teaspoon sea salt
- 1 cup canned pumpkin puree (not pumpkin pie filling)
- 1/4 cup pure maple syrup
- 1/4 cup almond butter (or cashew butter)
- 1 tablespoon ground flaxseed
- 1 teaspoon ground cinnamon
- 1/2 teaspoon ground ginger
- 1/4 teaspoon ground nutmeg
- 1/4 teaspoon sea salt

Directions:

1. In a food processor, blend pecans, dates, shredded coconut, and sea salt until finely ground and sticky.
2. Press the mixture firmly into the bottom of a mini muffin tin or silicone mold. Use the back of a spoon to press it down evenly. Chill in the refrigerator while preparing the filling.
3. In a bowl, combine pumpkin puree, maple syrup, almond butter, ground flaxseed, cinnamon, ginger, nutmeg, and sea salt. Mix until smooth.
4. Spoon the pumpkin filling over the chilled crusts in the muffin tin. Smooth the tops with the back of the spoon.
5. Refrigerate the bites for at least 1-2 hours, or until firm.
6. Gently pop the bites out of the mold. Serve chilled or at room temperature. Store in an airtight container in the refrigerator for up to 1 week.

Almond Butter Stuffed Dates

 Servings: 12   **Prep. time:** 10 min   **Total time:** 10 min

Nutritional Information (Per Serving):

Calories: 80, Protein: 2g, Carbohydrates: 11g, Fats: 4g, Fiber: 2g, Cholesterol: 0mg, Sodium: 1mg, Potassium: 180mg

Ingredients

- 12 Medjool dates (pitted)
- 1/4 cup almond butter (creamy, unsweetened)
- 1 tablespoon chia seeds (optional, for added crunch)
- 1 tablespoon chopped almonds (optional, for added crunch)
- 1/2 teaspoon ground cinnamon (optional, for extra flavor)

Directions:

1. Gently slit each Medjool date lengthwise to open them without separating the halves completely.
2. Using a small spoon or a piping bag, fill each date with almond butter. If desired, sprinkle chia seeds and chopped almonds on top of the almond butter for extra texture and nutrition.
3. Sprinkle ground cinnamon over the stuffed dates if using, for added flavor.
4. Enjoy immediately or chill in the refrigerator for a firmer texture. Store leftovers in an airtight container in the fridge for up to 1 week.

Coconut Rice Pudding

Servings: 4   **Prep. time:** 5 min   **Total time:** 30 min

Nutritional Information (Per Serving):

Calories: 320 kcal, Protein: 4 g, Carbohydrates: 50 g, Fats: 12 g, Fiber: 3 g, Cholesterol: 0 mg, Sodium: 80 mg, Potassium: 180 mg

Ingredients

- 1 cup uncooked jasmine rice
- 2 cups full-fat coconut milk (canned)
- 1 cup water
- 1/4 cup maple syrup or agave nectar
- 1 teaspoon vanilla extract
- 1/2 teaspoon ground cinnamon
- 1/4 teaspoon ground nutmeg
- Pinch of salt
- 1/4 cup unsweetened shredded coconut (optional, for garnish)
- Fresh berries or mango slices (optional, for serving)

Directions:

1. Rinse the jasmine rice under cold water until the water runs clear. In a medium pot, combine the rinsed rice with coconut milk and water. Bring to a boil over medium heat.
2. Once it reaches a boil, lower the heat to a simmer, cover, and cook for 20 minutes or until the rice is tender and has absorbed most of the liquid.
3. Mix in the maple syrup, vanilla extract, cinnamon, nutmeg, and a pinch of salt. Continue to cook on low heat for another 5 minutes, stirring occasionally, until the pudding reaches your desired thickness.
4. Remove from heat and let it cool slightly. Serve the pudding warm or chilled, topped with shredded coconut and fresh berries or mango slices if you like.
5. For a smoother texture, blend half of the pudding in a blender until creamy, then mix it back with the rest.

Orange & Almond Salad

Servings: 4   **Prep. time:** 15 min   **Total time:** 15 min

Nutritional Information (Per Serving):

Calories: 160 kcal, Protein: 2 g, Carbohydrates: 21 g, Fats: 8 g, Fiber: 4 g, Cholesterol: 0 mg, Sodium: 25 mg, Potassium: 360 mg

Ingredients

- 4 large oranges
- 1/4 cup raw almonds, sliced or slivered
- 1/4 cup fresh mint leaves, chopped
- 1/4 cup pomegranate seeds (optional)
- 1 tablespoon extra virgin olive oil
- 1 tablespoon freshly squeezed lemon juice
- 1 teaspoon maple syrup or agave nectar
- 1/4 teaspoon ground cinnamon
- Pinch of sea salt

Directions:

1. Peel the oranges, removing as much of the white pith as possible. Slice the oranges into rounds or segment them by cutting between the membranes. Arrange the orange slices or segments on a large serving plate.
2. In a dry skillet over medium heat, toast the almond slices or slivers until they are lightly golden and fragrant, about 3-4 minutes. Stir frequently to prevent burning. Remove from heat and let cool.
3. In a small bowl, whisk together the olive oil, lemon juice, maple syrup, cinnamon, and a pinch of sea salt until well combined.
4. Drizzle the dressing evenly over the orange slices. Sprinkle the toasted almonds, chopped mint leaves, and pomegranate seeds (if using) on top.
5. Serve the salad immediately as a refreshing and nutritious appetizer or light dessert.

Conclusion

As we reach the end of this plant-based journey, it's clear that embracing a diet rich in fruits, vegetables, legumes, and whole grains is more than just a trend—it's a lifestyle choice with profound benefits for your health, the environment, and even your wallet. Throughout this book, you've discovered a wide array of delicious, nutritious recipes that prove just how versatile and satisfying plant-based eating can be. From hearty breakfasts to vibrant salads, comforting main dishes, and indulgent desserts, the recipes provided are designed to nourish both body and soul.

One of the key takeaways from this cookbook is that plant-based eating doesn't require sacrificing flavor or satisfaction. On the contrary, with the right ingredients and a bit of creativity, you can enjoy meals that are not only healthful but also incredibly tasty and fulfilling. The recipes here emphasize whole, unprocessed foods, ensuring that every bite you take is packed with nutrients that support your overall well-being.

Now that you have this wealth of knowledge and recipes at your fingertips, it's time to put it into practice. Start by incorporating more plant-based meals into your daily routine, and don't be afraid to experiment with the recipes provided. Whether you're a seasoned plant-based eater or just beginning your journey, there's something in this book for everyone. Remember, the goal is not perfection but progress—each plant-based meal you enjoy is a step toward better health and a more sustainable lifestyle.

As you continue exploring the world of plant-based eating, we encourage you to share your experiences. If this book has been helpful to you, please take a moment to leave a review on Amazon. Your feedback not only helps others discover the joys of plant-based living but also supports the ongoing creation of resources like this one.

Here's to your health and happiness—one plant-based meal at a time!

Made in United States
Orlando, FL
18 November 2024